Disability, Hate Crime and Violence

CW01572585

This book provides a comprehensive and interdisciplinary examination of disability, hate crime and violence, exploring its emergence on the policy agenda. Engaging with the latest debates in criminology, disability and violence studies, it goes beyond conventional notions of hate crime to look at violences in their myriad forms as they are seen to impact upon disabled people's lives.

Despite a raft of relevant policy and legislation, few have attempted to draw together research on the disabled as victims of hate crime and violence. This innovative volume conceptualises issues of disability, hate crime and violence and connects empirical research with theoretical insights. Making links between criminal justice policy, social care and welfare, it highlights areas of best practice and makes suggestions for policy and legislative reform. *Disability, Hate Crime and Violence* is written in accessible language, with minimal jargon and an international focus. Each chapter is grounded in research and practice, with relevant policy and legislation clearly signposted throughout.

Disability, Hate Crime and Violence provides a much needed theoretical and practical investigation of the key issues around disabled hate crime and violence and is an important work for students and academics researching and studying disability studies, criminology, social policy and sociology, as well as those with an interest in domestic violence studies and broader historical and philosophical constructions of disability, violence and social harms.

Alan Roulstone is Professor of Disability Policy at Northumbria University, UK.

Hannah Mason-Bish is Senior Lecturer in Criminology at the University of Roehampton, UK.

Routledge Advances in Disability Studies

New titles

Towards a Contextual Psychology of Disablism
Brian Watermeyer

Disability, Hate Crime and Violence
Edited by
Alan Roulstone and Hannah Mason-Bish

Forthcoming titles

Intellectual Disability and Social Theory
Philosophical Debates on Being Human
Chrissie Rogers

Disability, Hate Crime and Violence

Edited by
Alan Roulstone and
Hannah Mason-Bish

Routledge
Taylor & Francis Group

LONDON AND NEW YORK

First published 2013
by Routledge
2 Park Square, Milton Park, Abingdon, Oxfordshire OX14 4RN
Simultaneously published in the USA and Canada
by Routledge
711 Third Avenue, New York, NY 10017

First issued in paperback 2014

Routledge is an imprint of the Taylor & Francis Group, an informa business

British Library Cataloguing in Publication Data
A catalogue record for this book is available from the British Library

Library of Congress Cataloging-in-Publication Data
Disability, hate crime and violence / edited by Alan Roulstone and
Hannah Mason-Bish.
p. cm. -- (Routledge advances in disability studies)
1. People with disabilities--Crimes against--Great Britain. 2. People with
disabilities--Violence against--Great Britain. 3. Hate crimes--Great Britain.
I. Roulstone, Alan, 1962- II. Mason-Bish, Hannah.
HV6250.4.H35D57 2012
362.4--dc23
2012004330

ISBN: 978-0-415-67431-7 (hbk)
ISBN: 978-1-138-82333-4 (pbk)

Typeset in Times
by Taylor & Francis Books

Contents

Acknowledgements

The editors would like to thank all of the contributors whose ideas and insights have made this book possible. With many demands on their time, we are grateful for their efforts which have made the book a success. Thanks also to Grace McInnes and James Watson at Routledge for their patient support and guidance. Alan wishes to thank Guy and Jo for their love and forbearance in providing the space for this and other projects. Hannah wishes to thank Alex for his love, support and encouragement during the book's development. We wish to remember those disabled people who have passed on during the completion of the book and whose efforts have created the terrain on which to tackle the wider barriers that have historically faced disabled people; your role will never be forgotten, Vic Finkelstein, Rowan Jade, Nasa Begum and Richard Smith. The lives of disabled people needlessly lost to hate crimes are of course central to this book and this collection aims to record the lives of those disabled people society should have done more to protect.

Abbreviations

ACPO	Association of Chief Police Officers
ASB/O	Anti-Social Behaviour/Order
BSL	British Sign Language
BCS	British Crime Survey
BCODP	British Council of Disabled People
BBC	British Broadcasting Corporation
CBT	Cognitive Behavioural Therapy
CDRP	Crime and Disorder Reduction Partnership
CJA	Criminal Justice Act (2003)
CJS	Criminal Justice System
COP	Community of Practice
CPA	Care Programme Approach
DDA	Disability Discrimination Act (1995, 2005)
DHCN	Disability Hate Crime Network
DoH	Department of Health
DPM	Disabled People's Movement
DPO	Disabled People's Organisation
DPP	Director of Public Prosecution
DRC	Disability Rights Commission
DWP	Department for Work and Pensions
EHRC	Equality and Human Rights Commission
ESRC	Economic and Social Research Council
FBI	Federal Bureau of Investigation
GAD	Greenwich Association of Disabled People
IPCC	Independent Police Complaints Authority
LGBT	Lesbian, Gay, Bisexual and Transgender
MoJ	Ministry of Justice
MPS	Metropolitan Police Service
NAO	National Audit Office
NGO	Non-Governmental Organisation
NHS	National Health Service
NPIA	National Police Improvement Agency
ODI	Office for Disability Issues

OfCOM	Office of Communications
OSCE	Office for Security and Cooperation in Europe
PiP	Personal Independence Payment
PMSU	Prime Minister's Strategy Unit
POVA	Protection of Vulnerable Adults
PPU	Public Protection Unit
PTSD	Post-Traumatic Stress Disorder
SCR	Serious Case Review
ULO	User-Led Organisation
UN	United Nations
UKCDP	United Kingdom Council of Disabled People

Introduction

Disability, Hate Crime and Violence

Alan Roulstone, Northumbria University, UK and Hannah Mason-Bish, University of Roehampton, UK

> Half a century old, the Holocaust still mocks the idea of civilization and threatens our sense of ourselves as spiritual creatures. Its undiminished impact on human memory leaves wide open the unsettled and unsettling question of why this should be so.
>
> (Langer, 1994: 184)

Introduction and aims

The question of disability, hate crime and violence has received little concerted attention in academic, policy and practice activity to date. The small quantity of work that has been completed has been largely in North America and often linked to wider oppressions – race, gender, sexual orientation. These intersectional issues are very important and this collection of works will continue in this tradition of acknowledging the multiple motivations to harm others based on their perceived difference. The advent of a collected edition that aims to bring together international perspectives, which foregrounds disability and which looks at issues and solutions to disablist hate crime, is therefore well overdue. The book aims to add to criminology, disability studies, sociology and policy studies in pulling together work from a range of disciplines and perspectives. A key message of the book is that there is no 'one best way' to reduce disablist hate crime. Education, self-empowerment, effective public protection, publicity campaigns, a responsive, timely and culturally sensitive criminal justice system are all important weapons in the fight against categorical, targeted crimes.

All crimes have victims and wider social costs; the authors of this collection share a philosophical view, however, that harming individuals simply because they belong to a socially stigmatised 'category' is especially heinous.

The book limits itself to hate crimes that are targeted at disabled people – which includes people with learning difficulties, manifest/known-about mental health problems, physical impairment and social learning difficulty (for example Asperger's/Autism). As stated above, writers do however draw down parallels with race, LGBT and gender hate crimes (Dunbar, E, 2006; Herek and Gillis, 1999; Iganski, 1999). Power relations in domestic violence are also drawn upon in some chapters where parallel dynamics are seen to exist with disablist hate crime or where domestic violence is perpetrated against a disabled 'friend', relative or partner. Hate crimes in institutional, high street and domestic contexts are all included in this collected work. We could have drawn on other forms of hate crime which highlight other stigmatised differences – for example, that made clear in the death of Sophie Lancaster, where sub-cultural differences were the pretext for horrendous violence; space, however, does not permit that analysis here. This in no way aims to create a hierarchy of importance, but simply reflects the expertise and focus contained in the book.

As some readers will be new to the field of disability-related work, a brief note on terminology is important. Following the social model of disability, authors distinguish between impairment – the difference of body, brain and intellect – and disability, which is seen as the range of barriers that confront people with impairments, including negative attitudes, structured disadvantage, a hostile media and internalised oppression that may result from these barriers. Where references are made to US work, the term 'people with disabilities' is sometimes used in the literature. We obviously respect this linguistic difference, but point out that it ostensibly equates to people with impairments in reality. For authenticity we have, however, kept this terminology intact in referring to some US-based work. In this broader vein the authors prefer the term disablist hate crime to make clear that our disablist hate crime and violence are part of a much broader set of exclusions that a disablist society exhibits. We include the term violence alongside hate as violence may take forms that are hidden, repeat or low-grade but which taken together make life intolerably difficult for disabled people – as was the case in the Pilkington-Hardwick deaths. The inclusion of violence also allows better links to be made to the wider violences literature which has been so important in framing this edited collection. The term 'hate' and 'hate crime' are of course deeply problematical and some authors choose to place the terms in scare quotes for that reason. The book explores alternative language and the morphing of the term in criminal justice practice into hostility at street level. For now, however, the term is a useful shorthand, whilst it is important to engage critically with current constructions of 'hate crime'. Alternatives are offered up – for example, targeted (EHRC, 2010), motivated (Berk, Boyd and Hamner, 1992); bias crimes (Murray, 1992).

The book aims to explore all contemporary forms of violence and hate directed at disabled people in 'advanced' societies. We do not argue that violence and abuse against disabled people is new; indeed there is much evidence of the historic violence against disabled people. One key factor in the shift to community-based social care was the outrage expressed over the severe and sustained abuse against disabled people in Ely, Farleigh and Normansfield hospitals. The twentieth century, of course, witnessed an attempt to exterminate those deemed to be *unnütze esser* or 'useless eaters' by the Third Reich. Together these are poignant reminders that deep-seated hatred of difference sits beneath the veneer of some aspects of civilisation. Economic crises seem in part to exacerbate these destructive binary viewpoints of useful and useless.

Current media discourses are making plain that people who would hitherto have comfortably been counted as disabled are now being highlighted as faux disabled or simply a drain on UK PLC (Garthwaite, 2011).

Hate crimes are diverse. The continued evidence of institutional violence in the recent Winterbourne View and related cases requires that such violence be accounted for despite the large-scale decarceration of many disabled people. Most of the hate and violence that is explored in this collection is, however, perpetrated in 'high street', local estates and domestic contexts. Although a small amount of evidence exists around disablist hate in the workplace, the evidence base is not sufficient to underpin a robust offering in this area currently. The evidence focuses on adult abuse and the book makes no claims as to offering evidence in abuse in childhood, although some evidence points to lifelong abuse for some disabled people.

The need to examine crimes of violence against disabled people is in part due to their neglect criminologically. As a field of study, criminology aims to examine constructions of crime and to provide a critical assessment of society's responses to crime. Disablist crimes have remained largely on the periphery of criminological inquiry. Where they have been considered, it has been in the wider context of 'crimes of the home', where some academics have begun to explore abuses occurring against vulnerable groups, including older people, children and, sometimes, disabled people. This has tended to be within an institution or care home setting. Typically this research has found a natural home within social care scholarship. What this has meant is that criminal justice responses to disablist crime have not been subject to critical examination until recently. While this collection does indeed examine crimes within 'private' settings, it also seeks to widen the boundary to 'public' settings and to look at the potential for criminal justice solutions and the need for change. It is hoped that this provides a more holistic approach to dealing with disablist crime which encompasses social care, criminal justice, health and social policy solutions.

Hate crime scholarship is one area where disablist crime has recently become more of a focus. Emerging as a response to the racist murder of Stephen Lawrence in 1993, the British Government sought to create legislation which would punish crime demonstrating racist hostility more harshly. This has since been expanded to include religion, sexual orientation and disability. The statutes were accompanied by a raft of policy designed to change policing practice and to encourage community cohesion and reporting of hate crimes generally. Since this development, academics have begun to examine hate crime more closely. Some of this research has taken the form of a critical assessment of the merits of punishing hate and a close inspection of the policy reforms. Others have been prompted to look at victims of hate crime and the harm caused to them by prejudicial and bigoted violence and harassment. Much of this research focused on racist crimes and it is only recently that disablist hate has featured in scholarly hate crime texts.

The reason for this omission could in part be due to the history of tensions between police and minority ethnic communities which sparked the emergence of hate crime legislation in the first place. Previous research into racist violence provided a backdrop from which scholars could make connections with new policy developments. However, academics who have looked at disablist hate have noted that it might have unique – or at least different – nuances when compared with other forms. The victim and perpetrator might have a personal relationship; the victim might have difficulty accessing the police; the perpetrator might perceive the victim as 'vulnerable' rather than being motivated by hostility. Furthermore, it is only in recent years that the larger charities have begun to examine disablist hate crime. Disability campaign organisations Mencap, Mind and Scope have all now carried out surveys and interviews with victims in an attempt to understand and highlight victim experiences. This collection is therefore a timely pursuit because disablist hate crime is now an area of academic, campaign and government interest. Yet our understanding of it is only in its infancy. A focus on disability and hate crime forces an examination of the construction of the category of hate crime; it challenges assumptions about the nature of violence and our responses to it.

The book also makes a contribution to victimology and theoretical understandings about the nature of victims (Williams, 1999; Williams and Goodman-Chong, 2009). The status of crime victims has changed significantly over the last fifty years, with governments initiating a raft of measures to give victims increasing rights to justice. A growth of victimology texts has documented the development of victim support services, campaign movements and high profile cases which have led to this shift in focus. There is also now a wealth of studies into specific forms of victimhood, including domestic violence victims, children and minority ethnic groups. Disability remains somewhat on the margins of victimology studies and few have looked at the position of disabled people within the wider discourse of victims' rights. As such this collection should be viewed as a critical victimology study in itself by seeking to examine the specific needs of disabled victims of hate and violence and to challenge essentialist understandings of disability. It seeks to understand the 'lived reality' of victimhood by including the words of campaigners and activists and recognising the importance of a recognition of the rights of disabled victims and the responsibility of the state to provide these.

The book's structure explained

This edited collection is constituted of two parts: the first part conceptualises disablist hate crime, while the second part explores the experience, impact and responses to disablist hate crime. Chapter 1 of **Part 1** is provided by Mason-Bish, who provides an overview of issues that relate to disablist hate crime – its form, significance and its social costs. Drawing on her own research, Mason-Bish highlights the reality that disablist hate crime appears last on the list for policy and criminal justice practitioner attention. She highlights the continued challenges if disablist hate crime is to get up to speed in the second decade of the twenty-first century. Chapter 2 by Roulstone and Sadique explores the jurisprudential limits of current hate crime constructions of disablist hate crime provision. They unpack discourses of vulnerability and hostility and highlight the urgent need to challenge both terms if disablist hate crime policy and practice are to mirror realities of disablist hate crime in wider society.

Chapter 3 by Perry offers a thoughtful reflection on the nature of prejudice and hate. This chapter uses insights from Galtung's typology of violence to critically examine 'disability hate crime' as a description and prescription for violence against disabled people. In so doing it asks for a broader reappraisal of the harms against disabled people more generally. Chapter 4 by Hollomotz explores the nature and responses to sexual violence and abuse against people with learning difficulties. Like Perry, Hollomotz argues that these institutional violences need to be read in the context of a broader loss of liberties, and abuse experienced by people with learning difficulties. Chapter 5 by Quarmby is a detailed content analyses of press coverage of disablist hate crimes. The chapter analyses how the media has reported disability hate crime and other targeted violence in the past. It also investigates whether media reporting has changed since 2007, and asks what effect the emergence of new forms of media is having on images of disability generally and disability hate crime in particular. Quarmby acknowledges that the media can be progressive, but that they currently are a part of the problem of unregulated negative portrayal of disability which may add to hate acts. Chapter 6 by the US writer Sherry provides a comparative appraisal of hate crime constructions and recording. His appraisal notes that hate crime has been recorded for much longer in the USA, but that both the USA and UK still have a long way to go in accurately comprehend disablist hate crime.

Part 2 explores responses to disablist hate crime. Part 2 of the book begins with Chapter 7, another US focused approach which explores the day-to-day realities and weaknesses of response to disablist hate crime. Levin explores parallels and differences in response to other hate crime streams such as race and religious hate crime. He argues that manifestations and responses to disablist hate crime are very different, whilst disablist hate crime gets little relative attention in the criminal justice system, despite good evidential systems. Chapter 8 by Thiara and Hague offers insights from three empirical studies conducted into domestic and gendered violence against disabled women. The chapter provides a very stark picture of the current threadbare infrastructure of support for disabled women and the notable lack of women's aid and refuge for disabled women who experience domestic hate crime. Chapter 9 is an exploration of Novis's important work with the Metropolitan Police's Independent Advisory Group (IAG) in responding to disablist hate crime. Novis, a disabled person who has faced repeated hate crime, relates her experiences of setting up and working with the IAG. Despite good work, she argues there is still a very long road to travel if disabled people are to be taken seriously in the reporting of, and in the criminal justice response to, disablist hate crime. Chapter 10 is also presented by a disabled person who has experienced disablist hate crime. Brookes explores the background to and development of the Disability Hate Crime Network (DHCN) in responding to disablist hate crime. He relates how the network aims to highlight good and poor practice and aims to hold the police, CPS and policymakers to account for decisions on sentencing. The network has had a key role in taking forward developments in hate crime policy.

Chapter 11 by Thomas explores the contentious notion of 'mate crime'. Mate crime is an as yet under-recognised phenomenon where non-disabled people deliberately befriend and often groom a disabled person in order to exploit them. Although the notion of mate crime divides critical opinion there are now a number of key cases in where disabled people have been serially abused via this method of grooming and pretence. Chapter 13 brings together notions of civil courage and critical theatre as tools for better responses to disablist hate crime. Brandon and Keyes, working with the disabled theatre company The Lawnmowers, explore the use of civil courage (and Good Samaritan principles) and their value in reducing hate crime. The innovative use of theatre to spread messages about and reduce crime make this a very novel addition to the field. Chapter 12 is provided by Balderston, who explores what works in reducing disablist hate crime. Drawing on gender, deaf studies and notions of intersectionality, Balderston makes plain the importance of victim support, which in turn requires a longer-term change in attitude to difference and tolerance if deeper held views and violence are to be confronted.

References

Berk, R. A., Boyd, E. A and Hamner, K. M (1992) 'Thinking more clearly about Hate Motivated Crimes'. In Herek, G. M and Berrill, K. T. Hate Crimes. London: Sage.

Burleigh, M (1994) *Death and Deliverance: Euthanasia in Germany 1900–1945*. Cambridge, England: Cambridge University Press.

Dunbar, E (2006) 'Race, Gender, and Sexual Orientation in Hate Crime Victimization: Identity Politics or Identity Risk?'. Violence and Victims. 21 (3) pp. 321–27.

EHRC (2010) 'Tackling the Challenge of Targeted Harassment'. London: EHRC. Available at: http://www.equalityhumanrights.com/key-projects/how-fair-is-britain/tackling-the-challenge-of-targeted-harassment/.

Garthwaite, K (2011) 'The language of shirkers and scroungers? Talking about illness, disability and coalition welfare reform'. Disability and Society, Volume 26, Issue 3, 2011, pp. 369–372.

Herek, G. M., Gillis, J. R and Cogan, J. C (1999) 'Psychological Sequelae of Hate Crime Victimization Among Lesbian, Gay, and Bisexual Adults'. Journal of Consulting and Clinical Psychology. 67 (6) pp. 945–51.

Iganski, P (1999) 'Why Make Hate a Crime'. Critical Social Policy. 19 (3) pp. 386–95.

Langer, L. L (1994) *Remembering Survival in Holocaust remembrance: the shapes of memory*. Cambridge: Blackwell.

Murray, J. G (1992) 'Bias Crimes: What do Haters Deserve?' Criminal Justice Ethics. 11 (2) pp. 20–23.

Williams, B. (1999) *Working with Victims of Crime: Policies, Politics and Practice.* London: Jessica Kingsley.

Williams, B and Goodman-Chong, H (2009) *Victims and Victimisation: A Reader.* Maidenhead: Open University Press.

Part I

Conceptualising disablist hate crime

1 Conceptual issues in the construction of disability hate crime

Hannah Mason-Bish, University of Roehampton

Introduction

In September 2011 the Equality and Human Rights Commission (EHRC) launched the findings of a comprehensive inquiry into disability hate crime. This long-awaited report, *Hidden in Plain Sight* (EHRC, 2011), recommended inter alia that greater understanding of, monitoring of, support in reporting, and residential service protections in hate crime are urgently required. The report also suggested an urgent need to review the extent to which 'special measures' are being embedded in criminal justice process and greater clarity on lead agencies in a given authority. This research comes four years after Fiona Pilkington killed herself and her disabled daughter Francecca Hardwick after suffering relentless abuse which went on for seven years. Despite the prolonged nature of harassment and evidence of targeting based on disability, the police failed to take action to stop the abuse and bring about justice for the victims. Central to this poor response was the failure to correctly identify the incidents as forms of disability hate crime. Speaking at the time of the inquest into their deaths, Mencap Chief Executive Mark Goldring said:

> This should be the watershed moment for disability hate crime, when the government and the police treat all disability hate crime as seriously as racist hate crime ... How many more defenceless people must die for these incidents to be treated as a crime rather than anti-social behaviour?
>
> (Mencap, 2009)

The Independent Police Complaints Commission (IPCC) inquiry into the case found a national lack of awareness by the police in recognising disabled people as targets of hate crime and a lack of understanding of sentencing provisions and evidence gathering (IPCC, 2011). This chapter therefore provides a useful examination of the reasons behind the slow responses to disability hate crime, the implications of this, and looks for potential remedies in terms of policy and practice.

There is evidence of a long history of poor treatment of disabled people by the criminal justice system and research also shows high levels of victimisation and low levels of reporting of crime (Cunningham and Drury, 2002; Quarmby, 2011). In this context it should be no surprise that disability hate crime mirrors this experience. When my own study of disability hate crime began in 2004 it would be fair to say that implementation of disability hate crime policy was patchy. Although included in the Association of Chief Police Officers (ACPO) manuals on hate crime in 2005, individual forces only had to collect data on it from 2008. The Crown Prosecution Service (CPS) did not issue their first disability hate crime guidance until 2007, whilst between April 2007 and March 2009, they prosecuted 576 defendants for disability hate crime. This is low when compared with 42,500 defendants prosecuted for racially and religiously aggravated crime (CPS, 2009).[1] When examining the police response there were 1,402 recorded disability hate crimes in the year ending December 2009, compared to 4,805 for sexual orientation and 43,426 for race (ACPO, 2009). Third-sector studies have shown that disabled victims of hate crime typically do not report it to the police for a number of reasons (Mencap, 1999: 'Living in Fear'). The EHRC reported that these include a lack of victim awareness of their rights, previous experiences of the police and fear of losing independence (EHRC, 2009: 73). Crucially, they found that disabled people would downplay the seriousness of the incidents against them and would not readily use the term hate crime to describe what had occurred. This means that the role of police in identifying disability hate crime is even more important if victims are to get adequate assistance and justice.

Hate crime and disability

This chapter is based upon the findings of qualitative research by the author (Mason-Bish, 2008) which involved interviewing campaign group activists, policymakers and criminal justice practitioners in an attempt to understand how hate crime policy in Britain has been developed. Fifty semi-structured interviews were carried out with a variety of 'key informants', ranging from activists to policymakers. These included leading policymakers, senior management and criminal justice officials and campaign group lobbyists.[2] The interviews focused on the strategies employed by activists in shaping policy on hate crime and the decisions made by policymakers about how policy would be formulated and implemented. The research revealed the way that the role of campaign groups has been critical in gaining legal recognition for hate crime victims. They have lobbied, gathered evidence and engaged with practitioners in the criminal justice system to try to create workable policy. Hate crime has been a useful banner under which to frame these efforts and to highlight the similarities between different forms of victimisation. This supports the suggestion that hate crime legislation represents a response to an identity-politics call for legal recognition of victimhood and an opportunity for government to appear 'tough on crime'. As many academics have noted, being included in hate crime legislation was designed to send a positive message to specific victim groups (Iganski, 1999; Hall, 2005). For the police it was a useful way to engage communities and to win their 'trust and confidence' (ACPO, 2000: 18). Aside from this, the term 'hate' suggested a level of ser-iousness which should mean that criminal justice agencies address it with some urgency. Academic contributions to the hate crime debate have tended to focus upon the concept of hate crime and how it should be defined. There is some consensus that hate crimes rarely occur because the perpetrator 'hates' the victim (Mason, 2005 abc).

For some, membership of a minority or oppressed group is a key criterion. Leslie Wolfe and Lois Copeland suggested that it was:

> Violence directed towards groups of people who generally are not valued by the majority of society, who suffer discrimination in other arenas and who do not have full access to remedy social, political and economic injustice.
>
> (Wolfe and Copeland, 1991: 8)

Their definition of hate crime suggests that victims are already marginalised by society and face injustice on many fronts. Barbara Perry concurs, suggest-ing that hate crimes reinforce structural inequalities and remind the victimised group of their position in society:

> [they] ... re-create simultaneously the threatened (real or imagined) hegemony of the perpetrator's group and the appropriate subordinate identity of the victim's group. It is a means of marking both the Self and the Other in such a way as to re-establish their 'proper' relative positions, as given and reproduced by broader ideologies and patterns of social and political inequality.
>
> (Perry, 2001: 10)

Key to Perry's explanation is the focus on victim groups rather than individual victims, which can be seen in the legislative response to hate crimes. Most legal statutes on hate crime have a definition of, and are accompanied by, a list of protected 'statuses'. In Britain these are race, religion, sexual orientation and disability, which represent groups with a shared history of oppression, statistical evidence of victimisation and a legacy of poor criminal justice responses. However, critics of hate crime legislation have warned against an identity politics which creates arbitrary divisions between groups and might be merely symbolic in nature (Jacobs and Potter, 1998; Fraser, 2003). Barbara Perry warns that the term 'hate crime' also 'tends to individualize bigoted violence, as the outcome of deeply personal dislikes' (Perry, 2004: 124). It suggests that the motivation for the offence is individual pathology and does not take into account the wider structural conditions that might be to blame for the behaviour of the offender. A further extension of this problem is in the way that hate crime conjures up images of violence committed by strangers. Kielinger and Stanko have used the term targeted violence because in their view:

> The term hate crime places the responsibility for the violence on strangers and therefore on individuals rather than society as a whole, the term 'targeted violence' places the incident inside the social context within which it occurs ... The term hate crime obscures the relational advantages or disadvantages that are ever present in society and which may underscore the motivation and the power of language and intimidation behind these incidents.
>
> (Kielinger and Stanko, 2002: 5)

It will be suggested that these issues are particularly pertinent to disability hate crime, where incidents might be more likely to be perpetrated by known offenders in a variety of public and private arenas.

An examination of hate crime as an approach to disablist violence is worthwhile, first due to the relative youth of the concept of hate crime and its influence on criminal justice policy. It emerged in Britain in the 1990s as a way of responding to racist instances of violence and harassment which had been drawn into sharp focus with the failures of authorities to respond to the racist murder of Stephen Lawrence. Hate crime legislation soon expanded to include enhanced sentences for religiously aggravated crimes in 2001, and in 2003 the Criminal Justice Act included a statutory aggravation for crimes where the perpetrator demonstrated hostility based upon the victim's perceived sexual orientation or disability (HM Government, 2003).[3] Furthermore, while incitement legislation has been developed to cover racist, religious and homophobic hatred, there is no legal coverage of disablist incitement.[4] Although the word 'hate' is absent from most legal definitions of hate crime, recently criminal justice agencies have adopted a shared definition:

> Any criminal offence which is perceived by the victim or any other person, to be motivated by a hostility or prejudice based on a person's disability or perceived disability.

Notable within this definition is that the perception of the victim or any other person is key in deciding whether or not a hate crime has occurred. Also key is the use of 'hostility', a rather wide term where the CPS provide this guidance:

> consideration should be given to ordinary dictionary definitions, which include ill-will, ill-feeling, spite, contempt, prejudice, unfriendliness, antagonism, resentment, and dislike.
>
> (CPS, 2010)

As this chapter progresses we will see the difficulties in creating an operational definition relating to disability hate crime.

A second justification for a focus on hate crime responses to disability-related violence is that it has been added to pre-existing legislation and policy previously applied to other victim groups. As Anne Novis notes in her chapter in this volume, when my research began in 2004 any campaign on disability hate crime was largely limited to smaller disabled people's organisations, and although the legislation had been enacted, few of the 'big' disability organisations were focused on the issue. Research interviews were carried out with key representatives of the main disability charities in Britain, including the Disability Rights Commission (DRC, now EHRC), Mind, Scope and Mencap. None of these were using the term hate crime in their literature at that time. The Director of Policy for one charity said that he did not think that the term hate crime was 'especially informative' and that it 'was quite telling that we haven't really thought about it'. A further complication was that a more general problem of hate crime had already been defined and implemented. The aforementioned legislation and policy was designed around racially aggravated offences and as a result of the murder of Stephen Lawrence and years of monitoring and research into the poor criminal justice response. Therefore, campaigners working on disability violence had to either *adopt* the term hate crime and attempt to prove how disabled victims suffer in a similar way or to *adapt* the term to encompass new forms of victimisation that disabled people experience. As this chapter will now demonstrate, this process has drawn light upon assumptions and misconceptions about the nature of disability hate crime.

The parameters of disability hate crime

One of the key barriers to correctly identifying disability hate crime lies in the perceived difference between hatred and vulnerability. Barbara Waxman identified hatred as the 'unacknowledged dimension' of violence against the disabled (Waxman, 1991). Criminal justice and social care agencies have traditionally looked to how they might be protected and 'helped', rather than how they might achieve justice. The research by the EHRC highlighted the need to move away from protectionism and towards a rights-based agenda which recognises the entitlement of disabled people to be secure and safe (EHRC, 2009: 80). The research supported this view and found that respondents – whether campaigners or practitioners – tended to fall into one of two 'camps'. Some felt that only crimes motivated by clear-cut hatred or hostility should be classed as hate crimes. Others felt that it did not matter if a perpetrator was motivated by perceived vulnerability because that too was evidence of an underlying prejudice about the victim (See Roulstone and Sadique's chapter in this collection). This dichotomy is also in evidence in the criminal justice system, with one police officer noting:

> We look at both victims who are disabled and victims who are targeted because of their disability. They are two distinct things. One is a disabled

person whose parking permit is stolen. Is that a disabled targeted hate crime? ... If a blind person is mugged is it because they are blind or because they know that the victim can't describe them visually?

The term hate crime conveys a definite motivation for the police. The ACPO manual described it as being caused by the 'perpetrator's prejudice' (ACPO, 2005). According to a senior police officer interviewed for the research, it is not about bias selection or vulnerability, but a distinct animus:

With hate crime we went along the lines of the perpetrator. Why are they targeting that victim? Is it because they are easy pickings or because they don't like that person because of who they are?

A disabled victim labelled as a vulnerable adult by the police might then find that they are pushed towards a solution involving social care and health services rather than criminal justice. It might also mean that any evidence of hostility at the time of the crime will not be recorded or looked for. Campaigners also noted this as an area of concern and the need to be clear. One noted:

What we have is that some criminal justice professionals are too willing to say that it was a vulnerability motive ... Sometimes criminal justice professionals will look for the obvious explanations without probing further and trying to find out about hostility.

Furthermore, they felt a need to be consistent themselves and would often express that they needed to be 'clear about what we mean by hate crime'. In their analysis of disability hate crime, Roulstone *et al.* noted that hate and vulnerability are often constructed as two opposing issues, rather than sitting on the same spectrum of motivations for violence and abuse (Roulstone *et al.*, 2009: 2). This has certainly been demonstrated when policymakers have sought to revise hate crime policy. In 2004, the Scottish Executive established a Working Group on Hate Crime with the aim of researching legislation relating to age, gender, sexual orientation and disability. They drew a similar distinction:

Crimes against disabled people or women living on their own may be motivated by the individual's real or perceived vulnerability, rather than by malice towards the social group of which they are a member.

(Scottish Executive, 2004a)

The Executive concluded that it would be for the police and prosecutors to determine whether a crime was motivated by hatred or vulnerability. They were keen to emphasise that if a crime was motivated by a stereotypical view or misconception of a victim, then that would be a hate crime. Some respondents interviewed for this research pointed out that surely the perceived weakness of a victim, and therefore their vulnerability, is based upon a stereotypical view. One campaigner interviewed said:

> Some of the cases that have appeared in the media have not been prosecuted as disability hate crimes because they are motivated by vulnerability to which my counter would be that you wouldn't do these horrific things to someone if you believed that they were a regular human being. That lack of empathy must have its roots in some sort of prejudice.

A gay man attacked because they are thought to be effeminate and an easy target would be a hate crime victim. A disabled person harassed because of the perception that they cannot defend themselves seems to be very similar. The distinction between vulnerability, stereotypes, malice and hate are not clear for some campaigners. Nevertheless, they are used to distinguish between types of incidents and whether or not they should be seen as hate crime. Such is the importance of this confusion that the CPS have moved to provide further guidance, noting that 'police and prosecutors often focus on the victim being "vulnerable", an "easy target" and no further thought is given to the issue of hostility. This approach is wrong' (CPS, 2010). It will take time and further research to see whether this directive filters down to operational policing approaches.

Disability hate crime is also not dealt with appropriately because it has introduced new forms of incident not traditionally associated with the hate crime model. Academic Mark Sherry pointed out that the sexual harassment of deaf people by nuisance callers sending obscene messages via text phones might be a form of hate crime harassment that was unique to disabled people (Sherry, 2000: 3). In addition to this is the fact that crimes against disabled people might happen in public or private situations. Traditionally, hate crime has been seen as 'stranger danger' – something which occurs in a public place (Ray and Smith, 2001). Therefore, there has been much debate about whether or not hate crimes that happen in care homes or institutions should be dealt with as domestic violence or abuse. One senior police officer interviewed for the research explained the decision to exclude age-related crimes from hate crime policy:

> We also talked about what crimes we are talking about and consistently people perceived two types of crime. One was abuse in care relationships, either by a family member or by a professional and the second was about bogus distraction burglaries. Both need addressing and I couldn't begin to think which would be motivated by hatred. ... So my view was and our recommendation that we shouldn't include it for those reasons.

It was specifically mentioned that where older people were abused in a care home, this was unlikely to be motivated by prejudice. If this is part of the reason for excluding certain victim groups from policy, then it is likely that disability hate crimes that take such a form may be overlooked. Many of the campaigners interviewed for this research felt quite strongly that disabled people attacked in institutions were often victimised because of hatred, hostility and power. There was also the added complication that if the perpetrator is a 'carer' within the home or institution then the incidents might take the form of controlling behaviour that might not appear criminal. It could be that this is control over finances, removing access equipment such as wheelchairs and acts of cruelty that are motivated by hostility towards their disability. In some situations, it might be relevant to at least investigate these as potential hate crimes by the police and for mechanisms to be put in place to encourage reporting in these instances. To draw a boundary around where disability hate crimes take place is arbitrary and not something applied to other victim groups.

As Pam Thomas notes in her chapter in this volume, another facet of disability hate crimes is that the victim might have been groomed by the perpetrators with the aim of perpetrating violence and abuse. After the death of Brent Martin there was a lengthy debate about the murder and about the veracity of claims that he was 'groomed' by a group of teenagers. Campaigners observed that many incidents involving disabled people exhibited this kind of befriending, where the offender was at least known to the victim or a kind of 'pseudo friend'. But instead of thinking of this 'grooming' as a new angle or new aspect to an understanding of hate crime, it has often led the criminal justice system to exclude it as a type of hate crime. In the Brent Martin case, the fact that he knew his attackers – even though they had befriended him with the purpose of murder in mind – meant that it was not classed as a hate crime. As the EHRC report demonstrated, in disability hate crime cases the perpetrator might even be the carer or a family member (EHRC, 2009). The fact that there might be a personal relationship of trust between victim and offender has been used by policymakers to exclude new categories of age and gender in hate crime policy (Mason-Bish, 2010). In the case of Steven Hoskin, the serious case review noted the length of the 'friendship' that he had with at least one of his attackers and suggested that this was one of the reasons that it was not a hate crime:

> The term 'disability hate crime' fails to recognise the duration of Steven's contact with his persecutors; the counterfeit friendship; the background to Steven's perilous disclosures to Darren; the joyless enslavement, or the motivations of all of his persecutors.
>
> (Flynn, 2007: 25)

These differences are used to frame the experiences of disabled victims as being different to hate crime. Once again we can see that the CPS has noted that a relationship between victim and perpetrator is a common trend among disability hate crime incidents (CPS, 2010). However, the perception of hate crime as 'stranger danger' has a long legacy that the criminal justice system needs to overcome, and this must involve aiding victim and public under-standing. The experience of other forms of interpersonal violence has shown that victim–perpetrator relationships create many problems in terms of reporting, access, trust and fear of retribution. Hate crime policy needs to do more than just recognise the likelihood of relationships in disability hate crime cases and develop supportive reporting mechanisms to suit this (Quarmby, 2008; EHRC, 2011).

Having examined two key areas where disability hate crimes are especially complex, there is a third issue which widens the problem beyond operational concerns. In her analysis of the legal recognition of violence against disabled people, Joanna Perry asks whether disability hate crime legislation might be merely symbolic and not help to achieve real change unless it is implemented (Perry, 2008: 1). The research revealed a similar concern, but campaigners went a step further to suggest that hate crime legislation had created a victim hierarchy, with disability at the bottom. This perception reinforced the idea that disabled victims were less worthy of receiving justice than victims of racist or homophobic crimes. Criminal justice practitioners interviewed for the research recognised this issue and one police officer admitted that 'in the hierarchy it is clearly, race, homophobia, faith and disability'. One campaigner interviewed for the research identified this as just one area where disabled people are not treated fairly within the criminal justice system:

> There has been a lot of progress but the fact is that people with disabilities are often not identified as vulnerable victims or witnesses by criminal justice professionals. They may be dismissed as being unreliable witnesses, they may be seen as liars. The response generally is poor and disability hate crime is just one crime that will inevitably be a part of that. It gets a poor response because any crime against a person with a disability is likely to get a poor response.

So hate crime legislation is symptomatic of a wider problem of injustice that disabled people – as victims, witnesses and perpetrators – experience. A fur-ther extension of this problem is that it can lead to victim blaming, whereby the victim is vulnerable because of their disability and should therefore take steps to protect themselves (Sobsey, 1994: 62). A more suitable approach would be for the justice system to think of vulnerable situations, where the victim is at risk of attack because of disablist hostility. This places the blame onto the offender for their disablism, rather than onto the victim for their disability. There has also been some evidence to suggest that perpetrators are aware that crimes against disabled people are not treated as seriously by the police as they see incidents going unpunished (EHRC, 2009; Balderston and Morgan, 2009). As Sorenson asserts:

> The general devaluation of people with disabilities in our society com-bined with a lack of public awareness of the epidemic of crime and

violence against people with a disability provides a fertile environment for bias or hate crimes (Sorenson, 2001: 3).

A further implication of hate crime policy is that it can create a rivalry between victim groups – a 'competition for suffering', as one activist put it. This is perhaps an unintended consequence of what Nancy Fraser calls a response which simplifies identity down to set groupings (Fraser, 2003, p. 22). Some race campaigners expressed concern that disability would become a primary focus for hate crime policymakers and that race would be lost. In this way there is a danger that hate crime policy treats victims as homogenous groups and does not recognise the nuances of the individual victim experience. Hate crime policy might oversimplify the identity of the victim by seeing each group as a neat, distinct category and not acknowledging intersectionality. In a recent article it was noted that separating victims via blunt titles – race, disability and so on – does not assist our understanding of the experience of victimisation (Mason-Bish, 2010). As one activist noted, 'I am disabled, gay and a woman. If I am targeted am I supposed to say which aspect was the most hurtful and damaging?' This experience illustrates how the victim experience might be very complex and a single-strand approach might over-look issues of risk, harm and access to justice. Research has shown that being a disabled person leads to higher levels of risk which can be compounded by other factors such as gender and age (ESRC, 2009: 33). The ESRC research pointed to an incident of a disabled Muslim who felt 'triply disadvantaged' as they had been attacked on the basis of racism, disablism and Islamophobia (ESRC, 2009: 33). An oversimplified understanding of the hate crime concept will miss the nuances and realities of being a disabled victim.

The potential for disability hate crime policy

This paper has shown how hate crime policy remains a relatively new way to combat disablist violence and harassment. Although some academics have labelled disablist hate crime nebulous and not fixed, this research has revealed that any changes are very slow and it retains a static nature (Iganski, 1999; Mason, 2005a, 2005b, 2005c; Ray and Smith, 2001). Implementation of policy shows that where any relationship exists between victim and perpetrator it means that it is less likely to be classified as disability hate crime. In the case of disability incidents, this is more often likely to be the case because the perpetrator might be a 'friend', carer or relative. Similarly, the notion that disabled victims are inherently vulnerable means that those working in the criminal justice system are less likely to record and prosecute it as a hate crime. Campaigners are faced with the difficulty of proving that different aspects 'fit' within the hate crime remit (Perry, 2008: 9). Hate crime is an umbrella term which encompasses a range of behaviours, but those behaviours which fit traditional notions of hate crime are more likely to be recognised within the criminal justice system. These notions were formed at the inception of hate crime policy, which was originally defined around racist and religious forms of violence and harassment. Disability hate crime campaigners have had to show how they are victims in a similar way, and deserving of protection, whilst also attending to the different experiences of disabled victims.

While the problems of hate crime policy are clear, the author would suggest that there are reasons for not discarding it in relation to disability and victimisation. After the deaths of Fiona Pilkington and Francecca Hardwick, politicians were criticised by campaigners for labelling this victimisation as 'anti-social behaviour'. This term obscures the disablist motivation that might lie behind their experiences. Hate crime offers a chance to reflect on the underlying societal and structural discrimination that led to them being targeted. In other words, we focus on the impact of the crime on the victim rather than on the offender and their 'yobbish behaviour'. Therefore, its strength is in its ability to be a banner under which we can gather to discuss the topic and in which we might focus more upon the discrimination which facilitates the violence that disabled people experience.

In terms of the problem of implementation of policy and practice, there are some specific recommendations that would greatly assist victims of disability hate crime. The first is to ensure that they are consulted directly and that disabled people's organisations are at the heart of consultation. The development of policy has been slow to recognise their work and victims need to have a voice through community engagement to ensure policy is workable and will encourage them to report. A second recommendation is that policy recognises issues of intersectionality and complex identity. This can be achieved by listening to what victims report, rather than assuming what has led to their victimisation. Conceptually, we might also move towards 'disablist' rather than 'disability' hate crime. All other forms of hate crime – homophobic and racist, for example, are titled according to the type of prejudice that causes them. The use of 'disability' points to the disability of the victim rather than the prejudice – disablism – of the offender. This might help in understanding the hostility that leads to hate crime.

There are signs that the criminal justice system is attempting to correct their preconceptions about disability hate crime. In March 2010, the CPS issued new guidance which stated that 'the vulnerable situation, within which a disabled person may find themselves, can provide the opportunity for an offender to demonstrate their hostility based on disability' (CPS, 2010: unpaginated). Undoubtedly some crimes are motivated by perceived vulnerability, but instead of seeing this in opposition to hate we need to understand it as being on a spectrum of motivations which might be interconnected. Disabled people are not vulnerable at all times; instead they might be in vulnerable or risky situations. The inclusion of disability within hate crime policy has presented many challenges, but has helped to highlight how no form of victimisation is straightforward – including racist and homophobic violence. It should be used as a chance to reflect on the hate crime policy domain and what it aims to achieve. The way forward is in developing policy with the victim at its centre.

Notes

1 It should be noted that the data provided for prosecutions of racially and religiously aggravated crime is for the four years up to 2009.
2 Interviewees included representatives from the Crown Prosecution Service, Police Service and Association of Chief Police Officers, Home Office. Campaign groups and charities included a range from Mencap, Mind, Action on Elder Abuse, The Monitoring Group, GALOP, Stonewall and many independent lobbyists. A snowballing technique was used, as well as directly seeking key people who were identified as having been involved in hate crime policy formation. These were selected from Parliamentary debates and government documents.
3 The Crime and Disorder Act of 1998 created specific offences for crimes that were racially aggravated and this was extended to include religion under the Anti-Terrorism, Crime and Security Act of 2001.
4 The Race Relations Act of 1965 and the Public Order Act 1986 stipulated that inciting racial hatred and distributing offensive racist materials would be outlawed. The Racial and Religious Hatred Act 2006 amended the Public Order Act 1986 to create a specific offence of stirring up hatred against people on religious grounds, and the Criminal Justice and Immigration Act of 2008 extended incitement provisions to cover homophobic hatred.

References

Association of Chief Police Officers. (2000) *Guide to Identifying and Combating Hate Crime*, London: ACPO.
——(2005) *Hate Crime: Delivering a Quality Service*. London: ACPO.
Balderston, S. & Morgan, T. (2009) *Mapping and Tackling Hate Crime in the North EastEngland*. Equality and Human Rights Commission and Vision Sense, Newcastle.
Berk, R., Boyd, A. and Hamner, K. (1992) 'Thinking More Clearly about Hate-Motivated Crimes', in Herek, G and Berrill, K.(eds) *Hate Crimes: Confronting Violence Against Lesbians and Gay Men,* Newbury Park, California: Sage.
Best, J. (ed.) (1989) *Images of Issues – Typifying Contemporary Social Problems*. New York: Aldine de Gruyter.
BBC (2007) 'Man jailed for urinating on woman', [online: 26 October 2007] at http://news.bbc.co.uk/1/hi/england/tees/7063366.stm. Accessed 27 May 2010.
BBC Online (2009) 'Murder mother's abuse "ignored"', [18 September 2009] at http://news.bbc.co.uk/1/hi/england/leicestershire/8263027.stm. Accessed 27 May 2010.
BBC (2010) 'Man, 64, collapses and dies after "abuse from youths"', [11 March 2010] at http://news.bbc.co.uk/1/hi/england/manchester/8561513.stm. Accessed 27 May 2010.
CPS (2010) *Disability Hate Crime – Guidance on the distinction between vulnerability and hostility in the context of crimes committed against disabled people*, London: Crown Prosecution Service.
——(2009) *Hate Crime Report 2008–9*, London: Crown Prosecution Service.
——(2007a) *Guidance on Prosecuting Disability Hate Crime*, London: Crown Prosecution Service.
——(2007b) *Guidance on Prosecuting Homophobic and Transphobic Crime*, London: Crown Prosecution Service.
——(2007c) 'CPS Launches Policy for prosecuting Disability Hate Crime' press release [27 February 2007] available at http://www.cps.gov.uk/news/pressreleases/archive/2007/114_07.htmldisability. Accessed 11 September 2008.

Cunningham, S. and Drury S. (2002) *Access All Areas. A Guide for Community Safety Partnerships on Working More Effectively with Disabled People.* London: Nacro.

Equality and Human Rights Commission (2009) *Disabled People's Experiences of Targeted Violence and Hostility,* EHRC: London.

——(2011) *Hidden in Plain Sight: Inquiry into Disability Related Harrassment.* London: EHRC.

Finch, E. (2001) *The Criminalisation of Stalking: Constructing the Problem and Evaluating the Solution,* London and Sydney, Cavendish Publishing.

Flynn, M. (2007) *The Murder of Steven Hoskin: A Serious Case Review,* Cornwall Adult Protection Committee.

Gerstenfeld, P. (2004) *Hate Crimes: Causes, Controls, and Controversies,* Sage, USA.

Greenhill, S. and Clarke, N. (2009) '"No excuses" Home Secretary attacks police and council over failures that led to deaths of tormented mother and daughter' *Daily Mail,* [29 September 2009] at http://www.dailymail.co.uk/news/article-1216065/Fiona-Pilkington-How-police-council-left-feral-families-terrorise-mother-disabled-daughter.html. Accessed 10 August 2010.

Hall, N. (2005) *Hate Crime,* Cullompton: Willan.

HM Government (2003) *Statute: Criminal Justice Act* (Part 12, Ch 1), London: TSO.

Iganski, P. (1999) 'Why make "hate" a crime?' *Critical Social Policy* 19 (3): 386–95.

IPCC (2011) 'IPCC report into contact between Fiona Pilkington and Leicestershire Constabulary 2004–7'.

Jenness, V and Grattet, R. (2001a) *Making Hate a Crime – from Social Movement to Law Enforcement,* New York: Russell Sage.

——(2001b) 'The Birth and Maturation of Hate Crime Policy in the United States' *American Behavioural Scientist* 45 (4) 668–96.

Kielinger, V. and Stanko, B. (2002) 'What can we Learn from People's Use of the Police?', in *Hate Crimes,* Criminal Justice Matters 48: 4–5.

Luckasson, R. (1992) 'People with Mental Retardation as Victims of Crime' in Conley, R. W., Luckasson, R. and Bouthilet, G. N. (eds) *The Criminal Justice System and Mental Retardation,* Baltimore: Paul H. Brookes.

Mason, G. (2005a) 'Can You Know a Stranger? Racist and Homophobic Harassment in the United Kingdom', *Current Issues in Criminal Justice* 17 (1): 185–201.

——(2005b) 'Hate Crime and the Image of the Stranger', *British Journal of Criminology* 45 (6): 837–59.

——(2005c) 'Being hated: stranger or familiar?' *Social and Legal Studies: An International Journal* 14 (4): 585–605.

Mason-Bish, H. (2010) 'Future Challenges for Hate Crime Policy – Lessons from the Past', in Chakraborti, N. (ed.) (2010) *Hate Crime: Concepts, policy, future directions,* Willan: London.

——(2008) 'Hate Crime in Great Britain: Examining, Expanding and Exploring a Policy Domain', unpublished PhD thesis.

Mencap (1999) *Living in Fear,* London: Mencap.

——(2009) 'Inquest into Fiona Pilkington and her severely disabled daughter Francecca Hardwick', press release, 29 September 2009.

Miller, P., Parker, S. and Gillinson, S. (2004) *Disablism – How to tackle the Last Prejudice,* London: Demos.

Mind (2007) *Another Assault,* London: Mind.

National Schizophrenic Fellowship (2001) *'Give us a break': exploring harassment of people with mental health problems,* Scotland: NSF.

Novis, A. (2010). *Snap Shot Report of Targeted Hostility Towards Disabled People in UK*. United Kingdom Disabled People's Council; London.

Oliver, M. (1990) *The Politics of Disablement*, Hampshire and London: Macmillan.

Perry, B. (2001) *In the Name of Hate*, London and New York: Routledge.

——(2004) 'The Semantics of Hate', *Journal of Hate Studies* 4: 121–37.

Perry, J. (2008) The 'Perils' of an Identity Politics Approach to the Legal Recognition of Harm, *Liverpool Law Review* 29 (1): 19–36.

——(2002) *Opening the Gateways*, London: Values into Action.

Quarmby, K. (2008) *Getting Away with Murder: Disabled People's Experiences of Hate Crime in the UK*, London: Scope.

——(2011) *Scapegoat: Why we are Failing Disabled People*, London: Portobello.

Ray, L. and Smith, D. (2001) 'Racist Offenders and the Politics of Hate Crime' *Law and Critique* 12 (3): 203–21.

Roulstone, A., Thomas, P., Balderston, S. (2009) 'Hate is a Strong Word: A Critical Policy Analysis of Disability Hate Crime in the British Criminal Justice System', Paper Presented at the Social Policy Association Annual Conference, Edinburgh, July.

Scottish Executive. (2004a) *Working Group on Hate Crime Consultation Paper*, Edinburgh: Scottish Executive.

——(2004b) *Working Group on Hate Crime Report*, Edinburgh: Scottish Executive. September.

Sherry, M. (2000) 'Hate Crimes Against Disabled People' [online] *Social Alternatives* 19 (4). Available at http://www.wwda.org.au/hate.htm. Accessed 5 September 2008.

——(2003) *'Don't Ask,Tell or Respond: Silent Acceptance of Disability Hate Crimes'* [online] available at http://www.farnorthernrc.org/mylifemychoice/Hate%20Crimes-Mark%20Sherry.pdf. Accessed 5 September 2008.

Sobsey, D. (1994) *Violence and abuse in the Lives of people with Disabilities: The end of Silent Acceptance*, Baltimore: Brookes.

Sorenson, D. (2001) 'Hate Crimes Against People with disabilities', presentation script, *Californian Coalition on Crime against People with Disabilities*, 18 May. Available online at http://www.farnorthernrc.org/mylifemychoice/Hate%20Crimes.pdf. Accessed 10 August 2010.

Stanko, E. (2001) 'Re-conceptualising the policing of Hatred: confessions and worrying dilemmas of a consultant' in Moran, Leslie (ed.) (2001) 'Hate crimes: Critical Reflections' Special Edition of *Law and Critique* 12 (13): 309–29.

Walker, P. (2009) Police errors contributed to the suicide of tormented mother Fiona Pilkington. *The Guardian*, 28 September.

Waxman, B. (1991). 'Hatred: The Unacknowledged Dimension in Violence Against Disabled People', *Sexuality and Disability*, 9 (3): 185–99.

Williams, C. (1995) *Invisible Victims: Crime and Abuse Against People With Learning Disabilities*, London : Jessica Kingsley.

2 Vulnerable to misinterpretation

Disabled people, 'vulnerability', hate crime and the fight for legal recognition

Alan Roulstone, Northumbria University, UK and Kim Sadique, De Montfort University, UK

Introduction

Disablist hate crime, violence and harassment have recently begun to receive academic, policy and legal recognition (Crown Prosecution Service, 2006, 2009, 2010; Equality and Human Rights Commission, 2009; 2010; Roulstone, Thomas & Balderston, 2011; Sherry, 2009). However, whilst the more specific notion of hate crime is now well established in the domain of race/ethnicity, religion, sexual orientation and gender identity in Britain (ACPO, 2011; Home Office, 2009), disabled people, as so often is the case, are late in being given statutory recognition in hate crime legislation, guidance and official statistics (compared to the US: Gratett & Jenness, 2001). The phenomenon of disabled people being 'last on the list' for policy attention and intervention is not new (Driedger, 1989). The exact reasons as to why disability, or for our purposes *disablist*, hate crime lags behind other areas is a moot point given that much anti-hate crime activity is relatively recent and largely stems from the Macpherson report (Macpherson, 1999). Much hate crime policy, practice and guidance therefore stems, not surprisingly, from the 'race hate' arena (Garland and Chakraborti, 2009; Iganski, 2008). This only partly explains why disability should take nearly 10 years to get full and almost comparable recognition. For example, hate crime ideas attached to sexual orientation and even transgender identity much earlier than to disability, with articles appearing in the academic literature as early as 1999 (Dittman, 2003; Dunbar, 2006 Herek *et al.*, 1999).

Arguably two other factors need to be borne in mind in an understanding of this 'attention lag'. First, disability is not a uniform, nor an uncontested concept. What on paper might look like two identical impairment profiles could lead one person to identify as disabled, to seek and receive statutory support (and accredited status) as a disabled person under the relevant legislation. Another person with the same objective impairment may categorically reject any disability label (Watson, 2002; Wendell, 1996). In this sense, notions of the boundaries as to who counts as disabled, how disability translates, say from Department of Health to Ministry of Justice definitions, is an important question. Notions of disability as a social construction and being 'in the eye of the beholder' make for yet further policy and practice challenges. However, the British Disability Discrimination Act (1995, as amended) (Gooding, 1995) makes clear that an inclusive definition is most appropriate and errs definitionally on the side of inclusion. By this definition disability takes over 10 million into its purview (Family Resources Survey, 2009). This is in itself a major challenge in applying ideas operationally in the criminal justice system.

However, in reality many of those that are subjected to hate crime (as opposed to incidents) are obviously and visibly disabled or are known by their attackers to have an unseen impairment (*Disability Now*, UKDPC & Scope, 2008). The major challenge, however, and one that has not been adequately documented to date, is the inherent legal contradiction that exists between constructions of hate/hostility *and* vulnerability (Roulstone, Thomas and Balderston, 2011). This, it will be argued, remains a deep and avoidable confusion and potential injustice perpetuated by the legal misunderstanding of hostility and vulnerability as opposites. The unproblematical use of the term 'vulnerable' in an era of rights and personalised choices has led some to critically explore the term (Keywood, 2010; Slater, 2004). Vulnerability is still used uncritically in much legal and criminal justice deliberation. This construction of disabled people as vulnerable has arguably weakened the impetus to introducing hate crime provisions and legal justice for disabled people, rather than strengthened them. This counterintuitive approach has arguably stemmed from a failure of key architects of hate crime guidance and law in listening to disabled people and their organisations as to the fundamental framing of both disability and hate/hostility.

Another possible explanation for the limited attention to disablist hate crime might be that the phenomenon is a rare one and that little attention is warranted. The evidence, however, points to a significant degree of disablist hate crime and hostility affecting a considerable number of disabled people (DRC & Capability Scotland, 2004; Higgins, 2006; Mencap, 2000; Mind, 2007; Quarmby, 2008; Shamash & Hodgkins, 2007). The keynote publication *Getting Away with Murder* (Quarmby, 2008) highlights a catalogue of hate crimes against disabled people, ranging from bullying and verbal abuse through to forms of bodily harm, torture and even murder. Although the term 'hate crime' is contentious, the evidence presented makes clear that disabled people are in some instances being actively targeted for abuse. The report, the findings of which are supported by the Ministry of Justice, details 17 deaths which are clearly attributable to what the author's term disablist 'hate crime'. Officially endorsed figures for 2009 point to 1,400 reported disability-related hate crimes in that year (ACPO, 2009a). In this context it is perhaps surprising that little explicit academic and policy attention has been given to disablist hate crime in Britain, despite a growth in interest in racist and anti-semitic hate crimes (Dixon, 2007; Dunbar, 2006; Garland and Chakraborti, 2009; Iganski, 2008; Levin, 2002).

Although the numbers are unreliable given the confusion as to what counts as a hate crime, only 141 cases of disability 'hate crime' had been successfully prosecuted in the English and Welsh courts by 2007/8 (Crown Prosecution Service, 2009). There is much official acknowledgment of significant under-reporting (ACPO, 2011). Although the British police and Crown Prosecution Service (the body formed to ensure fair, appropriate and consistent pro-secution decisions) have since 2006 taken increased note of disablist hate crime, it is noteworthy that in the case of the police, they prefer to construct the problem as largely impinging on people with mental health problems and learning disabilities (ACPO, 2010:7; See also Department of Health, 2009a: National Policing Improvement Agency, 2010; however, for a more progressive construction, see Home Office and ACPO, 2005). This is a very selective view of disablist hate crime, with one recent challenge to this official perception being the 'fashion' in some parts of Britain for tipping wheelchair users out of their chair or moving them to very dangerous locations against their will:

> An attack by yobs who tipped a disabled man from his wheelchair and kicked him as he lay on the ground has been branded a 'hate crime' by a community leader. The 50-year-old victim was set upon by three youths as he made his way along Charles Street last Wednesday (January 5) at around 7pm. They dragged the man from his wheelchair and threw him onto the ground and then kicked him before running off.
>
> (http://www.therugbyobserver.co.uk/2011/01/13/story-Wheelchair-man,-50,-is-hate crime-victim-32526.html, accessed 22 March 2010)

Experiences documented in Sherry's excellent account of disablist hate crime in the USA and UK add further evidence that disabled victims form a wide group in impairment terms and do not sit neatly with state and federal/national definitions of disability and vulnerability (Sherry, 2010).

A key factor in limiting prosecutions is the legal construction of disability hate crime and notions of hate/hostility in opposition to notions of targeted vulnerability that lie at the centre of the criminal justice guidance on disablist hate crime. To date, English law constructs hate crime as distinct from crimes targeted at those perceived to be 'vulnerable'. By definition if a crime is estab-lished to be motivated by perceived vulnerability then potential for establishing hate/hostility as a motivation for crimes against disabled people is severely reduced. Arguably, such constructions operate with stereotyped and untested notions of both 'hate' and 'vulnerability'. Indeed, as currently constructed, 'hate' and 'vulnerability' are implicitly formulated as opposites and cannot co-exist in the motivational repertoire of those who commit crimes against disabled people. This lack of clarity and indeed muddle as to both hate/hostility and perceived vulnerability need addressing if disabled people are to be afforded the protections they deserve. As with many areas of disability policy, pre-existing ableist constructions create inbuilt constraints on the enabling potential of disability-related guidance and legislation. In this vein, an urgent policy and practice review is now required to ensure disabled people gain the fullest protection of the law and that where hate crimes occur that they are accounted for in official statistics.

The legislative position

Hate crime against disabled people received its first official recognition in England with the provisions set out in Section 146 of the Criminal Justice Act (henceforth CJA) (HM Government, 2003: 54). Section 146 of the CJA affords an increased use of the 'tariff' where hate motivation can be established in a crime against a disabled person. This then, in strictly legal terms, strengthens the sentencing provisions attached to primary offences which are seen to be motivated by hate (Iganski, 2008). However, unlike race hate and religious hatred, no discrete new offences have been created, but simply the scope to add to the tariff attached to an offence where hate has formed part of the motivation for the crime and can be evidenced from judicial procedure. This might point to hierarchies of credibility attaching to certain forms of hate crime and the inadvertent positioning of disability as invisible where other excluded identities are foregrounded. Such a conscious development of hierarchies of credibility and worth is unlikely, indeed implausible. A better interpretation is that disability hate crime is constructed as less clear cut in jurisprudence (legal theory/conceptualisation) terms. Whatever the jurisprudential niceties, this categorical approach risks ignoring or downplaying the significance of intersectionality in understanding disablism, racism and homophobia (Vaughns and Eibach, 2008) as some hate crimes are motivated by a number of perceived differences. Indeed for key hate crime writers it is the categorical negative treatment of difference that lies at the heart of hate crimes (Levin, 2002).

One key challenge, then, in the area of disablist hate crimes attaches to wider constructions of disabled people as 'vulnerable' compared to say black, gay/lesbian and transgender victims. This unhelpfully ensures that safeguarding and adult-protection measures often take precedence over criminal justice responses where disabled identities are constructed as vulnerable. This risks denying many disabled people the right to be taken seriously in the criminal justice system, as having the fullest range of legal protections and rights (Perry, 2008). Interestingly, such 'safeguarding' approaches have been driven by learning-disability services, which in emphasising vulnerability serve to play down individuals' rights to independent living and full judicial rights. Such approaches also overlook the fact that people with a range of physical and intellectual impairments are victims of disablist hate crimes (DoH, 2000; 2007; 2009a; 2010). The risk of repeat offences is arguably made greater where social care rather than criminal justice agencies predominate in alleged hate crime/incident reporting.

Defining hate crime

In seeking to explore the current challenges and contradictions in disablist hate crime guidance and policy it is important to first explore definitions of hate crime as they apply to disabled people. The English Crown Prosecution Service (CPS) definition at the heart of their 'Guidance on Prosecuting Cases of Disability Hate Crime' establishes that hate crime is defined as:

> Any incident which is perceived to be based upon prejudice towards or hatred of the victim because of their disability or so perceived by the victim or any other person.
>
> (Crown Prosecution Service, 2006: 7)

This looks promising at first sight, its emphasis upon the perception of the victim of hate crime counting in the deliberations as to whether a primary offence reaches the threshold required in law that establishes that disability related hate crime has taken place. Other terms are in use, but less commonly so, for example the UK Equality and Human Rights Commission have used the terms 'motivated crime' and 'targeted crimes' to describe hate crime (Equality and Human Rights Commission, 2009). This is an interesting linguistic shift and may have greater legislative value in going beyond the terms hate and hostility. Hate 'crimes' and 'incidents' have more recently been separated to afford a better sense of the continuum of hate-motivated activity against disabled people. This also ensures that hate crimes and incidents are more easily distinguished in operational terms and that neither is overstretched, nor misapplied. One key issue that remains is that the CPS has to date refused to archive the term hate in their guidance. This is regrettable given the linguistic difficulties of reaching this threshold in case investigations. More recently, the CPS and Ministry of Justice have shifted their guidance and policy to operate with the term hostility in practice rather than hate:

> If someone pleads or is found guilty of a crime against you, and the court is satisfied that the crime was motivated by *hostility* because of your disability, then the court must treat this *hostility* as something that makes the offence more serious.
>
> (Crown Prosecution Service, 2010: 2)

This arguably does not move debates on further as it remains a unidimensional explanation of disability-related prejudice and simply the choice of a slightly less emotive term than hate (ODI, 2009). If hate is seen as being as strong a term in operational responses to such alleged crimes, why does it remain in continued use as the headline terminology in CPS and ACPO guidance (Association of Chief Police Officers, 2011; Crown Prosecution Service, 2010)? A useful shorthand that captures the public imagination – possibly. However, disabled people's organisations are increasingly sceptical about the term 'in use' as it were (Roulstone and Thomas, 2009). What terms are adopted else-where? In the USA, the term 'Bias Crime' attaches to what in Britain we dub hate crime (Centre for Criminal Justice Policy Research, 2000; Lawrence, 1999). The less-used term 'hate-motivated crime' also appears in the US literature (Craig, 2002). However, although hate crime policies have a longer heritage in the US, disablist hate crimes also appeared much later than other forms of officially acknowledged hate crimes (Jacobs and Potter, 1998). In England and Wales, however, even the more institutionally accepted term, racist hate crime, which predates by 20 years discussion of disablist hate crime, still had less than 6,000 convictions in 2007/2008 and less than a 1-in-35 incident to conviction rate (Gadd, 2009), which may point to wider difficulties with the term hate and hate crime.

Interpreting and constructing disablist hate crime

The strict interpretation of hate crime is provided by Section 146 of the Criminal Justice Act of 2003. This section makes provision for additional sentencing powers and use of the tariff for penalties where hate crime has been established against disabled people. As noted earlier, this does not create a primary offence, unlike sections 29 and 32 of the Crime and Disorder Act 1998 relating to racial or religious hatred. More simply, a sentencing provision is provided for aggravation of a primary offence. Section 146 then:

> imposed a duty upon courts to increase the sentence for any offence aggravated by hostility based on the victim's disability (or presumed disability).

> (HM Government, 2003: 54)

Here, the establishing of aggravation due to disability-related hostility must be treated as more serious than an incident where such factors are absent. An offender has to have either:

> Demonstrated disability related hostility ... or
>   Be seen to have displayed hostility based wholly or partly on a motivation particular to a person's disability [sic]

> (Ibid: 54)

Either point (a) or (b) can satisfy the legislation that disablist 'hate crime' has been established in law. For example, where hostility has been established through words or actions, there is no requirement for hate crime to be established through motivation. It is perhaps odd that having established the powers that attach to disablist hate crime responses, blanket exceptions come in to play where crimes are seen to be motivated not by hatred but by the perceived 'vulnerability' of a disabled person. Whilst safeguards are clearly required, it is concerning that vulnerability should weaken disabled people's right to legal redress, especially where institutional practices have helped cement notions of difference and where their categorical status is seen to weaken rather than strengthen such rights:

> However, not all crimes against disabled people are disability hate crimes. Some crimes are committed because the offender regards the disabled person as being vulnerable and not because the offender dislikes or hates disabled people.
>
> (Crown Prosecution Service, 2006: 9)

This then begs the question as to just what the motivations and perceptions are that do attach to aggravated crimes against disabled people? Indeed, does hostility not get closer to notions of bias, discrimination and differential treatment that are used effectively in the wider British legal system? Also, does vulnerability not point to a similar set of dynamics to discrimination? Unless we take the view that vulnerability, pity, tragedy are all benign assumptions about disability which are very different to discrimination, prejudice, hostility and hate, then we begin to question the edifice on which disablist 'hate crime' policy and law are built. Similarly, the notion of vulnerability, although not unique to disability, can be seen as categorically more pernicious when used in certain criminal justice policy debates. For example, if we assume that vulnerability in the criminal justice context is akin to saying someone was 'asking for it', or more generously was not as protected from crime as non-disabled people, it seems unjust to blame the individual. For example, there is a clear difference between arguing that an insufficiently protected house prone to burglary is equivalent to a blind person negotiating a quiet subway after dark. The imperative is to support community safety in such publically defined spaces.

Vulnerable to misinterpretation

The construction of categorical exclusions from disablist hate crime remedies based on notions of vulnerable adults is a serious concern. The notion of vulnerability has received critical attention in the disability studies literature. Primary concerns attach to whether vulnerability is a condition inherent to a given individual or whether a product of relationships and the production of vulnerable situations and failed protections on the part of mainstream ableist society (Roulstone, Thomas & Balderston, 2011; Sherry, 2009). Roulstone recently concluded that whilst some may be vulnerable in a range of contexts due to the severity of a profound impairment, it would be quite erroneous to extrapolate from this assertion to all disabled adults (Roulstone, 2009). Indeed to argue that vulnerability inheres in disabled people is to potentially blame disabled people for any attacks or nuisance that non-disabled people can protect against. We could also say that target hardening has not taken place following crime-prevention thinking as people are the source of a crime problem. This in essence is an inadvertent ableist extension of categorical and negative treatment which hate crime policy is supposed to be fighting against. At a policy level within the Department of Health, the 'Safeguarding Adults with Learning Disabilities: Information for Partnership Boards' provides insights to aid hate crime and incident minimisation and appropriate protection protocols (Department of Health, 2007). Here are some excerpts taken from the guidance:

> Ensuring that support workers and service managers know how to contact health and social care practitioners and make referrals, ensuring that individuals receive the support they need.
>
> When planning residential placements it is important to consider carefully who will be living together. Attending to issues of compatibility and ensuring residents are not at risk of being bullied, exploited or harmed by their peers is an important aspect of helping people stay safe.
>
> Helping people to learn about how to get in touch with self-advocacy groups or carers support groups. Helping people to access such groups can enable individuals to develop the skills and confidence to better protect themselves or their relatives.

What is interesting is that the safeguarding provisions assume institutional or managed packages of support as the baseline of disability status and of support. To put it bluntly, to gain protection or redress, one has to enter or seek to enter the social care and safeguarding system. This is some distance from the reality of much disablist hate crime that takes place in the mainstream of life, away from institutional and family contexts. In this sense, protection protocols are essentially being applied to those with the most significant impairments. Not only do most disabled people never come into contact with official care and protection agencies but also would 'run a proverbial mile' from such agencies where possible given the increasingly critical perceptions of both institutions and care professionals (Swain, French & Cameron, 2003).

The Protection of Vulnerable Adults Scheme (POVA) was established in Part 7 of the Care Standards Act (HM Government, 2000). Evidence from one key disablist hate crime study (Balderston and Morgan, 2009) points to these Safeguarding boards inadvertently perpetuating unhelpful constructions of vulnerability in their work, which may inadvertently exacerbate notions that perceptions of vulnerability form the basis of much criminal behaviour towards disabled people. A recent study by the Office for Public Management pointed to concerns that hate crime safeguarding interventions could well be viewed as risking disabled people losing, rather than gaining, independence (Office for Public Management, 2009). Rather than becoming a less-used term, 'vulnerable' has increasingly entered the lexicon of adult social care, with the expression 'vulnerable adults' often overshadowing the previously dominant term 'disabled adults' (Pritchard, 2008). The construction of vulnerability in relation to impairment is complicated within the field of disability policy. Notions of 'vulnerability' grate on the sensibilities of analysts committed to the social model of disability since the very admission of this status contradicts central tenets of equality. As a term, 'vulnerable' has connotations of weakness and is generally applied by members of a powerful majority to oppressed groups. There is arguably something inherently paternalistic in the act of designating another as 'vulnerable'. Public agencies which invoke this term may also fail to meet their substantive Disability Equality Duty to prevent harassment and promote equality.

The Serious Case Review following the deaths of Fiona Pilkington and her daughter Francecca Hardwick clearly demonstrates the unhelpful constructions of vulnerability held by the criminal justice and social care sectors. The Serious Case Review (SCR 2008) notes, 'This was a household consisting of individuals with varying degrees of vulnerability. Individual vulnerability was compounded by exposure to much anti-social behaviour'. Failure to put in place multi-agency procedures in this case was based on the problematic definition of vulnerability set out in the No Secrets (2000) safeguarding vulnerable adults guidance. Under these guidelines any multi-agency referral would have been seen as a request for services rather than as a safeguarding matter. This 'identified' vulnerability did not translate into an appropriate reaction as they were not deemed vulnerable enough, and therefore the response to this family was fragmented and piecemeal. The SCR (2008) further mentions that the police categorised most of the reported incidents in this case as grade 2 & 3 (grade 2 being where the person involved is in extreme distress or deemed to be *extremely* vulnerable) (emphasis added). However, the incidents were nonetheless recorded as anti-social behaviour, and the failure to gauge the level of hate/hostility and categorise these incidents as hate crime prevented a robust response and provision of appropriate support for Fiona & her daughter (SCR, 2008). These conflicting constructions lead to a grave misinterpretation of the levels of vulnerability and hate/hostility, which had a significant and detrimental impact on the risk assessment in this case.

Despite being couched in the language of human rights, the protection frameworks work on an assumption of a trade-off that protection would involve a person falling under the purview of a whole array of statutory authorities. The 'No Secrets' guidance (Department of Health, 2000) is an example of this. Deriving from a concern over institutional abuse, the guidance makes clear the inter-agency role in reducing the risk and ameliorating the effect of various forms of abuse:

> This document gives guidance to local agencies who have a responsibility to investigate and take action when a vulnerable adult is believed to be suffering abuse. It offers a structure and content for the development of local inter-agency policies, procedures and joint protocols which will draw on good practice nationally and locally. Coherent strategies should be developed, in all areas of the country, by all the statutory, voluntary and private agencies that work with vulnerable adults.
>
> (Department of Health, 2000: 7)

We can see from the above that to be classified as vulnerable creates a whole organisational identity that in reality is better able to respond to abuse than to prevent it. Local mainstream social dynamics, attitudes and behaviour are arguably not that susceptible to this organisational scrutiny. These ideas seem borne of an age before mainstreaming and personalisation of choices in disabled people's lives were asserted in policy (Department of Health, 2009b, 2009c). This is not to argue that these provisions are not important – they clearly can be for the most vulnerable – but community safety, civil dynamics and responsive services without recourse to vulnerability categorisation are what count for most disabled people (NACRO, 2002). Once again, it is worth restating that the assumption is that disability is equated in the guidance with learning disability or mental health problems, as the following suggests:

> ACPO recognises that people with mental ill health and learning disability experience an increased risk of being victims of crime. Police officers and staff are often the gateway to appropriate care and other services and therefore must be able to recognise and provide appropriate support to people with mental health difficulties.
>
> (ACPO, 2010: 7)

Hate and vulnerability revisited

As stated above, a key concern of this paper is to unpack the assumptions that lie behind criminal justice policy constructions of disability, hate, hostility and vulnerability. A recent study undertaken by one of the authors of this chapter noted that in practice much more complex disablist interpretations and motivations may be at work in hate crime:

> For many disabled people it makes no difference if our attackers think we are abominations who are unworthy of life, think that killing us is an act of kindness, or simply think they will get away with it because we are disabled people. The motives may be different but the fear is the same and the reason seems to be the same, we are different.
>
> (Roulstone and Thomas, 2009)

The above quotation highlights the inadequacy of current oppositions contained in established definitions between hate/hostility and vulnerability. Nowhere in disabled people's viewpoints here can a motivational clarity be discerned, or indeed separated. It is clear there is in fact a much more complex and challenging interplay of ideas of hate, hostility, prejudice, aesthetic shock, ontological or existential unease (Hughes, 2007), othering and at times opportunism based on perceived vulnerability. Indeed, contrary to oppositional notions of 'hostility' and 'vulnerability', the above quitation suggests perceptions of vulnerability and categorical treatment of difference may well sit together as the basis of opportunistic crimes on those perceived least likely to fight back or resist crime (See also Calderbank, 2000). Another quotation actually confronts ideas that disablist hate crimes cannot be equated with perceived vulnerability:

> [Disability hate crime is] when they know who to pick on and they pick on us because they think we will not fight back. They do it for the fun of it because of the way we are. We are not strong. People gang up on us. Some learning disabled people are frightened of getting on the bus. School kids call us names. Kids don't understand the situation a person is in. It becomes a hate crime when we heard them say they did it because we are disabled people. They do it when they are playing on us being disabled people.
>
> (Roulstone and Thomas, 2009)

The case details of many of the most disturbing allegations of hate crime point out that in practice the construction of disabled people as vulnerable is being interpreted by offenders and the criminal justice system alike in their actions against disabled people. In the Brent Martin case one offender made clear, 'I am not going down for a muppet.' This categorical and profoundly harmful construction of difference sat at the heart of their actions, and the offender's refusal to countenance going to jail for killing a mere disabled person (or 'muppet'). This was clearly a construction of vulnerability and an example of hate/hostility against a category in the same way as prejudice and ill treatment against any marginalised group through history.

In terms of criminal justice responses to cases of disablist hate crime, the evidence is just as unsettling. In the Brent Martin case no hate crime aggravation was instigated, and the case was not treated as a hate crime. This was mirrored in the Pilkington case. Police records identify the 32 incidents reported by Fiona Pilkington as anti-social behaviour. Yet as mentioned earlier, the police believed many of the incident reports reflected extreme distress or vulnerability on the part of Fiona Pilkington. The police management report for the SCR noted that it may have been more appropriate to have categorised these incidents as hate crimes. In the case of Donna Smith, a young woman who was a wheelchair user with a severe speech impediment, police responses highlighted a serious failure to follow practice guidance set out in 'Speaking Up for Justice' (Home Office, 1998) and 'Vulnerable Witnesses: A Police Service Guide' (Home Office, 2002). Donna experienced hate incidents/crimes over a period of months, which included robbery, burglary and verbal abuse and harassment. Following an incident where her handbag was stolen, she was asked to type up her own statement 'because of communication barriers with the police' (Pitt, 2009). The guidance set out in the above documents places a responsibility on criminal justice professionals to facilitate equal access to justice and equal treatment for those witnesses identified as vulnerable or at risk of being intimidated, but whilst vulnerability and hate/hostility continue to be variably defined this will not be achievable. These are clearly counterintuitive interpretations of hate/hostility and vulnerability, which dampen official responses and further 'dis-enable' victims of disablist hate crime.

Ken MacDonald QC, Director of Public Prosecution (2003–2008), in his speech in 2008 on prosecuting disability hate crime, stated that 'Hostility and vulnerability are not mutually exclusive':

> [an] inappropriate focus on vulnerability risks enhancing an already negative image of disabled people as inherently 'weak', 'easy targets' and 'dependent' requiring society's protection. Instead focus ought to be on enforcing the victims' rights to justice and scrutinising the offender's behaviour, prejudices and hostility so that the case is properly investigated and prosecuted for what it is.
>
> (CPS, 2010)

Conclusions

This paper has explored the key challenge of disabled people and criminal justice policy and professionals developing a shared understanding and language of 'hate crime' against disabled people. There is evidence from the above that presently this lack of understanding could severely limit disabled people's human rights in being afforded a safe, secure public space. Notions of vulnerability are still being used to negate claims of disablist hate crimes. The targeting of disabled people for hate crime needs further research and statutory bodies need to gain a better understanding of the context of discrimination in which disabled people live, by working with disabled people themselves in policymaking and appointing more disabled people into the criminal justice system and public life. The recent call for a review of the tariff for aggravated murder when applied to disablist hate crimes suggests that disability may begin to be recognised for a mandatory minimum life sentence to mirror provisions under Section 21 of the Criminal Justice Act on race and religious aggravated murders (HM Government, 2009:25). The mandated review of 'No Secrets' (DoH, 2000) and 'In Safe Hands' to build in disablist hate crime issues is a promising development (HM Government, 2009). Similarly, the emphasis in the Single Equality Bill and its Guidance on preventing hate crime against disabled people is also welcome (HM Government, 2009), although the extent to which that can be coordinated at ground level is questionable, especially in an era of public financial austerity where underlying inequality is unlikely to be addressed. The development of a cross-governmental Hate Crime Action Plan is also very welcome in seeking to join up departmental and frontline coordination in reducing hate crime in all key equality strands (ACPO, 2009b; Home Office, 2009). The extent to which preventive and partnership approaches to disablist hate crime can remain core business for criminal justice and social care organisations is an open question at this point – especially as major police reports point to their involvement in abuse issues due to the retraction of other social services (National Policing

Improvement Agency, 2009). In particular, the issue of vulnerability needs to be addressed; that disabled people may be targeted because of perceived vulnerability rather than a motivation of hatred should not lead to a reduction in response from the criminal justice system. There seems to be little, if any, well-funded, preventative work in this area of hate crime against disabled people.

References

ACPO (2009a) Total of Recorded Hate Crime from Regional Forces in England, Wales and Northern Ireland During the Calender Year 2009. Available at http://www.acpo. police.uk/asp/policies/Data/084a_Recorded_Hate_Crime_-_January_to_December_ 2009.pdf (accessed 22 March 2011).

——(2009b) ACPO Comment on Hate Crime Action Plan. http://www.cjp.org.uk/news/ archive/acpo-comment-on-hate crime-action-plan-14-09-09/ (accessed 27 January 2010).

——(2010) Response to the Equality and Human Rights Commission Call for Evidence. Available at http://www.acpo.police.uk/documents/edhr/2010/201010EDHREHR01. pdf (accessed 23 March 11).

——(2011) Statement By Professor John Grieve, Chairman of the Government's Hate Crime Advisory Group. Available at http://www.acpo.presscentre.com/Press-Releases/ Hate crime-data-published-for-the-first-time-a4.aspx (accessed 22 March 2011).

Balderston, S. & Morgan, T. (2009) *Mapping and Tackling Hate Crime in the North East England*. Equality and Human Rights Commission and Vision Sense, Newcastle. Unpublished Report.

Centre for Criminal Justice Policy Research (2000) *Hate Crime Statistical Report*. CCJPR, Boston.

Craig, K. M. (2002) 'Examining Hate Motivated Aggression'. In Perry, B., *Hate and Bias Crime*. Routledge, London.

Crown Prosecution Service (2006) *Guidance on Prosecuting Cases of Disability Hate Crime*. CPS, London.

——(2009) *Hate Crime Report*. London: HMSO.

——(2010) 'Disability Hate Crime: Guidance on the distinction between vulnerability and hostility in the context of crimes committed against disabled people (Annex A)'. CPS, London. Available at http://www.cps.gov.uk/legal/d_to_g/disability_hate_crime_/ #a04 (accessed 1 May 2011).

——(2010) *Policy for Prosecuting Cases of Disability Hate Crime*. CPS, London.

Department of Health (2000) *No secrets: Guidance on developing and implementing multi-agency policies and procedures to protect vulnerable adults from abuse*. Department of Health, London.

——(2007) *Safeguarding Adults with Learning Disabilities: Information for Partnership Boards*. Department of Health, London.

——(2009a) *Improving Health-Supporting Justice: The National Delivery Plan of the Health and Criminal Justice Board*. London: DoH.

——, (2009b) *Disability and Delivering Adult Social Care*, London, Department of Health. http://www.dh.gov.uk/en/SocialCare/Deliveringadultsocialcare/Disability/index.htm (accessed 14 February 2009).

——(2009c) *Putting People First: Personalisation Toolkit*. Department of Health, London.

——(2010) *Vetting and Barring Scheme Guidance*. Department of Health: London.

Disability Rights Commission and Capability Scotland (2004) *Hate Crime Against Disabled People in Scotland: A Survey Report*. DRC, Edinburgh.

Dittman, R. (2003) 'Policing Hate Crime: From Victim to Challenger: A Transgendered Perspective'. *Probation Journal*, Vol. 50, No. 3, 282–288.

Dixon, L. (2007) 'Current Issues and Debates in Race Hate Crime'. *Probation Journal*. Vol. 54 No. 3 pp. 109–24.

Driedger, D. (1989) *The Last Civil Rights Movement*. St Martin's Press, New York.

Dunbar, E. (2006) 'Race, Gender and Sexual Orientation in Hate Crime Victimisation: Identity Politics or Identity Risk?' *Violence and Victims*. Vol. 21, No. 3 pp. 323–37.

Equality and Human Rights Commission (2009) *Disabled People's Experiences of Targeted Violence and Hostility*. Office for Public Management, London.

——(2010) *Inquiry into Disability Related Harassment: Consultation Document*. Available at http://www.equalityhumanrights.com/legal-and-policy/inquiries-and-assessments/inquiry-into-disability-related-harassment/.

Gadd, D. (2009) 'Aggravating Racism and Elusive Motivation'. British Journal Of Criminology 49 pp. 755–771.

Garland, J. & Chakraborti, N. (2009) *Hate Crime: Impact, Causes and Responses*. Sage, London.

Gooding, C. (1995) *Disabling Laws, Enabling Acts*. Pluto, London.

Herek, G., Gillis, J. R., Cogan, J. C. (1999) 'Psychological Sequelae of Hate Crime Victimization Among Lesbian, Gay, and Bisexual Adults'. *Journal of Consulting in Clinical Psychology*. Available at http://psychology.ucdavis.edu/Rainbow/html/violence_pre.PDF.

Higgins, K. (2006) 'Some Victims Less Equal Than Others'. *SCOLAG Journal*, Autumn.

HM Government (2000) 'Statute: Care Standards Act 2003'. TSO, London.

——(2003) 'Statute: Criminal Justice Act 2003'. TSO, London.

——(2009) 'Single Equality Bill'. Available at http://services.parliament.uk/bills/2008–09/equality/documents.html.

Home Office & Association of Chief Police Officers (2002) *Vulnerable Witnesses: A Police Service Guide*. Home Office & ACPO, London.

——(2005) *Hate Crime: Delivering A Quality Service: Good Practice and Tactical Guidance*. Home Office & ACPO, London.

Home Office (1998) 'Speaking up for Justice: Report on the Interdepartmental Working Group on the Treatment of Vulnerable or Intimidated Witnesses in the Criminal Justice System'. Home Office, London.

——(2009) *The Cross-Government Hate Crime Action Plan*. Home Office, London.

Hughes, B. (2007) 'Being Disabled: Towards a Critical Social Ontology for Disability Studies'. *Disability & Society* Vol. 22, no. 7 pp. 673–84.

Iganski, P. (2008) *Hate Crime and the City*. Policy Press, Bristol.

Jacobs, J. B. and Potter, K. (1998) *Hate Crimes, Criminal Law and Identity Politics*. Oxford University Press, Oxford and New York.

Keywood, K. (2010) 'Vulnerable Adults, Mental Capacity and Social Care Refusal'. *Medical Law Review*. Vol. 18, no. 1 pp. 103–110.

Lawrence, F. M. (1999) *Bias Crimes: Punishing Hate Under American Law*. Harvard University Press, Harvard.

Levin, J. (2002) *Hate Crimes Revisited: America's War Against Those Who Are Different*. *Northeastern University Press, Boston*.

Macpherson, W. (1999) *The Stephen Lawrence Enquiry Report*. Report of an Inquiry by Sir William Macpherson of Cluny Presented to Parliament by the Home Secretary. CM 4262–1. HMSO, London.

Mencap (2000) *Living in Fear*. Mencap, London.

MIND (2007) *Another Assault*. Mind, London.

NACRO (2002) Access All Areas. A guide for Community Safety Partnerships on working more effectively with disabled people. http://www.nacro.org.uk/data/files/ nacro-2004120261-429.pdf. Accessed 3 October 2009.

National Policing Improvement Agency (2010) *Responding to People with Mental Ill Health or Learning Disabilities*. NPIA for the Association of Chief Police Officers and Department of Health. Available at http://www.npia.police.uk/en/docs/Mental_ill_ Health.pdf. Accessed 22 March 2011.

ODI (2009) 'Proceedings of the Office for Disability Issues Evidence Day'. London, ODI, 19 November.

Office of Public Management (2009) *Disabled People's Experiences of Targeted Violence and Hostility: Research Report for the Equality and Human Rights Commission*. Office for Public Management, London.

Perry, J. (2008) 'The Perils of an Identity Politics Approach to the Legal Recognition of Harm'. *Liverpool Law Review*, Vol. 29, No.1.

Pitt, V. (2009) 'Joint working call to tackle disability hate crime'. Communitycare.co. uk (16 October 2009) http://communitycare.co.uk/Articles/2009/10/16/112886/hate crime-action-plan-comes-under-fire.htm (accessed 30 April 2011).

Pritchard, J. (ed.) (2008) *Good Practice with Vulnerable Adults*. Jessica Kingsley, London.

Purdie-Vaughns, V. & Eibach, R. P. (2008) 'Intersectional Invisibility: The Distinctive Advantages and Disadvantages of Muliple Subordinate Group Identities'. Sex Roles, Vol. 59: No 5/6, pp. 377–91.

Quarmby, K. (2008) *Getting Away with Murder: Disabled people's experiences of hate crime in the UK*. Report for *Disability Now*, UK Disabled People's Council and SCOPE, London.

Roulstone, A. & Thomas, P. (2009) *Hate Crime and Disabled People*. Equality and Human Rights Commission and Breakthrough UK, Manchester. Unpublished Report.

Roulstone, A. and Morgan, H. (2009) 'Neo-Liberal Individualism or Taking Control? Are We All Speaking The Same Language on Modernising Adult Social Care?' *Social Policy and Society*. Vol. 8 pp. 333–45.

Roulstone, A. (2010) Review of Mark Sherry's 'Disability Hate Crimes: Does Anyone Really Hate Disabled People?' Ashgate, Farnham. In *Disability and Society* Vol. 24, No. 2 pp. 245–52.

Royal College of Psychiatrists (2002) *Acute In Patient Psychiatric Care for Young People with Severe Mental Illness*. RCP, London.

Shamash, M. and Hodgkins, S. L. (2007) *Disability Hate Crime Report*. Report for Disability Information Training Opportunity. DITO, London.

Sherry, M. (2010) *Disability Hate Crimes: Does Anyone Really Hate Disabled People?* Ashgate, Farnham.

Watson, N. (2002) 'I well I know this is going to sound strange, but I don't see myself as disabled'. *Disability and Society* Vol. 17, no. 5 pp. 509–27.

Wendell, S. (1996) *The Rejected Body: Feminist Philosophical Reflections on Disability*. Routledge, New York.

3 The wrong war?

Critically examining the 'fight against disability hate crime'

Joanna Perry

The 'battle' against 'disability hate crime' has been moving up the media and criminal justice agendas in Britain. Disability activism around the issue has been effective and strong (Disability Hate Crime Network, 2011) and there have been key policy successes since the implementation of 'disability hate crime' legislation in 2005 (ACPO 2005; CPS 2007) (Criminal Justice Act 2003. s 146(2)). Several high-profile and very serious cases of violence against disabled people have led the Equality and Human Rights Commission to hold an inquiry into whether and how public authorities have discharged their statutory duty to eliminate disability-related harassment (EHRC 2011).

This chapter uses insights from Galtung's typology of violence to critically examine 'disability hate crime' as a description and prescription for violence against disabled people. In addition, the approach of the EHRC inquiry into disability-related harassment will be assessed in the light of this theoretical analysis. Theoretical insights can also support a healthy interrogation of the hate crime concept itself. To recall a Tupac Shakur lyric – 'Instead of a war on poverty, they got a war on drugs so the police can bother me' – is the war against 'hate' the right war? Where do poverty and other structural problems feature in the fight against violence?

What is 'hate crime'?

As pointed out by Ray and Smith, 'the definition of hate crime is subject to a process of contestation and negotiation rather than being pre-given' (Ray and Smith, 2001, p. 211). While Britain, the US and other countries have passed a proliferation of 'hate crime laws', Iganski points out that 'hate crime' goes beyond the legal sphere, and is an area of policy, activism and scholarship as well as law (Iganski, 2008). Jenness's work focuses on how the 'hate crime canon' has been produced at the interface between social movements and the legislature, thus shaping which groups are 'protected' – and which aren't: 'The inclusion of state hate crime provisions in law is, in the first instance, an outgrowth of social movement mobilization, the presence of interest groups in the dynamics of law making' (Grattet & Jenness, 2001, p. 679). Barbara Perry's work describes the unique dynamic and impact of hate crimes: 'hate crime is about the assertion of the offender's own identity and belongingness over and above others – in short it is about power' (Perry, B. 2005, p. 125). 'Hate crime' can also be described as both a description of and a remedy for targeted, bigoted violence (Perry, J. 2008).

The hate crime concept has strongly shaped criminal justice policy and law in Britain. A clear legal framework recognises hate crime based on the following 'strands': race, religion, sexual orientation and disability (Crime and Disorder Act 1998, Section 28, as amended by the Anti-Terrorism, Crime and Security Act 2001, Powers of Criminal Courts (sentencing) Act 2000, Section 153; Criminal Justice Act 2003, Sections 145 and 146) and is underpinned by a comprehensive policy framework that adds gender identity as a hate crime category, an established shared definition of hate crime used across criminal justice agencies, specific policies relating to what victims and witnesses of hate crime can expect from the criminal justice system and published statistics of reported and prosecuted hate crimes (ACPO 2005; CPS 2001,2007a,2007b; 2008; 2010).

Internationally, the hate crime model has been enacted to varying degrees and in different forms, although there is little published data presenting the detail of international approaches in this area. *Hate Crimes in the OSCE Region – Incidents and Responses*, published by the Organisation for Security and Cooperation in Europe, is one of the few international reports containing figures for reported hate crimes and information about data-collection practices reported by governments across the OSCE region. In addition, the report contains incidents reported by non-governmental organisations (NGOs), which help provide further context to the phenomenon, especially in countries where no incidents of hate crime have been reported by the participating State. In 2010, 13 of the 56 participating States of the Organisation for Security and Cooperation in Europe reported that they collect data on disability hate crime offences. In comparison, 35 out of the 39 States that contributed to the findings of the final report reported that they collect data on hate crimes based on bias against ethnicity (OSCE, 2010, p. 19).

However, only two countries actually provided data on disability hate crime incidents for the 2010 report. These were the UK and Germany, with 1,569 and 20 incidents respectively. In addition, an NGO reported the murder of Jennifer Daugherty, a woman with learning difficulties who was 'held captive for 36 hours, during which time she had been forced to drink detergent, spices and urine, and was bound up with Christmas decorations'. She was stabbed and beaten to death with a towel rack. The report states, 'during the trial … one of the suspects was reported to have testified, "we knew her brain didn't work as well as everyone else's" and "we thought it was funny to make fun of her"' (OSCE, 2010, p. 84). As we have seen throughout this book, Jennifer's murder echoes a tragic and very disturbing pattern of violence that is experienced by many disabled people across society.

It is clear from this short review of available data that disability hate crime is seriously underreported internationally. Of course the relatively high number of incidents reported in the UK does not begin to reflect the prevalence of this type of violence. However, it does reflect a growing commitment in the UK by key agencies, with essential support from activists and NGOs, to develop an understanding of the prevalence of disability hate crime and to improve the confidence of disabled people who are victims to come forward and report what has happened to them.

In Britain, there have been specific legal and policy advances in relation to disability hate crime. Section 146 of the Criminal Justice Act 2003 gives the court the power to pass enhanced sentences where it can be proven that a crime was motivated by hostility towards real or perceived disability; or hostility was demonstrated immediately before, during or after an offence was committed. The criminal justice system has adopted a shared definition of disability hate crime: 'Any criminal offence which is perceived by the victim or any other person, to be motivated by a hostility or prejudice based on a person's disability or perceived disability' (CPS, 2007). The Crown Prosecution Service (CPS) developed its disability hate crime policy and performance framework in 2007, and the volume of hate crimes coming through from the police to the CPS for prosecution has increased year on year (CPS 2010). In addition, leaders within the criminal justice system, most notably Sir Ken Macdonald, Director of Public Prosecutions from 2003 to 2008, have also helped bring violence against disabled people out of the social policy ghetto by powerfully and unequivocally acknowledging the reality of disability hate crime and the responsibility of the criminal justice system to tackle it (CPS 2008).

The case at the level of policy has been made, and despite continued and significant barriers, progress is moving slowly in the right direction. There is, of course, a long way to go before the policy advances described above make a real impact on the ground. To give just one indicator of the journey that remains: the unsuccessful rate of disability hate crime prosecutions is still stubbornly high, at 24 per cent compared to 18 per cent for racist and religious hate crime, and the volume of cases charged by the CPS remains relatively low, at 506, compared with racist and religious hate crime at 9,214 (CPS 2010, p. 38).

It has been established that disabled people are victims of serious and widespread violence. Sin *et al.* (2009) have provided the most comprehensive review of the literature, as well as the most in-depth qualitative research into the issue to date, and found a broad spectrum of violence endured by disabled people on a daily basis. Katharine Quarmby's forensic investigation of several high-profile and extremely serious cases shares previously unexposed details of the circumstances of these individuals' lives and, very sadly, their deaths (2011).

The BBC documentary *Tormented Lives,* presented by Rosa Monckton, follows the struggles of several disabled individuals, and in some cases their families, who are targets of persistent harassment and violence (BBC 2010). In one scene, Christopher, a man with a dry sense of humour, a love of music, and a talent for computers, is showing Rosa his scars. A severe burn on his leg that required a skin graft, a head injury from a man who punched him, leaving a dent in his forehead from his rings, lost teeth from being stomped on the face by a man wearing Doc Martens, while asking him, 'What it is like to be a retard?'. Christopher needs to bring money with him every time he leaves the house to give to people who hassle him on the street. He is literally battle scarred; not because he has picked a fight, but because a battle is being waged against him.

In this context, the urgency of recognising much of the violence for what it is – hate crime, where it is the offender's hostility and bigotry that is the focus of investigation, prosecution and punishment – is important and justified. At the same time, however, the deep-rooted inequality, which makes people in these situations so vulnerable to this continuous hostility, must also be understood and addressed. It seems timely to examine what the hate crime model captures, and, importantly, misses when it comes to the most effective strategy to vanquish the pervasive violence that disabled people face.

Why theorise disability hate crime?

The fight against hate crime takes place at the grass roots of activism, policymaking and equality politics. It is a fast-paced world and gains speed with every publicised violent act. In this context, using theoretical approaches to interrogate current thinking and action in disability hate crime might appear too late, too high-level and, frankly, inaccessible. An immediate question that could fairly be asked by people concerned about hate crime is: What has 'theory' got to do with it? How's it going to help us in the fight?

In his classic work on violence, Johan Galtung points out that developing theoretical frameworks helps, 'indicate ... significant dimensions of violence that can lead thinking, research and, potentially, action, towards the most *important* problems' (emphasis added) (1969, p.168). Climbing a few steps above the grass roots of politics and activism, and past the tiers of law and policy, helps identify the connecting thread of action needed to dismantle those structures that produce and reproduce inequalities.

A model of 'violence'

While it is not possible to do justice to Johan Galtung's 'violence typology', with all of its facets and implications, his approach provides specific theoretical insights into what the most significant problems of violence affecting disabled people are, and how effective the hate crime model is in tackling them.

Galtung makes the following definitional points: 'Peace is an absence of violence' (1969, p. 168) and 'violence is present when human beings are being influenced so that their actual somatic and mental realizations are below their potential realizations' (ibid.). He explains what he means by the difference between the 'potential' and the 'actual' in the following way:

> Violence is that which increases the distance between the potential and the actual, and that which impedes the decrease of this distance. Thus, if a person died from tuberculosis in the eighteenth century it would be

hard to conceive of this as violence since it might have been quite una-voidable, but if he dies from it today, despite all the medical resources in the world, then violence is present according to our definition.

(Ibid.)

This point is illustrated by the evidenced disparities between the health status and life expectancy of people with learning difficulties compared to the general population in Britain. A recent investigation conducted by the then Disability Rights Commission found that people with learning difficulties are more likely to experience major illness, to develop serious health conditions at an earlier age, and are less likely to receive proper treatment or offered pre-ventative services than others (DRC, 2006). Mencap revealed the harrowing individual cost of this reality in its report *Death by Indifference* (Mencap, 2007), which details the deaths of six people with learning difficulties, con-cluding that they were avoidable and were caused, in part, by institutional discrimination. The report includes the story of Mark, a man who was admitted to hospital with a broken leg and died eight and a half weeks after the operation. The inability of hospital staff to meet his communication needs led to a failure to give him a blood transfusion, and his epileptic medication. Towards the end of his stay in hospital he acquired septicaemia and finally died of multiple organ failure. The report powerfully puts the question to the authorities concerned: 'How was it possible for someone to go into hospital with a leg injury and die? (2007, p. 9)'

Galtung defines the concept of 'structural violence': 'violence is built into the structure and shows up as unequal power, and consequently as unequal life chances'. As a group, disabled people enjoy significantly less economic and cultural power in our society (Sin, 2009; Quarmby, 2011, PMSU, 2009). Despite policies targeted at improving social inclusion (DoH, 2001; 2009) in 2007 only 29 per cent of disabled people had a job, compared with 76 per cent of nondisabled people (DWP, 2006). Social attitudes towards disabled people are relatively negative. For example, the British Social Attitudes Survey found, 'Eight out of ten respondents said they would be very or fairly com-fortable being in a club or team with someone with a mental health condition and nine out of ten with a person with a learning disability' (Office for Disability Issues, 2009, p. 10). A report by the Prime Ministers Strategy Unit into the 'life chances' of disabled people found 'The extent of the disadvantage is especially acute for some specific groups ... People with learning difficulties face particularly poor outcomes' (2005, p. 34). Thus *inequality* and *discrimination* are conceptualised as significant dimensions and problems of *violence*. This insight helps us to consider how these types of 'structural violence' are connected to other types, such as hate crime, and vice versa.

Galtung provides descriptions and distinctions between the 'direct' or 'per-sonal', and 'indirect' or 'structural' dimensions of violence. Direct violence takes place, 'where there is an actor that commits the violence', as compared with structural or 'indirect' violence, where there is no such actor (1969, p.

170). In addition, direct or personal violence is usually intended, in contrast to structural or indirect violence, the blame for which can rarely be traced to a single actor. Direct, or personal violence, Galtung explains,

> represents change and dynamism – not only ripples on waves, but waves on otherwise tranquil waters. Structural violence is silent, it does not show – it is essentially static, it is the tranquil waters.
>
> (1969, p. 173)

Importantly, Galtung's typology, hate crime, can be characterised as direct, personal and intended. However, Galtung identifies a risk here: 'ethical systems directed against intended violence will easily fail to capture structural violence in their nets – and may hence be catching the small fry and letting the big fish loose' (1969, p. 172).

Indeed, hate crime policies, laws and activism are concerned with criminal violence and focused on criminal justice solutions. As such they are mainly and necessarily skewed towards the investigation, prosecuting and punishment of the proven intentions of offenders who have committed single incidents of direct, personal violence, rather than aiming to remedy any underpinning structural inequality.

Letting the big fish loose?

Other commentators have expressed concern with decoupling approaches that address targeted violence from wider struggles against discrimination. Maroney points out:

> It is possible to support anti-hate crime measures without supporting the more controversial and resource-heavy demands of disenfranchised groups for equality in housing, education, wealth and sexual freedoms. Doing so allows government authorities to condemn the most extreme manifestations of prejudice without committing to eradication of ... more pervasive forms.
>
> (Maloney quoted in Macphail, 2003, p. 276;
> see also Jacobs and Potter, 1998)

The importance of establishing connections between acts of hate crime and power inequalities has also been established by Barbara Perry (2001). As she points out, 'hate crime ... must be understood as [a] mechanism by which deeply ingrained sets of power relationships are maintained' (2001, p. 97). Perry also describes these power relationships as 'almost invisible', echoing Galtung's 'still waters' description.

Recalling the example of Christopher above, he has applied for many jobs, and, despite his qualifications in computer-related studies and obvious skills, he has been rejected. He has been placed in sheltered accommodation in a deprived area of Hastings in a house, where the majority of his neighbours are much older people. The structures that keep him 'in his place', limiting his chances to achieve his potential, are the still waters in which he is a victim of regular direct violence. This picture is replicated across the world, and from this perspective it is clear that a purely criminal justice approach to tackling 'violence' will necessarily only capture a certain type. As such, winning the argument on hate crime and even securing high-profile, successful prosecutions is merely a battle, which must be connected to wider struggles.

However, Galtung points out that dealing with direct violence is still as important as addressing structural violence. He takes us a step forward by providing a framework that firmly situates hate crime as an issue of equality and tells us that the most important problems of this type of direct violence most probably most affect those with the least power and who are subjected to structural violence, or, in other words, broader, non-criminal discrimination. It seems to follow that the hate crime model could have a lot to offer as a methodology for connecting the dimension of direct violence with pervasive discrimination at the level of policy, community engagement and activism. Following this analysis, an important dimension of violence, worthy of action, could be described as: criminal violence that is committed in the context of discrimination and, specifically, 'disability hate crime' committed in the context of disability discrimination.

Equally, Galtung's model helps us further analyse the nature of the still waters of discrimination that define the treatment of and barriers faced by disabled people in relation to the criminal justice system as a whole, not just as victims of hate crime. It is established that disabled people and people with learning difficulties and/or mental health problems in particular are over-represented as suspects, defendants and prisoners (Mind 2007; Talbot 2009; Jacobson, 2008). At the same time, they are less likely to receive the necessary support from the criminal justice system to give evidence in court and help bring offences to justice. Thus Galtung's conceptualisation of 'violence' connects the diverse realities of disabled victims, witnesses, suspects, defendants and prisoners. Even while the characteristics of their experiences vary, the remedy of removing structural violence and discrimination is the same. Policies, laws and activism need to address the situation of disabled people in the round, not just from one policy perspective or another; without this, approaches are too narrowly drawn and will almost certainly miss the 'big fish'.

Crime committed in the still waters of discrimination

In practical terms, it follows that approaches to tackling 'violence' in the context of discrimination should be underpinned by both robust criminal as well as anti-discrimination laws, policies and activism. Section 146 of the CJA and related policies provide the framework to robustly mark the 'hate' element inherent in the direct violence of disability hate crime. Disability discrimination laws provide the framework for state agencies to assess and redress their impact in terms of victims, suspects and offenders (and staff).

This approach has been taken in relation to race in the UK, where Section 95 of the Criminal Justice Act 1991 requires the publication of annual statistics on race and the criminal justice system, detailing the representation of minority ethnic groups as victims, defendants, suspects and staff. Thus information about the direct violence of racist hate crime is presented in the context of evidence of the structural violence of discrimination (high rates of stop and search, higher imprisonment rates, lower satisfaction rates of victims and witnesses from ethnic minority backgrounds, and so on) experienced by ethnic minorities from other perspectives, providing a legal and policy model to connect and effectively address several aspects of direct and structural violence (MoJ, 2009).

Current developments

On 3 December 2009, the Equality and Human Rights Commission (EHRC) announced its intention to conduct a formal inquiry into the actions of public authorities to eliminate disability-related harassment and its causes. The inquiry is ongoing at the time of writing and due to report in September 2011. Its terms of reference are wide ranging and its methodology inclusive. Disabled people have been involved directly in its design and research and the EHRC team has heard from hundreds of people, including some of the most senior leaders in the criminal justice system.

Examining the inquiry from the perspective of Galtung's model, important points emerge. First, it focuses on the environment in which direct violence occurs, defining disability-related harassment as: 'unwanted, exploitative or abusive conduct that has the purpose or *effect* of violating the dignity, safety, security or autonomy of the person experiencing it, or creating an intimidating, hostile, degrading or offensive environment'. Second, it focuses on the actions, and importantly the lack of actions, of a wide range of public authorities far beyond the criminal justice system. Both of these points suggest a strong interest in getting to the structural aspects of violence that create the conditions for harassment to occur. In line with Galtung's model, the Commission is strengthening the net and keeping its eye on 'the big fish'. It may be this nuanced focus on direct violence in the context of structural violence is as a result of the Commission's own legal framework that is defined by anti-discrimination as opposed to criminal law.

The challenge for the EHRC will be to follow through on its commendably ambitious agenda, in the context of significant cuts to its resources. The issues it wants to address cut across a range of policy areas, including criminal justice, health, housing, transport and education, which have historically struggled to connect conceptually, let alone linguistically.

Further, it is submitted, the Commission should be even more ambitious in its approach and identify policy interventions, similar to the Section 95 requirements in relation to race, so that the experiences of inequality faced by disabled victims, witnesses, defendants, suspects and prisoners are clearly set out, connected and understood. Only then will the thread of action needed to be taken in order to achieve Galtung's and Tupac's peace be discerned.

From disability to disablist hate crime

The hate crime model has the power to connect direct, personal and intended violence with structural violence. In this sense, the term 'disablist', as opposed to 'disability hate crime', is most apt. Each incident of criminal, targeted hostility against a disabled person is inextricably connected with the historical oppression and current discrimination they face(d). It clarifies the role of the agencies of the state: to investigate, to prosecute and to apply the law equally to disabled victims and witnesses; to recognise the particular harm that discrimination commits: that of keeping people 'in their place'; in fear and at higher risk of experiencing violence.

A note about the 'mate crime' concept

A term being increasingly used in the context of disability hate crime is 'mate crime', which can be loosely described as the process by which someone purports to be a friend and then goes on to steal, assault and attack their 'mate', who is often a person with learning difficulties. This term is problematic. While the term 'disablist' hate crime anchors the direct violence of criminal, bias-motivated acts to the pervasive problem of discrimination and is also one that has been fully accepted by the criminal justice system at the policy level, the term 'mate crime' fails on both counts. Putting the focus on what is 'going on' between two people, it suggests an equality of power and agency that is, of course, absent. It is likely to be regarded with bewilderment by the criminal justice system, which has already been slow to get to grips with the hate crime concept and disability hate crime in particular.

Considering the drive behind the recognition of disability hate crime is to raise awareness among victims, their families, the criminal justice system and society about the hostility that disabled people face, and to obtain successful prosecution using section 146, this seems to be terminology that could take us in the wrong direction.

That is not to say that the behaviour that the term 'mate crime' aims to describe is not important. Befriending and grooming happen to people with learning difficulties; and this behaviour is an important dimension of hostility in disability hate crime cases. However, it is these terms that should be used in place of 'mate crime' because they better reflect what is really going on. 'Grooming', and '*be*friending', include an active component that focuses on the action of the offender, clearly situating the blame for the act and consequence of violence on him. It is part of the human condition to experience loneliness at times and to misjudge relationships and friendships. Terms that make it a 'peculiarity' of one group of disabled people should be avoided.

Conclusions

'Disablist hate crime' provides an important and legitimate description and prescription for particular types of direct violence against disabled people that should continue to be pursued by activists, policymakers, legislatures, law enforcement and the courts.

Our 'war' should also be waged against structural violence if Galtung's and TuPac's peace is to be achieved. To recall the words of a respondent to one of the very few studies of violence against disabled people: 'Money protects. For example, taxis, nicer environments, more choice about where you live. Living alone on a council estate might make you more vulnerable to abuse, for example being "befriended" by an abuser' (EHRC 2010, p. 6). The structural violence of disproportionate relative poverty experienced by disabled people as a group must be addressed.

The EHRC inquiry's broad approach to violence against disabled people seems methodologically sound and theoretically robust. The test will be whether it has the resources and can secure the political will to implement its recommendations, which will inevitably span a number of significant policy areas. Finally, it should go even further and suggest strong frameworks that connect a range of evidence of discrimination and violence experience by disabled people so that it can be understood and robustly addressed.

Bibliography

Berthoud, R. 2006 *The employment rates of disabled people, research report no. 298* Department for Work and Pensions, London, viewed 8 October, http://research.dwp. gov.uk/asd/asd5/report_abstracts/rr_abstracts/rra_298.asp.

Crown Prosecution Service 2007a, *Policy for Prosecuting Cases of Disability Hate Crime*, viewed 8 October 2011, http://www.cps.gov.uk/publications/prosecution/ disability.html.

——2007b, *Policy for Prosecuting Cases of Homophobic and Transphobic Hate Crime*, viewed 8 October 2011, http://www.cps.gov.uk/publications/prosecution/homophobia. html.

——2008a, *Policy for Prosecuting Cases of Racially and Religiously Aggravated Offences*, viewed 8 October 2011, CPS.http://www.cps.gov.uk/publications/prosecution/ rrpbcrbook.html.

——2010, *Annual Hate Crime and Crimes Against Older People Report*, viewed 8 October 2011, http://www.cps.gov.uk/publications/equality.

Department of Health 2001, *Valuing people,* Department of Health, London, viewed 8 October 2001, http://www.dh.gov.uk/en/Publicationsandstatistics/Publications/Pub licationsPolicyAndGuidance/DH_4009153.

——2009, *Valuing People Now,* Department of Health, London, viewed 8 October 2011, http://www.dh.gov.uk/en/Publicationsandstatistics/Publications/PublicationsPolicyAnd Guidance/DH_093377.

Disability Rights Commission 2006, *Equal treatment: Closing the Gap, A formal investigation into physical health inequalities experienced by people with learning disabilities and/or mental health problems.* Disability Rights Commission, London, viewed 8 October 2011, http://www.scie-socialcareonline.org.uk/profile.asp?guid=A146 A83A-4589-4074-827E-05A8C2BB7F5E.

EHRC 2010, *Promoting the Safety and Security of Disabled People*, EHRC, London, viewed 8 October 2011, http://www.equalityhumanrights.com/uploaded_files/research/ promoting_safety_and_security_of_disabled_people.pdf.

Grattett R. & Jenness V. 2001, 'Examining the Boundaries of Hate Crime Law: Disabilities and the "Dilemma of Difference"', *The Journal of Criminal Law and Criminology* Vol. 91(3), pp. 653–697.

Iganski, P. 2008, *Hate Crime and the City*. Bristol: Policy Press.

Jacobs, J. & Potter, K. 1998, *Hate Crimes: Criminal Law and Identity Politics*, Oxford University Press, Oxford.

Jacobson, J. 2009, *No One Knows: Vulnerable defendants in the criminal courts*, Prison Reform Trust, viewed 8 October, http://www.prisonreformtrust.org.uk/Publications/ vw/1/ItemID/89.

MacPhail, B. A. 2003, 'Gender-Bias Hate Crime: a review' in B. Perry (ed.), *Hate and Bias Crime: a Reader*, Routledge, pp. 261–279.

Mencap 2007, *Death By Indifference*, Mencap, London.

Mind 2007, *Another Assault*, Mind, London, viewed 8 October 2011, http://www. mind.org.uk/campaigns_and_issues/report_and_resources/894_another_assault.

Ministry of Justice 2009, *Statistics on Race and the Criminal Justice System 2008/09 A Ministry of Justice publication under Section 95 of the Criminal Justice Act 1991*, Ministry of Justice, London, viewed 8 October 2011, www.justice.gov.uk/downloads/ publications/statistics-and-data/mojstats/stats-race-and-the-criminal-justice-system- 2008-09c1.pdf.

Office for Disability Issues (2009), *Public Perceptions of Disabled People*, Department for Work and Pensions, viewed on 8 October, 2011, odi.dwp.gov.uk/docs/res/ppdp/ ppdp.pdf.

Perry, B. 2001, In the Name of Hate. Routledge, New York.

Perry, B. 2003, 'Accounting for Hate Crime: Doing Difference' in B Perry (ed), *Hate and Bias Crime: a Reader*, Routledge, London, pp. 101–107.

Perry, B. 2005, 'A crime by any other name: the semantics of "hate"', vol. 4, no. 1, pp. 121–37.

Perry, J. 2008, 'The "Perils" of an Identity Politics Approach to the Legal Recognition of Harm', Liverpool Law Review vol. 29, pp. 9–36.

Prime Minister's Strategy Unit 2005, Improving the life chances of disabled people, London, Prime Minister's Strategy Unit 2005, viewed 8 October 2011, *http:// webarchive.nationalarchives.gov.uk/+/http://www.cabinetoffice.gov.uk/strategy/work_ areas/disability.aspx.*

Quarmby, K. 2011, *Scapegoat: why we are failing disabled people*, Portobello Books, London.

Ray, L., and D. Smith 2001, 'Racist offenders and the politics of "hate crime"', *Law and Critique*, vol. 12, pp. 203–221.

Sin C. H., Hedges A., Cook C., Mguni N. & Comber N. 2009, *Disabled People's Experiences of Targeted Violence and Hostility*. Office for Public Management for the Equality and Human Rights Commission, London, viewed on 8 October 2011, http:// equalityhumanrights.com/key-projects/good-relations/safety-and-security-for-disabled- people/summary-of-the-research-findings.

Talbot, J. 2008, *No One Knows: Prisoners' Voices*, Prison Reform Trust, London, viewed 8 October, http://www.prisonreformtrust.org.uk/Publications/vw/1/ItemID/89.

Films

BBC 19 October 2010, *Tormented Lives*, viewed 8 October 2011, http://www.youtube.com/watch?v=xPsdtu1uIEE.

Speeches

Sir Ken Macdonald 2008, *Prosecuting Disability Hate Crime*, viewed 8 October 2011, http://www.cps.gov.uk/news/articles/dhc_dpp_speech.

4 Disability and the continuum of violence

Andrea Hollomotz, Manchester Metropolitan University, UK

A legacy of oppression

Throughout history, philosophers, scientists and medical professionals advocated for the differential treatment of disabled people. For instance, the practice of infanticide dates back to antiquity. In classical Greece people with learning difficulties were kept as slaves and fools by the aristocracy (Stainton 1994, cited in Parmenter, 2001: 269). Closer to our times, in the early decades of the twentieth century, the eugenics movement became concerned with a perceived 'drastic increase' of impairments amongst the population (Braddock & Parish, 2001). Eugenicists advocated the view that people with learning difficulties might reproduce 'excessively', threatening the national heritage of intelligence.

Many countries, such as the USA, Canada, Sweden and France, introduced sterilisation laws to reduce alleged 'gene depletion' and wider social risk (Parmenter, 2001). In the UK, population control was exercised by means of segregation in residential institutions, which was legally enacted by the 1913 Mental Deficiency Act (Weeks, 1989). Such 'total institutions' are characterised by barriers to social intercourse with the outside world, such as locked doors, high walls and barbed wire (Goffman, 1961). There is an immense imbalance of power between inmates and staff, who tend to express their superiority by harsh treatment of the inmates, whom they perceive to be less than human (Ryan & Thomas, 1987). Furthermore, the Nazi project included a strong eugenicist ideology to rid the 'Aryan race' of genetic 'deficiencies' (Burleigh, 1991).

In the last quarter of the twentieth century the way in which services were provided to disabled people in England and other advanced industrial societies changed from institutionally based to predominantly community-based provisions (Parmenter, 2001). Changes in provisions for people with learning difficulties were influenced by the 'normalisation' principle, which aims to make 'conditions of everyday life which are as close as possible to the norms and patterns of the mainstream of society' available to people with learning difficulties (Nirje, 1994 [1969], p. 19). Wolfensberger (2004 [1983]: 43) argued that 'the most explicit and highest goal of normalisation must be the creation, support, and defence of *valued social roles* for people who are at risk of social devaluation'. In order to achieve this aim the social image and competencies of individuals should be enhanced. This approach consequently focuses on changing the individual.

Within the last decade, UK government thinking has shifted from the broad aim of assimilation to a new vision. The White Paper *Valuing People* (Department of Health, 2001) and the *Valuing People Now* delivery plans (e.g. Department of Health, 2010a) are underpinned by the principles that the rights, choices and independence of people with learning difficulties must be promoted. Moreover, the Coalition Agreement (HM Government, 2010: 30) states that 'the government believes that people needing care deserve to be treated with dignity and respect'. In publishing its *Vision for Health and Social Care* (Department of Health, 2010b) the Government further outlines its plans for personalisation. Thus, they are adamant that individuals, not institutions, should take control of the support they need. Meanwhile, the *Equality and Human Rights Commission* (2011) continues to enforce and promote equality across nine 'protected' grounds, which include disability.

Yet, despite such apparent progress, this chapter demonstrates that patterns of ill-treatment, including oppression, disablism, violations of human rights, threats, intimidation and power imbalances, remain ingrained in the everyday lives of many disabled people. The discussion so far indicates that such contemporary experiences have their roots in disablist attitudes that arise from a legacy of oppression (Barnes, 1997). This chapter will outline how categorical treatment of disabled people continues beneath the thin veneer of rights discourses. The notion of a continuum of violence will be introduced to contextualise how intrusive processes that are not commonly viewed as harmful are linked to more severe acts of violence. The discussion draws on case studies of adults with learning difficulties, but broader observations can be made about the experiences of disabled people in general.

Violence on a continuum

We commonly use the term 'abuse' to describe violence against disabled adults (Saxton, 2009), older adults (Teaster & Anetzberger, 2010) and young people (Firth, 2009), but 'violence' to describe the experiences of non-disabled adults (Dutton, 2006). This differing terminology emphasizes the perceived differences between individuals who are accredited with adult social status (Priestley, 2003) and those who are not. This chapter therefore adopts the term 'violence' to offset this inconsistency. Carol Thomas (2007: 72) describes the 'intended or unintended "hurtful" words and social actions of non-disabled people' towards disabled people as psycho-emotional disablism. She argues that this can have profound effects, 'impacting negatively on self-esteem, personal confidence and ontological security'. This approach is equally applicable to some of the processes outlined in this chapter, as is Pam Thomas' concept of 'mate crime' (see her chapter in this volume). However, for the purpose of this chapter, the reader is invited to think of differential and derogatory treatment of disabled people as violence on a continuum.

The notion of a continuum was first suggested by Kelly (1988) in respect to gendered violence. She argues that men routinely control women and that contact violence is used only when other methods of control have failed. The threat of rape and the fact that it happens to some women create a climate of fear. According to Kelly (1988) all men benefit from this and thus benefit from the fact that some men rape women. However, it has been argued that such a broad use of 'violence' is inappropriate and that it should be reserved for physical coercions or their threat (Jacobs *et al.*, 2000). According to the *Oxford English Dictionary*, the term violence should be limited to describing 'behaviour involving physical force intended to hurt, damage, or kill' (OED online, 2011). Kelly (1988), however, asserts that we need to pay more attention to the language we use and to make the difference between emancipatory and 'common-sense' definitions apparent. A propensity for violence against disabled people continues to be 'ingrained in the relationships, institutions and cultural acts of our time' (Goodley & Runswick-Cole, 2011: 614). Violence should therefore not be understood as singular acts of physical or sexual assault. Those are merely more severe expressions of bigotry on a spectrum of routine intrusions.

In this chapter the term violence therefore refers to any restrictions that breach a person's rights under the *Human Rights Act* (HMSO, 1998), such as segregation, any acts of bigotry or derogatory treatment, such as dismissing what a person has to say, as well as contact incidents of violence, such as physical and sexual assaults. In line with Kelly's (1988) suggestion, these processes can be seen to be forming a continuum, as illustrated in Figure 4.1. (This is an adapted version of a figure which first appeared in Hollomotz, 2011.)

The reader should note that this continuum is not hierarchical. That means that it does not intend to indicate that, for example, not being listened to has a less damaging impact than name calling. One act is perhaps likely to be more frequently perpetrated than the other. Categories, furthermore, overlap and some facets on the continuum will occur simultaneously. In fact, the more facets occur at once, the more likely it is that contact acts of violence ensue. The notion of a continuum seeks to draw attention to the fact that boundaries between incidents of mundane intrusions, derogatory treatment and violence are blurred, which can make it difficult for an individual to

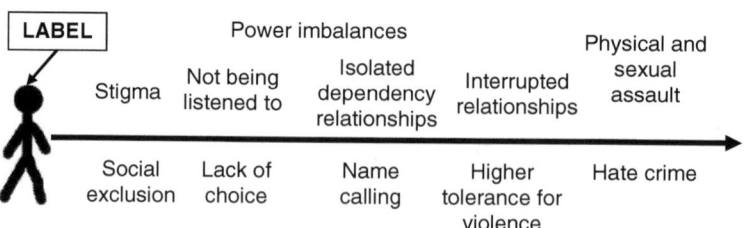

Figure 4.1 A continuum of violence

distinguish that which is seen to be 'acceptable' as part of the everyday from that which is seen, even by others and the law, as an act of violence.

Hate crime is the only facet on the continuum that is not explicitly discussed in this chapter. However, it is often made up of several features that appear on the continuum. For instance, perpetrators of hate crime assert power over their targets. They often use hate speech and disregard the target's pleas to stop the attack. Hate crime is at times allowed to continue, because victims are not sufficiently supported (Chakraborti & Garland, 2009). The purpose of this chapter is to highlight that, given the daily experiences of many disabled people, hate crime is not an extraordinary occurrence. Instead, it arises from prejudice that is deeply engrained in the fabric of society (Levin & Nolan, 2010).

This chapter will use case studies to illuminate how the continuum works in practice. Semi-structured interviews were conducted with 12 men and 17 women with learning difficulties. With the exception of one person with South Asian heritage, all of the participants were White British. Respondents were between 22 and 68 years old. They had labels of 'mild' to 'moderate' learning difficulties. About half of the respondents had additional impairment labels, such as physical impairments, epilepsy and 'Autistic spectrum' labels. Furthermore, half lived with their parents or other family members. About a quarter lived in residential group settings and another quarter lived on their own or with a partner. These figures are roughly representative for the accommodation arrangements for this population (Emerson & Hatton, 2008).

Becoming a subject with 'special' needs

The subsequent three sections will illustrate how facets on the continuum shape the lives of disabled people. Here, the focus is on labelling, segregation, restrictions to choices and barriers to maintaining important relationships. Emma (early 30s; all names used in this chapter are pseudonyms) had an impairment all her life, but she only became *disabled* when she was labelled and when services began to 'help'. Illich (1977: 11) claims that 'disabling professionals' may impose their services on individuals who do not want them. This appears to be the case here. Previously, she had been living independently with a partner and their two children. Nowadays Emma, who has lost custody of her children, lives in a residential group setting. Her care plan states that she needs support with many things she had managed independently before, such as shopping. Emma states:

> It upsets me cause I want to be like a normal, normal person [...] without having a carer or help [...]. I just wanna do it myself. [...] I'm still doing the same things as before, but ehm ... now I'm having help with it and I just ... it ... I just don't like. I, I don't like it cause it upset, like, cause, people are helping me and I wanna do it myself.

Britney (early 20s) used to live in her own flat with some support. However, four years ago a group of 'friends' threatened to harm her in a dispute over her reluctance to engage in illegal activities. Amongst other things, they wanted to store stolen goods in her flat and they attempted to engage Britney in their activities. This is not an uncommon experience. As Emerson *et al.* (2001) have pointed out, individuals in semi-sheltered accommodation are at greater risk of exploitation from people in their local community than those living in 24-hour residential services.

This is precisely why Britney was moved to a more controlled environment. She now lives in a large institutional complex and shares a unit with 14 residents, all of whom are at least 20, and some 40, years older than her. However, Britney believes that her current residential setting is not meeting her needs: 'It's not the right place for me. I'm too independent and it's the wrong age limit. They don't do fun stuff like we [young people] do.' Britney's 'protection' by segregation contradicts *Valuing People* (Department of Health, 2001, 2010a). It could be conceptualised as a form of violation, as it contradicts an individual's rights to 'full and effective participation and inclusion in society', 'equality of opportunity' and 'accessibility' (United Nations, 2006 (Article 3 (c, e, f), 19)).

Lack of choice in everyday life, both in respect to mundane issues and more significant decisions, such as that described by Britney, is a restriction that affected many respondents. This is perhaps surprising, given the current choice-based policy rhetoric in the UK (Department of Health, 2001, 2010a). This study found that such rhetoric was often used to present people with a pre-arranged 'menu of choices' (Hollomotz, under review). For instance, all of the women interviewed described how they opened their wardrobe every morning and selected the clothes they were going to wear by themselves (wardrobe: items on the 'menu'). Yet when it came to determining which clothes they would find whilst clothes shopping, the women had less control (shop: options beyond a pre-agreed 'menu'). Only five of the thirteen women who lived with family members or in residential services were able to choose whatever clothes they liked, even when others disagreed with this choice.

Clothes choices are an important way of expressing who we are and how we would like others to see us, and also when it comes to expressing a sexual identity (Gleeson & Frith, 2004). It was this sexual identity that others seemed to be eager to control. As Martha (early 30s) reports: 'If it's too – showing all your ... breast off. She won't let me have ... a top.' Similar accounts were noted over a decade earlier in McCarthy's (1998) study. For the respondents in this study, not much has changed since then. Making such an apparently mundane decision independently and seeing through the consequences (e.g. having to realise the purchase was a bad choice after all) is important practice at self-determination. As Hingsburger (1995) asserts, only those who practice decision-making in respect to mundane issues will feel confident enough to speak up about 'big' decisions, such as deciding whether they should speak up against derogatory treatment. Yet individuals in this study were often acutely aware of the boundaries beyond which they cannot exercise control. Some were eager to remain within these. Ryan (late 20s) asserts: 'I've always tried pleasing people in my life, cause that's with my difficulty, that's what I've always thought I've had to do.' This mindset leaves Ryan open to exploitation. Martha's clothes choices may initially appear trivial, but this interaction can be said to socialise her towards obedience.

Friendships can counteract such imbalances. They give an opportunity for social inclusion, as friends often share similar concerns or situations. Yet less than a third of the respondents (8 of 29) were able to meet up informally with friends. Participants of all ages told me about friends they had at school, but in most cases contact ceased as soon as they left. Gemma (early 20s) explains: 'I don't see them anymore. Now I moved on, you see. ... I still love them.' This breakdown of relationships is surprising compared to the experiences of non-disabled people, who mostly sustain some of their friendships from school into adulthood (Adams & Allan, 1998). Maintaining contact could be easily facilitated for many respondents, as most remained living in the same area as their friends. However, most of them had not socialised informally while they were at school and they did not take this up once they left. Due to limited opportunities to develop and maintain friendships, many people with learning difficulties rely on relationships with support workers to fulfil some of their social and emotional needs. This potentially increases dependency, which makes these relationships easily exploitable. In the following it is outlined how individuals' concerns are at times dismissed, something that would be less likely to happen amongst friends.

Disregarded incidents

Gemma told me that she was unhappy about attending one of her weekly activity groups at the day centre, because a woman in the group kept verbally assaulting her. We spoke to Gemma's key worker about this. However, the key worker was already aware of these issues. She reminded Gemma that she likes the group activity and that she should 'simply ignore' the woman. She could not be persuaded to change Gemma's group or indeed to talk to the woman who was upsetting her. When Gemma turned her back to us the key worker rolled her eyes at me. Later on she described Gemma as a 'drama queen'. Terms like 'drama queen' or 'challenging' were applied to a range of individuals in this study. This is potentially dangerous, as these labels may prevent individuals from being listened to and thus from accessing the support they require to protect themselves from harm. Some individuals may furthermore begin to display 'challenging' behaviour as a result of violent experiences (Hingsburger, 1995). Noting changes in behaviour and questioning their causes should therefore be an imperative aspect of adult protection work. The reaction by Gemma's key worker was not exceptional. Peter (late 50s) describes the following incident, perpetrated by another user of his day service, which took place during an arts and crafts activity group:

> He was teasing with his scissors. He says: 'I will cut your hair!' And then he came one time and put the point of the scissors in the back of my head […] And then you just, you just say: […] 'You've been warned. Stop it!' 'Why, would I go to prison?' I says: 'You did that outside.' I says: 'You would.' I said: 'If you did anything like that to anybody in [city centre] or round where you live', […] I says: 'They wouldn't put up with it!'

Peter implies that people who attend day centres have fewer rights to protection from threats of violence than people 'outside'. When Peter reported the incident he was told that the man who threatened him 'cannot help it'. As in Gemma's case, staff asked Peter to ignore the behaviour. Peter's observations mirror research findings of increased levels of violence within service settings (Strand *et al.*, 2004) and findings of some level of tolerance for violence amongst staff, who will weigh up whether they perceive an occurrence to be a 'serious' incident before reporting (Jenkins *et al.*, 2008). However, intimidating or violent behaviour should never be tolerated, even when it is perpetrated by a person with learning difficulties, as they, too, have a responsibility not to physically, emotionally or sexually hurt others (Cambridge, 1996). Furthermore, despite the drive to community inclusion (Department of Health, 2001, 2010a, 2010b), the conceptualisation of life 'in here' and 'outside' expressed by Peter bears resemblance to the 'total institution' (Goffman, 1961). Although the day centre is based in the community and not sectioned off by barbed wire, different rules apply within. These continue to perpetuate the divisions between disabled and non-disabled people (Barnes, 1990).

Crossing the line

Thus far the discussion considered case studies that are not commonly viewed as 'violence'. However, there is a thin line between mundane experiences of oppression and contact violence. In fact, mundane oppression paves the way that makes contact violence more likely to occur, as it becomes difficult for a person to discern when the line towards more serious intrusions has been crossed. In this section a sample of case studies that would be classed as violence within more conventional frameworks are discussed, with a view to highlighting how processes on the continuum underpin each incident. To begin with, a brief quantitative overview of the extent to which respondents in this study were affected by violence is given. Approximately half reported an incident of physical or emotional maltreatment, including intimate-partner violence and violence by family members. This figure excludes bullying at school, which was reported by three quarters of those who could remember that far back. Respondents asserted that impairment-specific name calling was rife in segregated schools and continued at adult day centres. Individuals were called names like 'backwards', 'terminator' and 'Mongol'. Five people described experiences of sexual violence. This incidence is likely to be lower than the actual prevalence of violence against the researched population, as about five individuals who were approached for participation decided not to take part in this study when they learned that violence would be discussed. They were explicit that they did not wish to talk about their personal experiences. Ann (early 40s) initiated talking about her experience of theft almost immediately, at the onset of the interview:

> ANDREA: Do you ever go out by yourself?
> ANN: No.
> ANDREA: You always go with–
> ANN: –with my mum.
> ANDREA: With your mum.
> ANN: Me meself outside. Boys nicked my ... all nicked my purse [...] 'Give me my purse back!' 'No!' And that I said. [...] He hit me over here.

Since this incident happened, Ann has not accessed the community unaccompanied. She is visibly shaken by the experience and makes repeated reference to it throughout the interview. At the same time she regrets not being able to talk to 'people outside': 'Outside don't know what to say ... People mean ... or they're saying: "Nut!" Or being away or, walking away ... Not talking to me. They no like it, that.' Ann reports such name calling is a regular experience. About a third of people with learning difficulties in Emerson & Hatton's (2008) study reported that someone had been rude to them within the last year because they are disabled. That includes, as outlined earlier, other users of services, but also members of the general public. It therefore appears that disabled people continue to be stigmatised. The experience of theft has led to Ann's further social exclusion. For instance, she no longer walks to the day centre on her own. Instead, she relies on the council bus. There are some distinct parallels to Britney's account, which was cited earlier. In both cases, dependency on supporters is furthered following an incident of victimisation in the community. However, supporting relationships can also be exploited, as the subsequent two accounts demonstrate. Mary (mid-50s) used to live with her nephew, who was physically and emotionally violent and exploited her financially:

> Many times I was locked in a room all day and all night. [...] I had a bucket [to go to the toilet]. And [...] he's taken all the money off me. He wouldn't let me have any money, unless I asked him for it and he'd be watching over while I had that.

Here, facets on the continuum can be seen to accumulate to characterise this violating relationship. First, Mary, who was experiencing increasing anxiety and depression, was living in a socially excluded setting with limited contact with the outside world. Her nephew exploited the resulting isolated dependency relationship. This initially hindered Mary from seeking help. He took choices away from her, including the choice of how to spend her money, and indeed he restricted her freedom by locking her in a room. Jessica (early 20s) had been sexually assaulted by a member of staff. 'At first I didn't tell anyone, but then […] the abuse went really bad. I told my parents and we went to the police. We took [violator] to court, but he walked away free.' Jessica was frustrated with the criminal justice system. Again, a set of facets on the continuum are notable here. First, the violence happened within a socially excluded setting and the violator exploited a caring relationship. Jessica felt that she had not been listened to by the criminal justice system and she has lost faith in speaking up within it. Tyler (early 20s) was sexually violated by a roommate at residential school:

> Basically what happened was, he was bi[sexual]. I didn't know what bi was when I was at this age. […] I think the phrase is 'give me a hand job' whilst I was playing on the games console. … I won't go down how it escalated from that. It did. […] and then you elbow them in the face to get them off you and they go and tell on you because they raped you. They say *you* raped *them*.

Again, this experience took place within an isolated social setting. The violator was in a more powerful position. He was older than Tyler and seems to have specifically groomed him. He possessed knowledge that Tyler did not have at the time. Tyler was therefore unable to make an informed choice about his participation in the sexual acts. He was not listened to when he reported the incident, leaving the violator unpunished and indeed free to roam within the residential school, making it likely that further incidents would occur. Rachel (early 30s) becomes disturbed whenever she speaks about her past relationship. She and her boyfriend had lived together. The couple were supported by an agency during daytime hours and allowed privacy at night. They were initially happy. After about a year her boyfriend became emotionally and physically violent towards her. Rachel recalls: 'He was throwing money round the living room … harassing me … getting into bed. Harassing me. Swearing at me. … Pushed me up the wall.' This is an incident of domestic violence, which is characterised by 'one person exercising power and control over another within the domestic setting […], through the use of coercion, threat and force' (Mays, 2006: 148).

This experience was painful for Rachel, but nobody had predicted this change in her boyfriend's behaviour. When Rachel felt unable to deal with the situation herself, she alerted a member of support staff and promptly received the assistance she asked for. The continuum was thus interrupted. She had been listened to. The violence was not tolerated. Rachel was able to make the choice to access support for herself and to break out of an imbalanced dependency relationship.

Conclusion

The reader should note that the data presented here focuses on problematic accounts, while respondents in this study also reported some very positive experiences of excellent support structures, as evident in the final case study presented. Nonetheless, overall it can be observed that differential treatment continues to affect some disabled people in some situations. At the onset of this chapter, it was argued that the use of 'softer' terms, such as 'abuse', in describing violence against disabled people is inappropriate. Some experiences that were outlined could be described as disablism (Thomas, 2007) or mate crime (Thomas, see chapter in this volume), but more likely than not they often go unnoticed. Such a patchy approach does not satisfactorily capture the severity, as well as the systematic impact, that differential and derogatory treatment have on disabled people. Describing them as acts of violence on a continuum creates a holistic picture, which has the advantage that shifting boundaries between that which is seen as 'acceptable' as part of the everyday and that which is classed as contact violence do not distract attention away from the fact that a range of processes act to systematically oppress and disempower, as well as to invade the human rights of many disabled people. In other words, it becomes evident how the legacy of oppression (Barnes, 1997) continues to have an impact on people's lives today. It should be noted that the continuum merely applies to individuals who are seen to be 'disabled'. This became evident in the case of a woman who had an impairment all her life, but who was labelled when she was in her early 30s. The processes on the continuum only started at that point. It is therefore not the impairment per se that determines whether individuals are subjected to specialised treatment. Instead, the cause lies with the social response to those who are conceptualised as different. This leads to the shaping of deviant realities. Most participants understood that they were treated differently as a result of their label. Many had been called impairment-specific derogatory names. Relationships with support workers were at times imbalanced and insufficient respect was given to other personal relationships that were of importance to a person. Some of those broke down due to a lack of support to facilitate contact. This furthers the socio-emotional reliance on support workers and family members and contributes to the creation of isolated dependency relationships, which are easily exploitable.

Some respondents spoke about a higher tolerance for violence within segregated settings. They reported that, when a person with learning difficulties perpetrated a violent offence against another user of their service, this did not always have consequences. This contrasts with mainstream settings, which often embrace zero tolerance of invasive and violent behaviour. For instance, many workplaces have bullying and harassment policies (see, for example NHS Employers, 2006). A heightened level of tolerance for violence within segregated settings is wholly unacceptable, as well as paradoxical, as these settings are deemed safe and protective. The mundane intrusions and violations to which disabled people are exposed on a daily basis also underpin incidents of contact violence. Having one's expressed wishes overruled, being unable to choose the people who are often involved in the most intimate aspects of one's daily routine, being made to feel less worthy and being unable to assert one's right not to be exposed to derogatory treatment are processes that are often engrained in disabled people's everyday life. This makes it difficult for individuals to decide when the boundary between routine invasions and violence has been crossed. Thus hate crime and contact violence can, as Kelly (1988) suggests, be seen as a mere extension on a continuum of habitual intrusions.

References

Adams, R. G., & Allan, G. (1998). *Placing friendship in context*. Cambridge: Cambridge University Press.

Barnes, C. (1990). *Cabbage syndrome: The social construction of dependence*. London: Falmer Press.

——(1997). 'A Legacy of Oppression: A History of Disability in Western Culture'. In L. Barton & M. Oliver (eds), *Disability Studies: Past, Present and Future* (pp. 3–24). Leeds: The Disability Press.

Braddock, D. L., & Parish, S. L. (2001). 'An Institutional History of Disability'. In G. L. Albrecht, K. D. Seelman & M. Bury (eds), *Handbook of Disability Studies* (pp. 11-68). London: SAGE.

Burleigh, M. (1991). *Death and Deliverance: 'Euthanasia' in Germany, c.1900 to 1945* New York: Cambridge University Press.

Chakraborti, N., & Garland, J. (2009). *Hate crime: impact, causes and responses*. London: SAGE.

Department of Health. (2001). *Valuing people: A new strategy for learning disability for the 21st century: A white paper*. Norwich: Stationery Office.

——(2010a). *Valuing People Now: The Delivery Plan 2010–2011*. London: Department of Health.

——(2010b). *A vision for adult social care: Capable communities and active citizens*. London: HMSO.

Dutton, D. G. (2006). *Rethinking domestic violence*. Vancouver: UBC Press.

Emerson, E., & Hatton, C. (2008). *People with Learning Disabilities in England*. Lancaster: Centre for Disability Research, Lancaster University.

Equality and Human Rights Commission. (2011). *About us*. Retrieved 13 June 2011, from http://www.equalityhumanrights.com/about-us/.

Firth, L. (2009). *Tackling Child Abuse*. Cambridge: Independence Educational Publishers

Gleeson, K., & Frith, H. (2004). 'Pretty in pink: Young women presenting mature sexual identities'. In A. Harris (ed.), *All about the girl: culture, power, and identity* (pp. 103–114). London: Routledge.

Goffman, E. (1961). *Asylums: Essays on the social situation of mental patients and other inmates*. Garden City, NY: Doubleday.

Goodley, D., & Runswick-Cole, K. (2011). 'The violence of disablism'. Sociology of Health & Illness, 33(4).

Hingsburger, D. (1995). *Just Say Know! – Understanding and Reducing the Risk of Sexual Victimisation of People with Developmental Disabilities*. Quebec/Canada: Diverse City Press.

HMSO. (1998). *Human Rights Act*. London: Her Majesty's Stationary Office.

Hollomotz, A. (2011). *Learning difficulties and sexual vulnerability: A social approach.* London: Jessica Kingsley Publishers.

——(under review). 'Are we Valuing People's choices Now? – Restrictions to mundane choices made by adults with learning difficulties'. *British Journal of Social Work.*

Illich, I. (1977). 'Disabling professions'. In I. Illich, I. K. Zola, J. McKnight, J. Caplan & H. Shaiken (eds), *Disabling professions* (pp. 11–39). New York; London: Marion Boyars.

Jacobs, S. M., Jacobson, R., & Marchbank, J. (2000). 'Intoduction: States of conflict'. In S. M. Jacobs, R. Jacobson & J. Marchbank (eds), *States of conflict: gender, violence and resistance* (pp. ix, 246). London: Zed.

Kelly, L. (1988). *Surviving sexual violence.* Cambridge: Polity.

Levin, J., & Nolan, J. (2010). *The violence of hate: confronting racism, anti-semitism, and other forms of bigotry* (3rd ed.). London: Pearson Education.

Mays, J. M. (2006). 'Feminist disability theory: domestic violence against women with a disability'. *Disability & Society*, 21(2), 147–158.

McCarthy, M. (1998). 'Whose body is it anyway? Pressures and control for women with learning disabilities'. *Disability & Society*, 13(4), 557–574.

NHS Employers. (2006). *NHS Employers guidance – Bullying and harassment.* Leeds: The NHS Confederation (Employers) Company Ltd.

Nirje, B. (1994 [1969]). 'The normalization principle and its human management implications (Classic article from 1969)'. *SRV-VRS: The International Social Role Valorization Journal*, 1(2), 19–23.

OED online. (2011). *Oxford English dictionary* [electronic resource]. Retrieved 20 June 2011, from http://oed.com.

Parmenter, T. R. (2001). 'Intellectual Disability – Quo Vadis?' In G. L. Albrecht, K. Seelman, D. & M. Bury (eds), *Handbook of Disability Studies* (pp. 267–296). London: Sage Publications.

Priestley, M. (2003). *Disability: A life course approach.* Oxford: Polity.

Ryan, J., & Thomas, F. (1987). *The politics of mental handicap* (rev. ed.). London: Free Association.

Saxton, M. (ed.) (2009). *Sticks and Stones: Disabled People's Stories of Abuse, Defiance and Resillience.* Oakland; CA: World Institute on Disability.

Teaster, P. B., & Anetzberger, G. J. (2010). 'Elder Abuse in Contemporary Society: Programs, Policy, and Politics'. *Journal of Elder Abuse & Neglect*, 22(1), 3–5.

HM Government. (2010). *The Coalition: our programme for government.* London: Cabinet Office.

Thomas, C. (2007). *Sociologies of disability and illness : contested ideas in disability studies and medical sociology.* Basingstoke: Palgrave Macmillan.

United Nations. (2006). *United Nations Convention on the Rights of Persons with Disabilities.* New York: United Nations General Assembly.

Weeks, J. (1989). *Sex, politics and society: The regulation of sexuality since 1800* (2nd ed.). London: Longman.

Wolfensberger, W. (2004 [1983]). 'Social Role Valorisation – A proposed new term for the principle of normalization'. In D. R. Mitchell (ed.), *Special educational needs and inclusive education : major themes in education* (pp. 42–50). London: Routledge.

5 Media reporting and disability hate crime

Katharine Quarmby, journalist, researcher and activist, London

Introduction

The criminologist Professor Robert Reiner puts it well: 'The mass media are saturated with news and fiction stories graphically portraying the violence and anguish suffered by those experiencing crime.' He explains that crime stories have 'long been sources of popular spectacle and entertainment, even before the rise of the mass media' but that in recent years, with the rise of 'info-tainment' and the police turning to the media to assist their investigations, the 'media and criminal justice systems are penetrating each other increasingly' (Reiner, 2007). Reiner's theory has been backed up and confirmed, of course, by recent events in Britain, where it has become clear how closely one tabloid news-paper in particular, the *News of the World* (and its owner, News International), was linked to the Metropolitan Police (BBC, 2011)

This media saturation theory holds very true of crime stories involving disabled people, which are often reported extensively, in the tabloid and broadsheet press, radio and TV, particularly when they involve sexual overtones, torture or, as is too often the case, culminate in murder. The role of the media in highlighting crimes, and sometimes challenging the criminal justice system's response to them, is also generally accepted as being potentially powerful. One particularly powerful example is that of the observational documentaries made by Roger Graef, documenting police officers from the Thames Valley force, in his words, 'aggressively interviewing' an alleged rape victim (Graef, 2008). The resulting press furore about the documentary series kick-started a process of reform within the police service which has, as a result, overhauled the treatment of women alleging sexual assaults and rape (Gregory and Lees, 1999).

Another example is the growing disquiet of the media, albeit over an extended time period, about the botched investigation by the Metropolitan Police into the murder of Stephen Lawrence in 1993 – one that I, and others, would argue was the first crime to be identified in the public eye as a hate crime in the UK (Iganski, 2008). It is also likely that the media's role in highlighting social injustice could become even more powerful, as social networking has created new forms of journalism, including both 'citizen journalism' and 'blogging', accessible to all, including the victims or friends of victims. However, despite the increasing influence of the Internet and social networks that can give victims unmediated access to public opinion, it is important to state that older forms of media, in particular print (tabloids and the middle-market newspaper – I avoid naming a particular paper for legal reasons), TV and radio remain extremely powerful. They both shape public opinion and can put pressure on those in positions of power to bring about reform.

The influence of the media

Theories about the influence of the media on audiences have developed over the last ninety years. The first such theory, known as the Hypodermic Needle or Magic Bullet Theory, suggests that the media can directly, and powerfully, influence the general public. It was developed after academics studied the influence of propaganda during the First World War (and after others studied the effect of a broadcast by Orson Welles of H.G. Wells' classic *The War of the Worlds*). It suggests that a media message is effectively injected into the brain of a largely passive audience, whose members all behave in the same way. Although the theory has been discredited by subsequent academic research, it remains popular in the media itself, where commentators often directly link the effect of violent video games to heightened levels of aggression in children (Berger, 1995). Paul F. Lazarsfeld's book *The People's Choice* was published soon after, and was about, the 1940 presidential election; he argued that peer group influence was more powerful than that of the media. Lazarsfeld claimed that so-called 'opinion leaders' were aware of the mass media and then interpreted it to others, and called this observation The Two Step Flow Theory (Lazarsfeld, Berelson and Gaudet, 1944). Perhaps a more helpful interpretation in understanding the role of the media on disablist hate crime is the 'Agenda Setting Function Theory'. The theory was developed by Maxwell McCombs and Donald Shaw, from their observations of voters in North Carolina in the 1968 presidential campaign, and asserted that based on their study the media was able to set an agenda, but cannot dictate how or what they think about that agenda – i.e. what they do with the information they are given by the media (McCombs and Shaw, 1972).

No one theory, of course, can explain how society (particularly British, rather than American, society, where most studies have been carried out), interprets what the media itself decides is important. All of the theories above hold sway to some extent. However, they interact with cultural and historical archetypes of disability which are also extremely influential – they can be mirrored in what journalists write. So how has the power of the media worked in the field of disability hate crime thus far? I argue in this chapter that although it is a potentially powerful tool which could be used to set a new and more positive agenda to reframe disability and bring about positive change, it is also one that has, until recently, remained largely unharnessed. Indeed, I also argue that the media can also create new 'harms', by creating new, pernicious stereotypes of disabled people that make them more likely, rather than less, to experience more crime. But pressure has been exerted to some extent; the criminal justice system, in particular, has started to respond to media and activist pressure to reform its response to disability hate crime.

Aims

In this chapter I analyse how the media has reported disability hate crime and other targeted violence in the past. I also investigate whether media reporting has changed since 2007, and I ask what effect the emergence of new forms of media is having on images of disability generally and disability hate crime in particular. I also deconstruct some of the most enduring images of disabled people in the media, and ask whether those stereotypes are impairing our ability to challenge disability hate crime. In order to illustrate my points I carried out a number of content analyses of the British media, on key occasions over the last few years, to examine how particular stories involving disabled people were treated, and whether reporting has changed since disability hate crime has been more widely understood in the media. I looked at a wide range of stories from the broadsheet, tabloid, local and online press.

I conclude that media reporting of disability hate crimes is changing, albeit slowly, but that reporting of disability in other fields (particularly around disability benefits) is creating new, negative stereotypes of disabled people (Garthwaite, 2011) which in turn, I argue, creates new opportunities for hate crimes to occur. I also conclude that the Internet, whilst being a potential force for good, is also being used by some unscrupulous individuals to perpetuate damaging stereotypes of disabled people, and in many cases to mock, or even torture, them for pleasure and broadcast the results with virtual impunity

History

I was the first British journalist to investigate the social problem of disability hate crime. I started my investigations in the summer of 2007, when I looked at the case of a young man with epilepsy, Kevin Davies, who was tortured and kept in a shed until he died. His assailants escaped murder charges, were charged with lesser offences and are now out of prison. That crime, like so many others I have identified, was never investigated, prosecuted or sentenced as a hate crime. The first article I wrote about this subject, identifying the similarities between the violent deaths of five men with learning difficulties, was headlined: 'If these are not hate crimes, what are?' (Quarmby, 2007). Since covering Kevin's case and those four others, I have written around thirty articles on this subject. In 2008 I wrote the first pan-disability report on disability hate crime, *Getting Away with Murder*, for the UK's Disabled People's Council (UKDPC), *Disability Now* magazine and Scope. In 2011 my book *Scapegoat: Why We Are Failing Disabled People* was published. It offers a critical analysis of the history of violence against disabled people, including recent cases and reaction to them in the press. In the book I also look at how pernicious images of disabled people, including the scapegoat, the sinner, the freak, the victim, and, more recently, the scrounger, are disseminated by the media and, as a result, remain extremely powerful (Quarmby, 2011).

When I first started investigating such crimes, they were never described as disability hate crimes – it was an invisible concept in the media, despite its existence in criminal law. I had to start from scratch and search under other words, which were concealing disability hate crimes from general view. These included 'bullying' for people with learning difficulties', 'vulnerable' for almost all disabled people, and 'motiveless' for almost all crimes against them. As I wrote in *Getting Away with Murder*, I identified a striking pattern in how newspapers report crimes against disabled people – and in how police, prosecutors and the judiciary choose to describe such crimes in press releases, in court and directly to journalists in interviews.

The judge presiding in the case of hate crime victim Barrie-John Horrell, who was killed in July 2006, dubbed him 'vulnerable and defenceless' (BBC, 2006). Mr Horrell was abducted from his house by people he considered to be friends, hit with a brick, robbed, falsely called a paedophile and strangled, a crime the judge called 'senseless'. Detective Inspector Geoff Brookes, who investigated the torture and death of Kevin Davies in September 2006, said that only the guilty trio could say 'exactly what motivated them', (BBC, 2007) with the judge dubbing Kevin 'vulnerable, gullible and naïve'. The judges sentencing those responsible for the murder of Rikki Judkins (*Lancaster Guardian*, 2007) and the manslaughter of Raymond Atherton also called both men 'vulnerable'. This pattern held true for almost all other crimes against disabled people I identified in that report, and in *Disability Now*'s Hate Crime Dossier, which was published some months earlier (Quarmby, 2008a).

I also looked at language, such as 'bullying', which is often used to describe attacks on people with learning difficulties. I wrote in *Getting Away with Murder*:

> This is then reflected in media reporting, where reporters will often describe people with learning difficulties as 'having the mental age of a child' (Quarmby, 2008b). Such language encourages the infantilisation of disabled victims of crime within the criminal justice system and masks the gravity of their experiences. It can lead to front-line police officers, faced with a victim saying that they are being 'bullied', failing to take a crime seriously and then record or investigate it appropriately.
>
> (Ibid.)

Unfortunately, little has changed – the language used to describe disabled people, and what happens to them, remains limited and stereotyped.

To illustrate and test the assertions I have made above in greater depth, I carried out a content analysis of news stories in the mainstream media about the case of Brent Martin, a young man from Sunderland with learning difficulties who was robbed, beaten, chased and eventually kicked to death in 2007 by three people who he considered to be his (new) friends. I chose this case because it was a very clear example of a disability hate crime, in my view, but was not viewed as such by police, prosecutors or the judiciary. For example, the senior investigating officer in that case, Barbara Franklin, referred to local children 'bullying' disabled people. Brent Martin had, in fact, been a victim of a sustained, sadistic attack – the full extent of which could never be adequately conveyed by the schoolyard term 'bullying' (Quarmby, 2008b).

I examined newspaper reporting of the murder trial, between the dates of conviction and sentencing, to look at what language was used to describe Brent, what happened to him, his attackers, and how the murder was described in the press. I accessed newspaper articles from the *Telegraph* (1 March 2008) the *Sun* (1 March 2008), the *Mirror* (23 January 2008), the local press, *Journal Live* (23 January 2008), the *Express* (29 February 2008), the *Sun* (22 January 2008), BBC Online, (22 January 2008) and *The Times* (1 March 2008). In *Journal Live*, Brent was described as 'suffering' from his disability and as being a 'trusting disabled man'. The murder was described as 'sickening'. The *Express* described Brent as a 'vulnerable disabled man'; the *Sun* also described him as 'vulnerable' and 'defenceless' and the crime as 'brutal'. BBC Online (2008) also described Brent as 'vulnerable'. *The Times* described Brent as 'suffering' from his impairment and the *Telegraph* also described him, in the words of the judge, as 'an extremely vulnerable victim'.

This content analysis clearly supports my conclusions in *Getting Away with Murder* and *Scapegoat*: that using euphemisms to describe harassment and assault as 'bullying', rape and torture as 'abuse', or victims as 'vulnerable' results in crimes against disabled people being seen as fundamentally different to those experienced by non-disabled people. These crimes are not, despite newspaper reports and handwringing by police and prosecutors, 'motiveless' acts carried out on 'vulnerable' people who should be tucked away at home or in institutions – but they are, far too often, described as such. Indeed, as I argued at the time,

> The fact that so few disability hate crimes are named as such in court means that the true motive behind these crimes is not acknowledged. Those who commit such crimes are not challenged in their offending behaviour, unlike those committing racially motivated offences or domestic violence, which can be compelled to attend courses that address their hostility. As a result, society is unaware of the scale of the problem of disability hate crime – fuelling the common belief that the crime does not exist.
>
> (Quarmby, 2008b)

I contend, instead, that identifying potential hate crimes as such, and calling them hate crimes, as well as describing crimes, where appropriate, as 'targeted', would be more helpful. The term 'vulnerable' should be used more sparingly and appropriately, and not as a synonymous term for disability. Other crimes of targeted violence are also regularly described, instead, as anti-social behaviour (ASB) or safeguarding issues by police, prosecutors and local authorities. One of the most notorious cases where disability hate crime was, in my view, wrongly categorised as ASB was that of Fiona Pilkington and her children, who were targeted by neighbours for eleven years in Barwell, just outside Leicester. Indeed, the Independent Police Complaints Commission report into the case establishes that neither hate crime nor anti-social behaviour co-ordinators were called on by Leicestershire Police (IPCC, 2011).

To illustrate this point, I carried out a further content analysis of the mainstream media at the time of the verdict reached by the inquest into the death of Fiona Pilkington and her daughter Frankie Hardwick. I looked at the media coverage in the *Independent*, (29 September 2009), BBC Online on the same date, the *Mirror* (28 and 29 September 2009), *The Times* (29 September 2009), the *Express* on the same date, the *Guardian* (28 September 2009) and the *Daily Mail* (29 September 2009). I wanted to analyse whether media reporting had taken on the notion of 'disability hate crime' since I first used it, two summers earlier.

All the newspapers expressed their horror at the story, with extensive coverage and, in a number of cases, comment articles as well as news reporting. The *Daily Mail* led with the Home Secretary's attack on anti-social behaviour, which he linked with the case. The newspaper also named a family that is said to have been behind the 'torment', describing the youths who harassed her as 'cretinous' (Greenhill and Clarke, 2009). The newspaper also said that Frankie had a 'mental age' of just four. Its comment piece opined that the story illustrated a 'tragic lesson in official neglect' (*Daily Mail*, 2009).

The *Independent* took a different line. It included comments from disability charities which (rightly) called the case a disability hate crime and included a comment piece from Alice Maynard, chair of the disability charity Scope, on the issue, as well as profiling the family said to be behind the problems and the apology of the police chief in the area. In its comment piece, it referred to comments by some that the tragedy should have been treated as a hate crime, but concluded that the affair illustrated the 'inadequate competence of public servants charged with upholding the rule of law and protecting the vulnerable' (*Independent*, 2009). BBC Online also covered comments from charities about the tragedy being a hate crime, as well as the issue of anti-social behaviour. The *Mirror* said that the police had not picked up on the 'vulnerability' of the family and stressed the anti-social nature of the 'abuse' the family had endured. One of its headlines ran: 'Backlash over bullied family deaths' (BBC, 2009). *The Times* also covered the story and called the gang responsible 'thuggish', also referring to the apology of the police chief for not responding better to 'low-level anti-social behaviour' (*The Times*, 2009). The *Express* blamed the deaths on Britain's 'yob culture' and ran a 'Have Your Say' special, asking 'Are yobs on Britain's streets out of control?' (which produced no less than six pages of reader comments) (*Express*, 2009). The *Guardian* reported the case extensively, asking whether it was a 'Stephen Lawrence moment for disability hate crime' in its headline, but also reporting on the threat of anti-social behaviour (*Guardian*, 2009). Lastly, the *Telegraph*, which also covered the case in detail, concentrating on whether it was anti-social behaviour and also running a 'Have Your Say' section on the matter, ran a comment piece claiming that the case should not be captured by hate crime activists, but should be seen as a plea for 'equal respect', not special treatment (*Telegraph*, 2009).

This relates to a wider issue, which is that public discourse on disability remains very restricted. There is a paucity of work analysing representations of disabled people in the media, but what there is suggests that disabled people are represented in a number of ways, all of which are stereotypical and most of which are negative (Cumberbatch and Negrine, 1992). This is particularly true in the few cases where persons with a disability appear in the media. The Canadian Association of Broadcasters report found that disabled 'individuals are viewed as the objects of pity and depicted as having the same attributes and characteristics no matter what the disability may be' (CAB, 2005). Similarly, the website Media and Disability, a partnership organisation advocating for broader representation of people with disabilities, points out that 'disabled people, when they feature at all, continue to be all too often portrayed as either remarkable and heroic, or dependent victims' (Media and Disability, 2007).

Not only are disabled people routinely stereotyped, but the full range of disabilities is not reflected in media portrayals. Lynne Roper of Stirling Media Research Institute, in her article 'Disability in Media', notes that 'wheelchairs tend to predominate ... since they are an iconic sign of disability. Most actors playing disabled characters are, however, not disabled. The wheelchair allows the character to be obviously disabled, whilst still looking "normal", and does not therefore present any major challenges for audience identification' (Roper, 2006). This, of course, means that when a victim of hate crime has an impairment which the media is not so well aware of (such as autism, or a learning difficulty), journalists find it hard to see that they, too, could be targeted for their impairment. To test whether these images were represented in media reporting in the UK, I conducted another content analysis of newspapers on and around 28 June 2010, when the Chancellor of the Exchequer, George Osborne, announced a crackdown on incapacity benefit fraud (an out-of-work benefit paid to many disabled people based on a medical assessment of eligibility).

I looked at coverage of the so-called crackdown in the *Independent* (28 June 2010), the *Telegraph* (26 and 28 June 2010), the *Guardian* (28 June 2010), the *Mirror* (28 June 2010), BBC Online (28 June 2010) and the *Daily Mail* (28 June 2010). I found that two images were particularly prevalent: that of the 'villain' – the disabled person who didn't deserve state help and was falsely claiming it – and that of the disabled person as 'victim', unable to speak for themselves and wholly dependent on public alms.

The *Daily Mail*, for instance, made much of the fact that many people on Incapacity Benefit were receiving it for being obese or having headaches. 'Following an admission by the last government that one million of the

2.6 million claiming incapacity benefit were actually fit to work, Mr Osborne said the issue could no longer be "ducked"' (*Daily Mail*, 2010). The newspaper illustrated its coverage with an image of one Martin Crowson, handling an alligator whilst claiming he was too sick to walk more than 50 yards (a story that was judiciously recycled from five years earlier, when the *Daily Mail* first ran it, ibid.). Other headlines in that day's coverage included: 'New figures reveal payouts of £1.8bn for stress and depression', '1,000 claimants got £5m for being "too fat" to work' and '£10m went to those incapacitated by headaches'.

The *Daily Telegraph* also covered the issue in some detail, reporting Mr Osborne saying that incapacity benefit could no longer be 'ducked', and reported on the drive to test 10,000 claimants a week 'to determine exactly how many genuinely need state help'. It also reported the data that claimed that 1.8bn was paid to those suffering from 'depression, anxiety and stress' (*Telegraph*, 2010). Its leader described the initiative as the start of a 'welfare revolution' in a headline and praised the astuteness of the Chancellor in tackling 'the most politically sensitive' welfare cut (i.e. incapacity benefit) first of all (*Telegraph*, ibid.). The *Guardian* covered the issue in detail, explaining the history behind the initiative (New Labour had also tried to cut the incapacity benefit bill). Its headline read: 'Welfare crackdown begins with drive to reduce incapacity benefit claims' (*Guardian*, 2010). The *Mirror* described the plans in a short article as 'another attack on benefit claimants ... The Chancellor said he would use the summer to work out cuts to incapacity benefit and other welfare payments ... The latest focus will be on 2.6 million incapacity benefit claimants' (*Mirror*, 2010). BBC Online reported Mr Osborne as saying: 'We have got to ... make sure it [benefit] protests those with disabilities and protects those who can't work but also encourages those who can work into work' and reported what the opposition was saying in equal detail (BBC, 2010a). Taken as a whole, it is important to note that the excoriation of those receiving disability benefits has continued unabated, despite the fact that all of those facing reassessment were once assessed as eligible for the benefit – and that the National Audit Office has also admitted that it had previously overestimated claims of disability benefit fraud (National Audit Office, 2009).

Coalition politicians have made much of people falsely claiming disability benefits. This has had two effects. Last August, shortly after the crackdown was announced, two newspapers, the *Sun* and the *Express*, launched campaigns, or wars, on 'scroungers'. The *Sun* declared 'war on benefit scroungers', saying: 'They cannot be bothered to find a job or they claim to be sick when they are perfectly capable of work because they prefer to sit at home watching wide-screen TVs – paid for by you' (*Sun*, 2010). This was followed, a couple of weeks later, by the *Express* warning that 'scroungers who play the benefits system to milk incapacity benefit' will be put back on the dole and forced out to work' (*Express*, 2010). This is part of an increasing number of negative reports calling people on incapacity benefit and disability living allowance 'benefit cheats'. Such rhetoric fuels anxiety amongst disabled people and their families, but as of yet there is no definitive evidence that it has led to physical violence. However, the charity Mind, which supports people with mental health conditions, says that it has received 'numerous calls' suggesting that such rhetoric is creating a witch-hunt against those dubbed by many in the media 'scroungers and cheats' (Corlett, 2010). This, in turn, Mind argued, in its submission to the Equality and Human Rights Commission inquiry into disability-targeted harassment, is creating a 'biased, unjust and misrepresented view of a group who are already vulnerable and marginalised in society'. One person with a mental health condition told the charity: 'Tabloids [...] are actively [...] encouraging people to shop the apparent easy-to-spot cheats directly to the paper. With mental illness, it is not that easy and this targeting feels unacceptable. I fear this will increase hate crime and further alienate those with mental illness who are on benefits.' Another said, movingly, that life was now 'barely tolerable' and added that they felt like an 'object of hate and derision with no escape. I worked for as long as my body could stand it and I do not need someone with no comprehension of my daily life, telling me that I am a "scrounger" and languishing on benefits', adding that many with hidden disabilities now find themselves 'the victims of an orchestrated hate campaign and what I can only describe as institutional bullying' (MIND, 2010).

But there was also a more direct reaction by the public to the launch of the 'crackdown' in June 2010. George Osborne called for members of the public to contribute their own ideas about how to save benefits money by contributing to the Spending Challenge pages on the Treasury website. The general atmosphere of hostility towards disabled people, created, at least in part, by media reporting and newspaper campaigns, then spilled over into downright hate language. The Spending Challenge website, which was not moderated, opened for business on or around 9 July 2010 (Treasury, 2011). It was soon displaying vicious comments about disabled people, a few weeks after the crackdown had been announced. One writer argued that all disabled people should be sterilised. Another said, 'depression is not a disability, neither is stupidity'. Many suggested that disabled people got too many perks and were particularly exercised about disabled car-parking spaces (Pring & Novis, 2010). Many others described disabled people as either 'too lazy to work' or as 'spongers'. Some were even more vicious (Pring, 2010). Another suggested, extraordinarily, that disabled people should be used as weapons of war:

> Those who can work that upon rigorous medical examination turn out to be just thick or bone idle to undertake intesnive (sic) course in employability, where they will learn to be punctual, meticulous, smartly dressed, articulate, and gain working attitude. Those who repeatedly fail the course to be deployed in Afghanistan as IED deterrents.
>
> (Ibid.)

It says something about how seriously the government took such comments that it took several days before they were removed. The website was finally suspended on 15 July, after the Equality and Human Rights Commission passed the comments to its legal enforcement team for 'consideration' and after the Treasury had been criticised by many disability groups.

The influence and role of the Internet

When I was drawing up recommendations for my report *Getting Away with Murder*, I talked to police officers and politicians about whether the law on incitement – particularly relating to inciting hatred using the Internet – should be broadened to include crimes against disabled people. At that time I was unable to find evidence that the Internet was being used routinely to mock, taunt, bully or harass disabled children and adults – and to incite others to similar acts or to physical violence. So I didn't include a recommendation that the legislation be broadened, as there wasn't evidence that the law was needed.

This isn't true any more. Four years on, during the course of research for my book *Scapegoat*, I came to the conclusion that there is increasing evidence that the Internet (and, to a lesser extent, television) is being used as a very modern freakshow where disabled people can be mocked, as well as being a place where disabled children are being bullied, and disabled people harassed, with virtual impunity. As in the past, when disabled men and women were exploited for the amusement of society as freaks, they are being used, now, as unwilling stars in virtual reality shows – then transmitted to millions without any regulation. Disabled people who also use chat rooms, Facebook and other social networks are often targeted for the amusement of others.

In November 2010, I came across a website, based in the US, on which anonymous users were encouraged to add to a so-called 'torture thread' about disabled people. The webmaster asked for 'stories how you maltreated, bullied or tortured your retarded friends, classmates, children'. Contributors came back with accounts of theft, assaults, putting faeces in milk for a schoolmate and throwing rocks at disabled people. Some contributors boasted of serially raping other classmates with learning difficulties. (I passed on details about this site to the police, and it is being investigated, as is another site which had encouraged attacks on deaf people.) In another case, a deaf woman, Jane Williams, who is confined to her house, has reported a two-year campaign of harassment conducted through a well-known social network. She was targeted by a fellow user. He created a website in her name, captured her account details, and started to spread rumours about her. Tim McSharry, head of disability at the charity Access Committee for Leeds, which has supported her, says that although the perpetrator was convicted of harassment, he did not stop: 'The perpetrator then took action to report Jane to the DWP for fraudulently claiming benefits' (of which she was completely cleared).

In another example, the charity Index on Censorship expressed its alarm and horror when three executives for the Internet service provider, Google, were convicted in February 2010 of violation of privacy laws in Italy. The charity denounced the court's 'flagrant disregard for free expression'. The case had been brought by a disability charity which claimed that Google was culpable for not gaining the consent of all parties in a video before it was uploaded to Google Video. The video showed a young boy with autism being beaten, humiliated and insulted by a group of youths at a school in Turin, Italy. The charity also claimed that Google had been slow to react when asked to remove the clip. The video was, briefly, rated as the funniest video in Google Italia, and was one of the most downloaded before it was removed (Mendez, 2010). In another recent case, communicated to the Disability Hate Crime Network's founder, Stephen Brookes, a young man with Aspergers was bullied so badly, first at school, then on the Internet by the same people, that he hanged himself. Police are investigating.

It is very difficult, though not impossible, to regulate Internet service providers (Index on Censorship, 2010). Google, YouTube (also owned by Google), Facebook and other sites have, just in the last two years, become major broadcasters and publishers – with unmoderated content being uploaded by the public every day – videos, audio, animations, and blogs. But they are almost completely unregulated – unlike terrestrial broadcasters and publishers. This lack of regulation allows broadcasts of attacks on disabled people without serious fear of prosecution.

For instance, Christine Lakinski, a disabled women, was filmed as she was urinated on and covered with shaving foam. The man who filmed it yelled: 'This is YouTube material!' He was arrested before the film could be uploaded. The phone has never been found. In another incident, in Melbourne, Australia, around the same time, a group of high school students assaulted a disabled girl, urinated on her, set her hair on fire, sexually assaulted her and then posted their exploits on YouTube (Militec, 2006). In another case, a group was created on Italian Facebook suggesting that children with Down's Syndrome should be used for target practice. Online harassment is pernicious, can be long-lasting, and many police forces are still playing catch-up in their knowledge and training of how to tackle it. However, if the online evidence trail is preserved, it can be investigated and prosecuted. It has, in the past, been difficult to get Internet service providers and social-networking sites to act, when abuse is alleged. This is partly because many are based in America, and UK court orders have to be dealt with there, causing delay. But it is far from impossible, and the CPS has recently published new guidance on harassment, including cyber-stalking (Crown Prosecution Service, 2010).

The role of regulation

Regulation of the media is key if we are to protect groups that are either (correctly) described as vulnerable, such as children, or those who have traditionally been targeted for harassment, such as disabled people, minority ethnic groups, gay people and certain religious groups. It is imperfect, but it helps, as the regulation of TV shows clearly. In 2010, on Channel 4's *Big Brother's Big Mouth*, ex-footballer and actor Vinnie Jones mocked presenter Davina McCall, saying that she walked like a 'retard'. Channel 4 was initially unrepentant, claiming that participants had the right to freedom of expression 'without censure'. However, after numerous complaints by disabled people and charities, the broadcaster eventually apologised, admitted its initial defensive stance was a mistake and cut the offending item from its recorded programme. Vinnie Jones also saw the error of his ways, with his spokesman saying: 'On behalf of Vinnie Jones I'd like to apologise for any offence caused by comments made on *Big Brother's Big Mouth* on January 29th 2010. While the show was live and the conversation was unscripted and off the cuff, Vinnie in no way meant to upset anyone and fully appreciates the choice of word was inappropriate' (Quarmby 2010).

The complaints also went to the broadcasting regulator, Ofcom. It ruled against the first complaint by Nicky Clark, a mother of two disabled children and a promoter of disabled talent on-screen. Ofcom said that although the matter was 'sensitive' the word was not aimed against people with a learning disability. But the matter didn't end there. Undeterred by the ruling, Louise Wallis, from a charity for people with learning difficulties, Respond, and a group of disabled people, demonstrated outside Ofcom's headquarters. Backed up with an energetic online campaign by Mencap, Ofcom eventually back-tracked, and ruled against Channel 4. The situation in the mainstream media is better because of regulation. Broadcasters can, and are, censured, both by the regulator and the mainstream media. But this is not so on the Internet. The new de facto broadcasters and publishers are hiding behind the 'right to free expression'.

Positive progress

Despite so many setbacks, I am, on the whole, optimistic that there has been progress within the media to understand disability hate crime and to put pressure on institutions responding to it. Journalists have become much more au fait with the term and some have helped to expose the problem, with a number of documentaries and articles. In January 2010 Simon Green's documentary *Why Do You Hate Me?*, about his life as a wheelchair user in Bridgend, Wales, showed in unflinching detail just how many insults he has to endure going about his everyday business (BBC, 2010b). Rosa Monckton's documentary, *Tormented Lives*, broadcast on BBC1 on 19 October 19 2010, looked at everyday life for people with learning difficulties and concluded that many lived under what amounted to siege conditions (BBC, 2010c). As I argued above, social media/networks do allow for victims to communicate with each other and to seek help from those they trust. The Disability Hate Crime Network, an online forum for those affected by and challenging disability hate crime, now has nearly 2,000 members. It is an increasingly important forum for debate, case sharing and challenge.

Conclusion

I believe that the media can be a great force for good in exposing the harms of disability hate crime. Some journalists have started to expose the issue: that, in turn, puts legitimate pressure on the criminal justice system to respond. In my role as one of the (volunteer) co-ordinators at the online forum on Facebook, The Disability Hate Crime Network, I play a part in publicising cases and allowing a safe place where disabled people can get advice on where to go if they need help, as well as getting those in power to respond. That's the good side of the Internet revolution.

But the media can be a force for harm too, in that newspapers and broadcasters are tremendously powerful in their ability to perpetuate and create new, negative stereotypes of disabled people. Disabled people, regulators and politicians all have a role in holding the media to account. However, journalism holds up a mirror to attitudes in society. Until our attitudes towards disabled people change in society, discrimination and prejudice will continue to flourish and the crimes that they foster, crimes of hate, will not be eradicated.

References

Adams, S., (2008) 'Jail for disabled man's "sadistic" murders', *Telegraph*, available at http://www.telegraph.co.uk/news/uknews/1580367/Jail-for-disabled-mans-sadistic-murderers.html.

BBC (1999), 'Stephen Lawrence: Timeline of Events', BBC Online, 1999, available at http://news.bbc.co.uk/hi/english/static/stephen_lawrence/timeline.htm [accessed 20 July 2011].

BBC News Online, 2007, 'Hillside murderers get life terms', available at http://news.bbc.co.uk/1/hi/wales/south_east/6624515.stm [accessed 23 March 2011].

BBC, (2007), 'Three jailed over shed prisoner', available at http://news.bbc.co.uk/1/hi/england/gloucestershire/6284184.stm [accessed 23 March 2011].

——(2008), 'Boy convicted of "£5 bet" murder', BBC Online, 22 January, available at http://news.bbc.co.uk/1/hi/england/wear/7202351.stm.

——, (2010a) 'Duncan Smith denies sickness benefit test to triple', 28 June, available at http://www.bbc.co.uk/news/10431024 [accessed 20 July 2011].

——, (2010b), 'Secret film uncovers "disabled hate crime" in Wales', BBC News Online, available at http://news.bbc.co.uk/1/hi/wales/8437523.stm.

——, (2010c) *Tormented Lives*, broadcast on BBC1 on 19 October 2010. http://www.bbc.co.uk/programmes/b00vhls2. The stories were all accessed 31 January, 2011.

BBC News, (2011), 'Q& a: News of the World phone-hacking scandal', available at http://www.bbc.co.uk/news/uk-11195407 [accessed 20 July 2011].

Berger, A. A. (1995). *Essentials of Mass Communication Theory*. London: SAGE Publications.

Bird, F., Jenkins, R., Ford, R., (2009) 'Pilkington inquest: police failings blamed in car blaze deaths', *The Times*, 29 September, available at http://www.timesonline.co.uk/tol/news/uk/crime/article6852880.ece [accessed 20 July 2011].

Brown, M., (2010) '500,000 benefits scroungers will be made to seek work', *Daily Express*, available at http://www.express.co.uk/posts/view/200030/500-000-benefit-scroungers-will-be-made-to-seek-work, [accessed 31 January 2011].

Burleigh, M., (2002), *Death and Deliverance*, London: Pan, 43.

Canadian Association of Broadcasters (2005) *The Presence, Portrayal and Participation of Persons with Disabilities in Television Programming*. Toronto:CAB/ACR http:// www.cab-acr.ca/english/research/05/sub_sep1605.htm.

Chapman, J., (2010) 'Osborne begins crackdown on incapacity benefit cheats with plans to treble assessments', *Daily Mail*, 28 June, available at http://www.dailymail.co.uk/ news/article-1290165/George-Osborne-begins-crackdown-incapacity-benefit-cheats.html [accessed 20 July 2011].

Corlett, S (2010) 'Personal communication', Mind, 16 November 2010.

Crown Prosecution Service (2010) 'CPS introduces "ground-breaking" legal guidance on stalking'. Available at http://www.cps.gov.uk/news/press_releases/138_10/index.html.

Cumberbatch, G. & Negrine, R., (1992), *Images of Disability on Television*, London: Routledge.

Daily Express, (2009) 'Are yobs on Britain's streets out of control?' 29 September, *Daily Express*, available at http://www.express.co.uk/posts/view/130787 [accessed 20 July 2011].

Daily Mail, (2009) 'A tragic lesson in official neglect', 29 September, *Daily Mail*, available at http://www.dailymail.co.uk/debate/article-1216800/MAIL-COMMENT-A-tragic-lesson-official-neglect.html [accessed 20 July 2011].

Daily Mail, (2010) 'Too ill to work ... but not to grab an alligator: "Disabled" soldier who claimed £17,000 in benefits is caught out by holiday snap', 28 June. http://www. dailymail.co.uk/news/article-352515/Benefit-cheat-snapped-alligator-wrestling.html.

Garthwaite, K (2011) 'The Language of Shirkers and Scroungers: Talking about Illness, Disability and Coalition Welfare Reform'. *Disability and Society.* Vol 26, No.3 pp. 369–72.

Graef, R., (2008), 'Don't blind-drunk women who cry rape bear any responsibility for what happens to them?', *Daily Mail* [online], 13 August, available at: http://www. dailymail.co.uk/news/article-1044160/Dont-blind-drunk-women-rape-bear-responsi-bility-happens-them.html [accessed 20 July 2011].

Greenhill, S., Clarke, N., (2009) 'No excuses': Home Secretary attacks police and council over failures that led to deaths of tormented mother and daughter', *Daily Mail*, 29 September, available at http://www.dailymail.co.uk/news/article-1216065/Fiona-Pilkington-How-police-council-left-feral-families-terrorise-mother-disabled-daughter. html [accessed 20 July 2011].

Gregory, J., and Lees, S., (1999), *Policing Sexual Assault*, London: Routledge.

Haller, B., (2010), *Disability in an Ableist world*, Louisville, KY: Avocado Press; http:// media-and-disability.blogspot.com/2010/09/highlights-of-2010-survey-of-people.html.

Hands, L., (2008) 'Judge calls for figures on spiralling youth homicides', Journallive, 23 January; available at http://www.journallive.co.uk/north-east-news/todays-news/ 2008/01/23/sickening-murder-has-jurors-in-tears-61634-20382381/.

HM Treasury (2010) *The Spending Challenge* http://www.hm-treasury.gov.uk/spend_ spendingchallenge.htm.

Iganski, P., (2008), *Hate Crime and the City*, Bristol: Policy Press.

Independent newspaper, (2009) 'Tragic lessons of a shameful saga', the *Independent*, 29 September, available at http://www.independent.co.uk/opinion/leading-articles/leading-article-tragic-lessons-of-a-shameful-saga-1794719.html [accessed 20 July 2011].

Jenkins, R, (2007), '"Feral" youths beat victim to death after months of abuse', April 4, *The Times*, available at www.timesonline.co.uk/tol/news/uk/crime/article1610309.ece.

Lancaster Guardian (2007), 'The killers who boasted of their senseless crime', 22 February, *Lancaster Guardian*, available at http://www.lancasterguardian.co.uk/news/lancaster-and-district news/the_killers_who_boasted_of_their_senseless_crime_1_1168 887 [accessed 23 March 2011].

Lazarsfeld, Paul F.; Berelson, Bernard; and Gaudet, Hazel. (1944). *The People's Choice: How the Voter Makes Up His Mind in a Presidential Campaign.* New York: Duell, Sloan and Pearce. http://www.agendasetting.com/res_theory.php.

McCombs, M. E., and D. L. Shaw. (1972) 'The Agenda-Setting Function of Mass Media'. *Public Opinion Quarterly*, Vol. 36 pp. 176–187.

Mendez, R (2010) 'Responsibility For Privacy Violations In User Generated Content Providers'. Master's Thesis. Available at http://www.chiefprivacyofficers.com/uploads/2/6/6/5/2665080/thesis.pdf,http://blog.indexoncensorship.org/2010/02/25/google-italy-disability-privacy/.

Militec, D (2006) 'Outrage over teenage girl's assault recorded on DVD'. Available at: http://www.theage.com.au/news/national/outcry-over-teenage-girls-assault-recorded-on-dvd/2006/10/24/1161455722271.html.

Mind (2010) *Response to the EHRC Targeted Harassment Inquiry.* London: Mind.

Mirror newspaper (2009) 'Backlash over Bullied family death', 29 September, *Mirror*, available at http://www.mirror.co.uk/news/latest/2009/09/29/backlash-over-bullied-family-deaths-115875-21709008/ [accessed 20 July 2011].

Mirror newspaper (2010) 'George Osborne warns incapacity benefits to be slashed', *Mirror*, 28 June, available at http://www.mirror.co.uk/news/top-stories/2010/06/28/incapacity-benefits-to-be-slashed-115875-22366143/ [accessed 20 July 2011].

National Audit Office (2009) *NAO Resource Account.* London: NAO.

Parton, D. (2011) 'People on benefits open to abuse or attack, Mencap fears' Learning Disability Today (website). http://www.ldtonline.co.uk/2011/04/people-on-benefits-open-to-abuse-or-attack-mencap-fears/.

Porter, A., (2010) 'Millions face incapacity benefit cuts as welfare reforms speed up', *Telegraph*, 28 June, available at http://www.telegraph.co.uk/news/politics/7858141/Millions-face-incapacity-benefit-cuts-as-welfare-reforms-speed-up.html [accessed 20 July 2011].

Pring, J. & Novis, A. (2010) Personal communication, 16 November 2010. http://www.disabledgo.com/blog/2010/07/treasury-fails-to-remove-disablist-comments-from-cuts-website/.

Quarmby, K (2007) 'If these aren't hate crimes what are?' Added Available at http://archive.disabilitynow.org.uk/search/z07_09_Se/hatecrimes.shtml.

Quarmby, K., (2008a) 'No hiding place', January, *Disability Now* magazine, available at http://www.disabilitynow.org.uk/the-hate-crime-dossier [accessed 20 July 2011].

Quarmby, K., (2008b), *Getting Away with Murder*, London: Scope.

Quarmby, K (2010) 'The Retard Controversy Over the Water'. Huffington Post, February 18. Available at http://www.huffingtonpost.com/katharine-quarmby/the-retard-controversy-ov_b_467766.html.

Quarmby, K., (2011) *Scapegoat: why we are failing disabled people*, London: Portobello Press.

Reiner, R (2007)., Media-made criminality: the representation of crime in the mass media. In Maguire, M. and Morgan, R. and Reiner, R. (eds) *The Oxford handbook of criminology.* Oxford University Press, Oxford, UK, Roper, L (2006) Available at http://www.mediaed.org.uk/posted_documents/DisabilityinMedia.htm.

Sloan, J.,(2010) 'Help us stop £1.5bn benefits scroungers,' *Sun*, available at http://www.thesun.co.uk/sol/homepage/features/3091717/The-Sun-declares-war-on-Britains-benefits-culture.html, accessed January 31, 2011 [accessed 20 July 2011].

Sun newspaper, (2008) 'Yobs killed disabled man', *Sun*, 22 January, available at http://www.thesun.co.uk/sol/homepage/news/article713830.ece [accessed 20 July 2011].

Telegraph newspaper (2010), 'The welfare revolution is only just beginning', 28 June. Available at http://www.telegraph.co.uk/comment/telegraph-view/7859619/The-welfare-revolution-is-only-just-beginning.html [accessed 20 July 2011].

West, S., (2009) 'The Pilkington case was a murder, not a hate crime for Guardian readers to fuss over'. *Telegraph*, 29 September, available at http://blogs.telegraph.co.uk/news/edwest/100011932/the-pilkington-case-was-murder-not-a-hate-crime-for-guardian-readers-to-fuss-over/ [accessed 20 July 2011].

Williams, R., (2009) 'Pilkington case may be a Lawrence moment for disability hate crime', 29 September, *Guardian*, available at http://www.guardian.co.uk/uk/2009/sep/28/fiona-pilkington-inquest-disability-hate [accessed 20 July 2011].

Wintour, P., Elliot, L., Sparrow, A., (2010) 'Welfare crackdown begins with drive to reduce incapacity benefit claims', 28 June, *Guardian*, available at http://www.guardian.co.uk/politics/2010/jun/28/welfare-incapacity-benefit-claimants-assessment [accessed 20 July 2011].

6   International perspectives on disability hate crime

Mark Sherry, University of Toledo, USA

Introduction

Disability hate crimes are a global phenomenon, but there are major differences in the way they are defined, prosecuted and reported in the US and the UK. The disability movement in the UK also has a different role in publicizing hate crimes and becoming incorporated into the policy-making process than its US counterpart. The UK movement has been far more active in organizing the disability community through local-level campaigns, whereas the US movement has been more concerned with lobbying in the legislative arena. Additionally, record-keeping on disability hate crimes is different in the US compared to the UK: statistics on hate crimes have been kept in the US much longer than the UK. Of course, one must be very cautious in relying on official figures about disability hate crimes because the vast majority of disability hate crimes are not reported. Finally, the incidence of disability hate crime in both the US and the UK must be understood against a background of entrenched disablism, a system of power which must be challenged in order to make the world safer for disabled people.

Aims

This chapter aims to outline some of the differences in language between the UK and the US in terms of disability hate crimes. It will also discuss some of the differences in political and legislative responses to disability hate crimes in the US and the UK, describing differences in the role of the disability movement in publicizing disability hate crimes and lobbying for their legislative recognition. As well, the chapter will identify similarities in hyperviolent and hypersexual disability hate crimes in both the US and the UK. The under-reporting of disability hate crimes in both the US and the UK will also be analyzed. Finally, the chapter will outline the broader context of disablism in both the US and the UK, which provides a cornerstone for negative assumptions and stereotypes about disabled people.

Language differences

There are major differences between the language used to describe disability hate crimes in the US and the UK. Within the UK, the social model of disability has become a dominant (almost hegemonic) framework for the disability movement (Sherry, 2006). The social model of disability relies on a strict divide between impairment (a recognized medical condition) and disability (negative social responses to such conditions). The rationale for this heuristic distinction is to distinguish between the experience of biological, cognitive, sensory or psychiatric difference and the prejudice, discrimination and other negative social consequences that many disabled people experience (Sherry, 2007). The collective experiences of disabled people are often discussed in terms of 'oppression' (Oliver, 1990) – necessarily requiring large-scale social change – and the collective term 'disabled people' has been the dominant language adopted by the disability movement.

In the US context, however, disability (like 'race', gender or religion) is regarded as an identity – albeit one with individual as well as collective dimensions. Within the overarching American cultural emphasis on individualism, disability has usually been framed as an individual identity, and not necessarily linked to any broader themes of oppression. When discussed as a collective experience, it is usually discursively positioned within a collective 'civil rights' framework as a 'minority' identity (Carey, 2009; David, Hill, Siegal, & Michael, 2004; Scotch, 2001; Shapiro, 1994). The language of 'oppression' is absent within this discursive framework and the term 'ableism' (which incidentally centers the nondisabled self) is far more likely to be used than 'disablism'. Underlying the individualist tones of the broader culture, the preferred language in the US context is 'person with a disability'.

These differences are significant for the study of disability hate crime because the crimes must be understood within their own particular social context. The cultural construction of disability is not a universal process; it is a continually changing, culturally specific social dynamic. For instance, if disability is understood as an individual identity, understood within a broader cultural emphasis on individualism, the appropriate remedies for hate crimes are individual ones – individual punishment for offenders, and assistance for individual victims. On the other hand, if disability is assumed to be a form of social exclusion and oppression which happens to a large group of people, then disability hate crimes are more likely to be regarded as the most heinous expression of wider social dynamics, and large-scale social change is necessary – true, but I don't think there's an explicit anti-individualist response to hate crimes from the UK Disabled People's Movement.

Not only do different cultural interpretations of disability influence the responses to hate crimes, but the targets of disability hate crimes involving vandalism often reflect culturally specific developments in the built environment. As an example, the vandalism of accessible vehicles and universal access signs (Sherry, 2010) only occurred after disability discrimination laws in the US required a certain number of accessible spaces in public car parks, and accessible vehicles became more common. Such crimes began in the US before the UK – in part, reflecting the fact that the Americans with Disabilities Act was signed in 1990, five years before the UK Disability Discrimination Act. They were also recognized legislatively in the US well before similar legislation occurred in the UK. In the US, disability hate crimes began to be recognized in State legislation in 1979 (Sherry, 2000b), whereas in the UK it was not until 2005 that Section 146 of the Criminal Justice Act only specifically recognized disability hate crimes.

There are also major differences in the ways in which disability hate crimes are defined and reported within the UK and the US. One UK poster on disability hate crime developed by the Lothian and Borders Police states 'Verbal Abuse. Swearing. Threats. Intimidation. Harassment. Bullying. Physical abuse. Vandalism. Graffiti. You don't have to be hit for it to be hate crime.' (Lothian and Borders Police, 2010). This approach to hate crime is very different from that adopted in the US, where verbal abuse and swearing would usually be protected under the Constitutional protection for freedom of speech. Such language might be used as evidence of anti-disability bias in the context of another crime such as assault, but would not be regarded as disability hate crime in its own right. This inclusion of verbal abuse in some UK definitions of hate crime has significant consequences for reporting: it may result in much higher figures than the US, where hateful language around disability would not be included in official reports.

Nevertheless, there are significant similarities between hate crime legislation in the US and UK. All hate crime legislation is rooted in identity politics. Particular groups campaign for recognition of hate crimes against them, and if successful they receive protected status within hate crime legislation, which usually results in sentence enhancement provisions for offenders. Hate crime legislation, in both the UK and the US, is therefore more akin to the US approach to disability than the UK social model: disability is regarded as an identity which may be targeted for criminal victimization, and hate crime legislation usually seeks individual remedies for victims and individual punishment for offenders. Collective remedies, such as broader social change that aims to challenge social inequality between disabled and nondisabled people, are largely absent from the individualist framework of the criminal justice system.

It is not a coincidence that British criminal justice organizations such as the Crown Prosecution Service use the language of 'disability hate crime' rather than 'disablist hate crime' (Crown Prosecution Service, 2007). The former implies an individualistic approach which is premised on demonstrating that an individual victim who was (or was perceived to be) disabled was victimized because of that identity. The latter approach suggests a broader connection to social exclusion and marginalization of disabled people, and connects individual crimes to broader forms of power and prejudice. Given that this chapter reviews particular legal cases in the UK and the US that have involved judicial determinations about 'disability hate crimes', rather than 'disablist hate crimes', this is the language which will be adopted here. However, the broader elements of disablism will be discussed in the final part of the chapter, in order to contextualize the crimes and to identify broader social dynamics which contribute to a cultural climate which is hostile to disabled people.

One of the major problems with the identity politics inherent in hate crime legislation is its reductionism – the complexities of multiple identities (and multiple forms of power) are largely ignored as a group presents a united front within its lobbying activities. However, such identity politics faces immediate problems in the context of an intersectional analysis of power. The following case – which could be represented as a disability hate crime or a racial hate crime – illustrates such reductionist tendencies. Billy Ray Johnson, an African American man with a developmental disability, was the victim of a life-threatening attack in 2003 (*Billy Ray Johnson v. Christopher Colt Amox*). He was called a 'crazy nigger' – a term which could be used to describe both racial bias and anti-disability bias. Within the identity politics approach that dominates hate crimes, the racial motivation was emphasized by prosecutors. This is typical: prosecutors in hate crime cases tend to reduce the motivation of perpetrators down to one identity of the victim. It is a serious shortcoming within the identity politics of hate crime laws that there is little room for the recognition of multiple identities and multiple biases.

In Waterford, England in 2007, a disability parking sign used by an openly gay black disabled man was the target of homophobic and racist graffiti. One handicapped parking sign (a symbol of disability) was removed and another was vandalized. Graffiti on the second parking sign included hateful slurs such as 'dick sucker', 'fudge packer' and 'nigger lover' (Michael, 2007). Unfortunately, the reductionist tendencies of hate crime legislation tend to result in such crimes being labelled racist hate crimes, or homophobic hate crimes, or disability hate crimes, but never do they incorporate all three simultaneously. Such reductionist tendencies occur both in the UK and in the US hate crime legislation and in prosecutorial practice. Multiple identities – which may result in increased or decreased chances of victimization for particular groups – are largely ignored in favor of simplistic, individualist, single-identity protection.

Simplistic and reductionist identity politics have also spilled over into the advocacy campaigns of disability groups. For instance, the (UK) *Getting Away With Murder* report on disability hate crime states:

> Comparisons with sentencing for crimes against other minority groups reveal that those motivated by religious, racial and homophobic hatred are more likely to be recognised as such and are therefore punished more harshly than crimes against disabled people.
>
> (*Disability Now*, The United Kingdom's Disabled People's
> Council, & Scope, 2008: 15)

Implicit in such comments is the simplistic, flawed and reductionist distinction between 'disabled people' and those people with racial, sexual or religious identities who might be victims of hate crimes. The overlapping nature of identities (and of power more broadly) is ignored within such perspectives.

Role of the disability movement

A personal disclaimer is necessary before this discussion begins. The author wrote the first Australian studies of disability hate crimes in 1999 and the first US study in 2000 (Sherry, 1999, 2000b). The author also gave conference presentations on the topic in the UK around 2002. As both an academic and an activist at the time, it could be argued that these were a part of the disability movement's response to the problem. However, to give such an impression would be misleading. It was not until years later that the disability movement in any of these countries began to collectively prioritize the problem of disability hate crimes in a large-scale fashion. In those years, the author felt virtually alone in moving away from the discourse of 'abuse' and instead conceptualizing the problem as 'disability hate crime'. Papers by the author were published by two disabled women's organizations and one Australian academic journal, but in general, responses to the author's research from disability organizations involved disbelief, disagreement and denial. These feelings of isolation occurred despite the fact within a few years, the Capability Scotland and the Disability Rights Commission reported that 73 per cent of disabled respondents reported experiencing verbal abuse and intimidation, usually from strangers (Capability Scotland and the Disability Rights Commission, 2004). 'Stranger crimes' have long been recognized as a potential sign of a hate crime (Sherry, 2004).

Disability hate crime

In the years 2006-2011, however, disability hate crimes became widely recognized in the UK – particularly in the period after 2007 when disability organizations began to actively prioritize this issue and mobilize around it, publicizing hyperviolent disability hate crimes in particular. Since that time, the disability movement in the UK has taken a much more activist position than its US counterpart. Okay – this responds to a previous query – I wonder if a more historically specific language could be adopted – I read the above rejection by the UK DPM to be fairly universal/timeless. It has focused a great deal of its attention at the grassroots and local level, whereas the US movement has not. Indeed, disability hate crimes are still largely ignored by most disability organizations in the US. On those rare occasions where disability organizations in the US have recognized the issue, they have simply been concerned with lobbying at the governmental and policy level, not actively campaigning through local-level education and organizing campaigns. That is not to suggest that the US disability movement has been unsuccessful – in fact, in 2009, the *Matthew Shepard and James Byrd, Jr. Hate Crimes Prevention Act* explicitly included disabled people in Federal hate crime law. But this did not result from a longstanding campaign; disability was simply one of a number of identities that was added to hate crime law at that time, including racial and sexual identities.

In contrast, the UK disability movement has told hundreds of stories about hate crime, held hundreds of community meetings, and has worked with the police in establishing regional task forces to address disability hate crimes. It has not only lobbied the Government for more effective prevention, protection and reporting of disability hate crimes, but has also worked to raise community awareness and to encourage disabled people to report their experiences of hate crime. Such activities have not occurred at all in the US context. There have been several (usually unacknowledged and unauthorized) reprints of the author's papers by US disability organizations on their websites, but no disability organization in the US has ever even held a disability hate crime conference.

This raises another difference between the two movements. The lobbying of the disability movement in the UK has been so effective that a number of activists from the disability hate crime movement have received prestigious government honors, have been given senior policy positions and have been appointed to various task forces. While this does not particularly mean that the advocacy of any particular individual will be compromised, and indeed, they may be able to effect significant policy change through such positions of power, such moves do raise the spectre of assimilation and co-option of some key members of a social movement. Broader studies of social movements suggest ' ... institutionalization is not like other tactical shifts or movement innovations that may be accomplished without significant costs to the movement and its goals; it also includes well-established drawbacks for social movements, not the least of which is cooptation and demobilization' (Coy & Hedeen, 2005: 405).

Hyperviolent and hypersexual crimes

Not all disability hate crimes involve interpersonal violence – many crimes involve theft or vandalism (Sherry, 2010). But a significant proportion of disability hate crimes are particularly sadistic. These hyperviolent, hypersexual crimes have sadly occurred on many occasions in both the US and the UK, frequently resulting in death. A few examples – from both the UK and the US – will give a sense of the viciousness of these crimes. The reasons why these are described as hate crimes, rather than homicides, will become evident in this discussion. Factors such as multiple perpetrators, repeat victimization and discriminatory language used in the commission of a crime all point towards a particular act being considered a hate crime.

The case of Eric Krochmaluk was the first disability hate crime ever prosecuted anywhere in the world. Krochmaluk's case, which occurred over 15 days in New Jersey in 1999, contained many features that have been repeated in other violent disability hate crimes, both in the US and the UK: multiple perpetrators, repeated victimization, destruction of property, hyperviolent behavior by the perpetrators (he was hit repeatedly, assaulted with many weapons, burned and so on) and sexual violence (for instance, Krochmaluk was stripped and was sexually assaulted with a string of wooden beads) (*The*

State of New Jersey v. Jennifer Dowell, Brandon Crz, Marni Soloman, William Mackay, Christal Lavary, Daniel Vistad, David Allen Jr. and Jessica Fry). Ashley Clark was another US victim who experienced a hyperviolent attack. She is a woman with an intellectual disability who was born without limbs. Over an eight-hour period, Clark was tied and gagged, punched and kicked, and was hit with a baseball bat, prompting Ohio legislators to enact disability hate crime legislation (Driehaus, 2008). Another case involved Lloyd Sterns, a 44-year-old developmentally disabled man from Iowa. This case also involved multiple perpetrators (between two and four at various times), repeat victimization, and hyperviolent behavior (they pushed Sterns into a running shower, duct-taped his arms together, forcefully poured mouthwash into his mouth, tried to spray insecticide into his eyes and tried to shove him into a lake). Property destruction (rather than theft of something that is valuable) is another common feature of such disability hate crimes. The perpetrators burned some of Sterns' property, including books, magazines, a coffee basket, and coffee percolator parts. They also threw kitchen knives in a door and broke some of his upstairs windows. Sexual degradation and dehumanization is often present in hyperviolent crimes. In this case, one of the perpetrators repeatedly pulled Sterns' shorts down and also pinched his nipples. As well, the perpetrators defecated on a table and urinated on the floor. Then they rubbed faeces in Sterns' hair, claiming it was good for him.

Hyperviolent and hypersexual attacks have also been an alarming element of disability hate crimes in the UK. The brutal murder of Brent Martin is a case in point. Though not *officially* recognized as a disability hate crime, the case became a rallying point for disability activists who felt that the absence of such official recognition denied the reality of hate in the lives of disabled people. Like the US cases discussed above, Martin's death also involved multiple perpetrators, vicious brutality, multiple locations, and degradation of the victim (in this case, one of the perpetrators urinated on the dying victim and the perpetrators took a number of trophy photographs over Brent's dead body) (Pearson, 2008). The death of many victims of hate crimes means that the language of 'victim', rather than 'survivor', is appropriate when discussing disability hate crimes. One cannot be a dead 'survivor'; the language also underlines the seriousness of the crimes, and connects to a broader discourse on criminal victimization. Raymond Atherton, another victim, was terrorized for months before his death. This pattern of repeat victimization is common in hyperviolent disability hate crimes. The offenders not only beat Atherton repeatedly (including attacking him with a plank of wood when they killed him) but they had also set his hair alight, urinated in his drinks, poured bleach over him, and had often broken into his apartment to vandalize it. Kerri Delacruz was another disability hate crime victim in the UK who was the victim of a hyperviolent attack. Delacruz, from Liverpool, was repeatedly victimized over a six-month period. Her dog was killed and she was slashed with a knife by multiple perpetrators, requiring 14 stitches to her breasts, face, back and hands (Johnson, 2009; Staff Mail Online, 2009).

While these powerful narratives are an important testimony to the hyper-violent nature of many disability hate crimes, it is also important to consider the broader data on such crimes in order to identify large-scale patterns in disability hate crimes in general.

Data on disability hate crimes

Data on officially recorded disability hate crimes has been collected in the US for a much longer period of time than in the UK. Of course, there are problems with such data – most disability hate crimes (in both countries) are unreported, and even if they are reported, law-enforcement officers have a poor track record in terms of recognizing them as 'hate crimes' (Sherry, 2002). Nevertheless, the figures on disability hate crimes that have been recorded in the US for the last 10 years do provide an insight into some patterns of disability hate crimes. The overall figures have been discussed in some detail elsewhere (Sherry, 2010), but the patterns can be briefly summarized here. Basically, the data on interpersonal violence in disability hate crimes suggests that simple assault is the most common form of criminal victimization, followed by intimidation. Importantly, there are much higher rates of simple assault in disability hate crimes than in other types of hate crimes, though the rate of aggravated assault is higher among people with physical impairments. In terms of property crimes, the most common disability hate crimes involve destruction, damage and vandalism, as well as larceny/theft. The overall patterns within property crimes that are motivated by anti-disability bias are somewhat different from other hate crimes. There is a relatively lower rate of property destruction/damage/vandalism compared to other hate crimes, and a much higher rate of theft and burglary. Such longitudinal data is not available in the UK. However, the Crown Prosecution Service has produced three years of hate crime data (from 2008-2010) and some broad patterns are emerging. Similar to the US data, crimes against the person are the most common form of disability hate crime, and again the incidence of theft and handling, burglary and robbery are much higher for victims of disability hate crimes than for other types of hate crimes (Crown Prosecution Service, 2008, 2009, 2010). However, the relatively short period of time for collecting this data, as well as the fact that most disability hate crimes are not reported, means that one should be cautious in making generalizations from these sources.

The under-reporting of disability hate crimes is a complex and multi-dimensional problem. It has many causes, including fear of not being believed, learned helplessness, disabling barriers in the criminal justice system, inappropriate assumptions by law enforcement officers that disabled victims are not reliable witnesses and will not be believed in court, and many other reasons. Many disabled victims, like victims of sex crimes, feel that the court system can be a form of 'repeat victimization' – feeling like they are on trial, rather than the offender. Indeed, there are many parallels and overlaps between disability hate crimes and sex crimes in general. Essentially, disabled victims of hate crimes have felt disempowered and disillusioned at all levels of the criminal justice system, from initial reporting of a crime to the (generally untried, unsuccessful or inadequate) prosecution of cases. This is an ongoing cycle of injustice. Most cases are not reported, and if they are reported they do not go to court, but if they do go to court, the offender is likely to be either found 'not guilty' or receive an incredibly lenient sentence (Sherry, 2010).

Links between disability hate crimes and disablism

Disability hate crimes must be understood in their broader social and cultural context – one where disabled people experience widespread social exclusion, marginalization, prejudice and vilification. Eugenics and Social Darwinist themes have a long cultural history in the devaluation of disabled people (and in the propagation of racism), and still receive widespread circulation. Of course, it would be a mistake to overemphasize the continuity of these ideas, and not to recognize the way they have changed and adapted over time. For instance, the rise of computer technology has led to the hacking of epilepsy websites, where flashing images have been deliberately inserted in order to provoke seizures. To unproblematically link such crimes with Darwinist ideas may miss their postmodern dimensions. Nevertheless, it is still important to recognize that such historical prejudices still contribute significantly to a cultural climate in which disabled lives are devalued and disrespected.

The source of such ideas is a matter of contestation. For some, disablism is interpreted within a framework of 'stigma' and 'prejudice', ideas that are best explored through the perspective of social psychology. This perspective is best summarized in the following quote: 'I believe stereotyping is a universal means of coping with anxieties engendered by our inability to control the world' (Gilman, 1985: 12). Gilman's assumption that stereotyping is an ahistorical cultural universal is problematic because it does not explain why particular stereotypes develop against particular groups. Likewise, Goffman's concept of 'stigma' is widely used (particularly in the US) to explain cultural attitudes towards disabled people (Chemers, 2008; Mittan, 2010; Schweik, 2010; Valeras, 2010). Like Gilman's analysis of stereotypes, the key theoretical flaw of Goffman's concept of stigma is that it leaves the relationship between stigmatizing ideas and wider processes of social inequality unexplored. For instance, it is insufficient to note that certain women, disabled people, or members of ethnic minorities may have stigmatized identities without acknowledging that stigmatizing ideas might be generated by unequal power structures, such as sexism, disablism and racism.

Other scholars, particularly in the UK, suggest that the link between disability and economics is paramount – in particular, the historical and ongoing exclusion of disabled people from the primary labour market (Oliver, 1990). Despite the economic reductionism of this approach, it does recognize that disablism does not simply lie in the realms of 'culture' and 'ideas'; it has material dimensions. The cultural devaluation of disabled people is deeply connected to broader social, economic and political systems of power (Sherry, 2000a). Likewise, such analyses suggest that attitudinal changes must be accompanied by material ones. The exclusion of disabled people from the workforce and from educational opportunities, the continuing segregation of disabled people in group homes and institutions isolated from 'mainstream' society, and the lack of supports, safeguards and advocacy for many disabled people must all be addressed in order to have an environment that is safe for disabled people.

Both these approaches to disability can be applied to the study of disability hate crimes. Undoubtedly, there are stereotypes about disability (and about particular impairments) which devalue disabled lives. Attitudinal changes are undoubtedly needed, stigma must be challenged, and longstanding prejudices against disabled people must be dismantled. But the disempowered economic position of many disabled people – which often places them in a position of having few supports and feeling as though they have few choices (even in abusive situations) – must also be addressed.

Some of the cases discussed here have underscored the importance of recognizing multiple forms of bias in the commission of hate crimes. The case involving Billy Ray Johnson was an excellent example. Hatred towards disability should not be studied in isolation; attitudes towards disability are always simultaneously infused with notions of race, class and gender (Sherry, 2007). Some subgroups of disabled people may be more likely to be targeted than others. An intersectional analysis of disability hate crimes is urgently required, demonstrating how racism, sexism, classism and disablism may influence victimization rates. It is particularly important to remember that impairments are not evenly distributed; their social distribution is deeply affected by the broader social structures of race, class and gender (Sherry, 2008). Disabled people are more likely to come from poor backgrounds; disability hate crimes often involve the targeting of people who were already socially marginalized by the combination of their class position and their disability identities.

Conclusion

Disability hate crimes are a serious and life-threatening form of criminal victimization. In both the UK and the US, they often have hyperviolent and hypersexual dimensions. These crimes need to be recognized, reported, investigated and prosecuted. Fortunately, legislative recognition has occurred in both the UK and the US in recent years; but that is only the first step. Victims must be encouraged and supported to report these crimes, and barriers in the criminal justice system must be dismantled. But individualist responses that simply respond after a crime has occurred (seeking to support a victim and prosecute an offender) by themselves are inadequate. Preventing disability hate crimes requires challenging disablism in all its forms. Deep-seated prejudices must be confronted. The collective economic and social position of disabled people must also be improved. The links between disablism and other forms of power (such as racism, sexism and classism) must also be explored in more detail, because some groups may be more likely to be victimized than others. Overall, there is a desperate need to empower disabled people, so that cases are reported, victims are supported, and offenders are punished. Safer communities are possible. But this requires a strong disability movement that demands the collective empowerment of disabled people. Empowered disabled people will not internalize learned helplessness, and will not accept social exclusion and marginalization; disempowered disabled people may not even report hate crimes. The fact that most hate crimes are not reported demonstrates that most disabled people are not empowered, and there is a long way to go in ensuring disabled people are safe.

References

Billy Ray Johnson v. Christopher Colt Amox (District Court of Cass County, Texas 5th Judicial District 2006).

Capability Scotland and the Disability Rights Commission. (2004). *Hate Crime Against Disabled People in Scotland: A Report.* Edinburgh: Capability Scotland.

Carey, A. C. (2009). *On the Margins of Citizenship: Intellectual Disability and Civil Rights in Twentieth-Century America.* Philadelphia, PA: Temple University Press.

Chemers, M. M. (2008). *Staging Stigma: A Critical Examination of the American Freak Show.* New York, NY: Palgrave McMillan.

Coy, P. G., & Hedeen, T. (2005). 'A Stage Model of Social Movement Cooptation: Community Mediation in the United States'. *The Sociological Quarterly, 46*(3), 405–435.

Crown Prosecution Service. (2007). *CPS Policy for Prosecuting Cases of Disability Hate Crime.* London: Mangagement Information Service, CPS.

Crown Prosecution Service. (2008). *Hate Crime Report 2007–2008.* London: Management Information Branch, CPS.

Crown Prosecution Service. (2009). *Hate Crime Report 2008–2009.* London: Management Information Branch, CPS.

Crown Prosecution Service. (2010). *Hate crime and crimes against older people report 2009–2010.* London: Management Information Branch, CPS.

David, B. P., Hill, E., Siegal, C. D. S., & Michael, W. (2004). *Disability Civil Rights Law And Policy: Cases And Materials.* St. Paul, MN: West.

Disability Now, The United Kingdom's Disabled People's Council, & Scope. (2008). *Getting Away with Murder: Disabled people's experiences of hate crime in the UK.* London: Scope.

Driehaus, B. (2008, 27 February). 2 Teenagers Are Accused Of Torturing Ohio Woman. *New York Times.*

Gilman, S. (1985). *Pathology and Difference: Stereotypes of Sexuality, Race, and Madness.* Ithaca, NY: Cornell University Press.

Johnson, A. (2009, 17 February). 'Woman tells of hoodie stabbing ordeal'. Retrieved 15 November 2009, from http://www.clickliverpool.com/news/local-news/122909-woman-tells-of-hoodystabbing-ordeal.html.

Lothian and Borders Police. (2010). 'You don't have to be hit for it to be a hate crime'. Retrieved 5 May 2011, from http://www.lbp.police.uk/disability-hatecrime/index.asp.

Michael, J. A. (2007, August 2). Mentally challenged man and his advocate target of racist and anti-gay vandalism. *Between the Lines Newspaper August 2.*

Mittan, R. J. (2010). 'Understanding and Coping with Stigma'. *Exceptional Parent,* 40(5), 37–41.

Oliver, M. (1990). *The Politics of Disablement.* London: Macmillan.

Pearson, A. (2008, January 9). Two admit murdering Brent Martin for 'sport'. www. journallive.co.uk.

Schweik, S. (2010). 'Marshall P. Wilder and Disability Performance History' [electronic version]. *Disability Studies Quarterly, 30.* Retrieved 5 May from http://www.dsq-sds. org/article/view/1271/1294.

Scotch, R. (2001). *From good will to civil rights: transforming federal disability policy.* Philadelphia, PA: Temple University Press.

Shapiro, J. P. (1994). *No Pity: People with Disabilities Forging a New Civil Rights Movement.* New York, NY: Random House.

Sherry, M. (1999). *Hate Crimes Against People With Disabilities.* Paper presented at the Hate Crime Conference.

Sherry, M. (2000a). 'Examining the Social and Political Dimensions of Access'. In M. Clear (ed.), *Promises, Promises: Disability in New South Wales* (pp. 126–137). Leichardt, NSW: Federation Press.

Sherry, M. (2000b, 1 July). 'Talking about Hate'. *Bent: A Journal of Crip Gay Voices* Retrieved 5 May, 2011

Sherry, M. (2002). *Don't Ask, Tell or Respond: Silent Acceptance of Disability Hate Crimes.* Paper presented at the Ed Roberts Post Doctoral Fellowship in Disability Studies at the University of California at Berkeley Public Lecture Series 21 November.

Sherry, M. (2004). 'Exploring Disability Hate Crimes'. *Review of Disability Studies: An International Journal, 1*(1), 51–60.

Sherry, M. (2006). *If I Only Had A Brain.* New York, NY: Routledge.

Sherry, M. (2007). (Post) Colonizing Disability. *Wagadu: A Journal of Transnational and Women's Studies, 3,* 10–23.

Sherry, M. (2008). *Disability and Diversity: A Sociological Approach.* New York: Nova Science.

Sherry, M. (2010). *Disability Hate Crimes: Does Anyone Really Hate Disabled People?* London: Ashgate.

Staff Mail Online. (2009, 17 February). 'Agony of disabled woman living in fear after sick gang butchers her Yorkshire terrier … then tortures HER for an hour'. Retrieved 15 November 2009, from http://www.dailymail.co.uk/news/article-1147822/Agony-disabled-woman-living-fear-sick-gang-butchers-Yorkshire-terrier–tortures-HER-hour.html

The State of New Jersey v. Jennifer Dowell, Brandon Crz, Marni Soloman, William Mackay, Christal Lavary, Daniel Vistad, David Allen Jr. and Jessica Fry (Monmouth County Court 2000).

Valeras, A. B. (2010). 'We don't have a box': Understanding hidden disability identity utilizing narrative research methodology [electronic version]. *Disability Studies Quarterly, 30.* Retrieved 5 May from http://www.dsq-sds.org/article/view/1267/1297.

Part II

Responses to disablist hate crime

7 Disablist violence in the US

Unacknowledged hate crime

Jack Levin, Northeastern University, USA

In February 2010, Jennifer Daugherty, a 30-year-old woman with a learning disability from Greensburg, Pennsylvania, was brutally murdered by six people pretending to be her good friends. Holding her hostage for days, the perpetrators allegedly tortured Daugherty, shaving her head, binding her with Christmas decorations, beating her with a towel rack and vacuum cleaner, feeding her detergent, urine, and various medications, and then forcing her to write a suicide note before stabbing her to death (Martinez, 2010). The sadistic attack on Daugherty was anything but unique, yet few Americans are aware of the special vulnerability of people with emotional, intellectual, and physical disabilities to extraordinary violence. Thinking of crimes inspired by hate or bias, they may conjure up an image of a burning cross on the lawn of a black family, or swastikas scrawled on the walls of a synagogue. They might recall the name of James Byrd, the black American in Jasper, Texas, who was dragged for miles to his death behind a pickup truck by three white supremacists, or they might have a memory of Matthew Shepard, the gay college student who was viciously beaten and then tied to a fence where he was left to die in the desert outside of Laramie, Wyoming. The same Americans who are acutely aware of violence perpetrated against victims because of their race, religion, sexual orientation or gender have 'tunnel vision' when it comes to the brutal murder of Jennifer Daugherty, who was apparently singled out only because of her intellectual deficit.

Vicious attacks on people with disabilities may be overlooked by those individuals who focus more on violence based on a victim's race, religion, gender, or sexual orientation and simply have not considered the extreme vulnerability to maltreatment that comes with such disorders as cerebral palsy, autism, multiple sclerosis, learning disabilities, and mental illness. Yet, according to anonymous victim accounts from the United States Bureau of Justice Statistics, Americans with disabilities experience serious violence at a rate nearly twice that of the general population. As indicated in Figure 7.1 below, violent victimization rates for people with disabilities are especially high for children, teenagers, and young adults. Moreover, the differences in rates by disability status tend to decline with advancing age (Harrell, 2011).

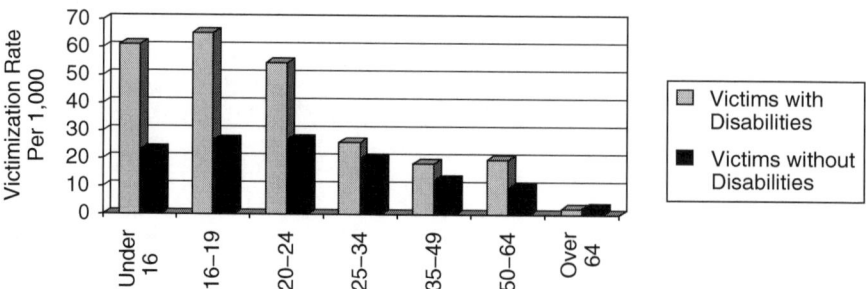

Figure 7.1 Violent victimization rates by age and disability status, 2010

Comparing particular offences, the risk of being a victim of either sexual assault or assault and battery with a deadly weapon is more than four times higher among individuals with disabilities than among those without disabilities. In 2010 alone, Americans with disabilities were victims of about 35,000 rapes, 98,000 robberies, 150,000 aggravated assaults, and 285,000 simple assaults (Harrell, 2011).

Estimating prevalence

Over the years, police departments around the United States have increased their sensitivity to hate crimes based on race, religion, gender, and sexual orientation, but they still may not recognize disablist bias in the motivation for an assault. For the year 2010, a total of merely 24 anti-mental-impairment and 22 anti-physical-impairment – of the 7,699 hate crimes recognized by the police in FBI data – reportedly targeted people with disabilities (Federal Bureau of Investigation, 2011). When the US Department of Justice asked persons with disabilities anonymously why they believed they had been targeted for violence, however, some 17 per cent, representing almost 100,000 victims, suggested it was because of their disability (Harrell, 2011).

The FBI data clearly represent a tremendous underestimate, but it is only part of a larger problem regarding the reporting of hate offences generally. The FBI hate crime count is based on a voluntary reporting system to which many local police jurisdictions refuse to contribute, causing hate offences of all kinds to be under-reported and less likely to be prosecuted when they go to court. In 2010, for example, only two hate crimes were reported for the entire state of Wyoming. Mississippi reported 11; Georgia 17; and Louisiana 13. By contrast, those states whose police departments are more willing to cooperate with the FBI have typically reported hundreds of hate crimes – for example, Massachusetts, 316; New Jersey, 543; and California, 1,087 (Federal Bureau of Investigation, 2011).

Moreover, an offence may not be recorded as a hate crime because of a lack of independent evidence that it was motivated by bias, even when victims are convinced that they were singled out for abuse because of some difference (Levin & McDevitt, 2002). The perpetrators might not have used a slur or written hate graffiti on a wall or sidewalk, might never have confided their intent to the police or an acquaintance, or might remain unknown to law enforcement. In October, 2006, for example, a mother of six, wearing a hijab (the head scarf of a devout Muslim woman) and carrying a three-month-old infant in her arms, was gunned down while walking on an affluent residential street in Fremont, California. Because her assailant has not yet been apprehended and did not leave any indication of his intent at the crime scene, the motivation for this murder cannot be definitively identified. Yet relatives of the victim, as well as local Muslim leaders who have been able to rule out such other possibilities as robbery and revenge, are convinced that the motive was hate (Kuruvila & Lee, 2006). Similarly, domestic violence counsellor Kimberly Black Wisseman (Wisseman *et al.*, 2011) attributed her selection as an appropriate victim of robbery and rape to her quadriplegia. On a Friday evening, four men invaded Wisseman's apartment, climbing through an open bedroom window and locking her attendant in an adjoining bedroom. Brandishing a knife and a gun, the assailants repeatedly threatened Wisseman's life during their sexual assault. If the victim had had 'normal' mobility, their crime might have been vastly more difficult. The victim's tormentors were very much aware of their advantage. Wisseman was convinced that she had been targeted for the attack. But proving that the assault was motivated by the victim's disability is not so easy to do. The four rapists have never been apprehended.

It isn't only law enforcement personnel who are reluctant to report hate attacks. Even the victims themselves probably provide a vast underestimate of the actual prevalence of hate offences. There are apparently numerous victims who also prefer not to inform anyone, and especially not the police, that they have been targeted. Based on a history of animosity, black and Latino victims may see law enforcement as an 'army of occupation'; immigrants may identify the police with a tyrannical regime in their home country or may be concerned about being deported; gays and lesbians may perceive, rightly or not, that police officers are generally homophobic and therefore unsympathetic to their victimization (Levin & McDevitt, 2002; Levin & Nolan, 2011).

According to Veronica Robertson, a staff member of the advocacy group Access on Living, fear may discourage individuals with disabilities from reporting their victimization to the authorities. She cites the case of a 30-something quadriplegic man who, whenever he leaves his apartment, is beaten and verbally abused by the same perpetrator, who calls him a 'cripple' and warns him not to inform the police. As a result, the victim is afraid to venture outside. He refuses to report the hate crimes committed against him (Wolfe, 1995).

Many victims with disabilities are extremely reluctant to report attacks out of fear that their tormentors will retaliate. They may have a psychiatric or intellectual deficit which seriously interferes with their capacity to recognize false friendships or to report a crime to a formal agency. Or they may assume a position of dependence in a relationship with caretakers who conceal their sadistic urges in the high credibility of their institutional roles. In October

2008, for example, five staff members in a Louisiana psychiatric facility were arrested for allegedly battering their patients with hand weights and inserting bleach into their open wounds. The victimized patients had complained bitterly, but were perceived to be out of touch with reality and undeserving of being taken seriously (Wolfe, 1995).

Even observers may be reluctant to report attacks against people with disabilities. Jean Parker, founder of Colorado's Cross-Disability Coalition and a blind person, was waiting for a bus when someone deliberately kicked her guide dog in the kidneys. It was easy to rule out motives such as robbery or rape. The attack was inspired strictly by hatred of disability, nothing else. Afraid of retaliation, a bystander who had witnessed Parker's dog being kicked refused to give the police a description of the assailant (Wolfe, 1995).

Violence against people with disabilities differs in important ways from other hate crimes, making disablist attacks even less likely to be reported or acknowledged. Unlike racially and religiously motivated offences, attacks against people with disabilities tend to be committed less by strangers and more by family members, neighbours, employees, and friends who may also be caregivers. According to Department of Justice statistics for the year 2010, only 33 per cent of violent victimizations against persons with disabilities were committed by strangers to the victim (Harrell, 2011). However, some of the most brutal hate-motivated disablist attacks have been perpetrated by individuals who have only a tenuous relationship with their victim (Farquhar, 1999). In January 1999, eight men and women tortured a 23-year-old man with learning disabilities who worked as a cook at a local fast-food restaurant. Apparently imitating the horror movie *Scream*, which they had recently viewed, the group persuaded their victim to attend a 'party' and, when he arrived, tormented him for almost three hours. They stripped their victim to his underwear, slapped and kicked him, and taped him to a chair which they dragged around the room. One of the perpetrators attempted to shave the victim's eyebrows and head with a razor; another completed the job with electric hair clippers. Members of the group then whipped him with rope knotted with a series of plastic beads so that his naked back, face, and chest were covered by a network of cuts and bruises. Cutting their victim out of the chair, they forced him to wear a bra and a woman's suit, while they dragged him into a van and drove him into the woods. Having reached a desolate area, they repeatedly punched him and slammed him to the ground. Finally, the victim was able to escape. He staggered to a nearby property, where he convinced a security guard to summon the police, who drove him to a local hospital, where he was treated and released.

Ignoring hate offences is particularly unfortunate, because the level of sadism and brutality is frequently greater in the case of disablist hate crimes than in their racial and religious counterparts. Disablist hate crimes are especially violent, containing major aspects of overkill not usually found to the same degree in hate attacks based on other kinds of bias. According to Department of Justice figures for 2010, the injuries suffered by people with disabilities are substantially more serious than for able-bodied victims, requiring medical treatment at a much greater rate, in 20 per cent versus 12 per cent of violent attacks (Harrell, 2011). Another source of under-reporting is associated with the special difficulty of identifying what is and what is not a crime based on hate or bias. Unlike other criminal acts, it is essential for the successful prosecution of a hate crime to establish a bias motivation in the perpetrators' mindset. Blacks may be regarded as 'mud people' who are lower than whites in the phylogenetic order, Jews as the children of Satan, Muslims as international terrorists, gays as perverts and paedophiles, and people with disabilities as stupid or deformed animals. The problem is that offenders don't usually confess; nor do they always leave eyewitnesses who are familiar with the offender's biases (Levin & McDevitt, 2002; Levin & Nolan, 2011).

In the United States, slurs espoused by the perpetrator at the crime scene represent the most widely employed evidence for establishing the commission of a hate attack (Levin & McDevitt, 2002). Racial and religious epithets are widely recognized to exist, even by those individuals who themselves would never use them in a conversation and are repulsed by those who do. The nasty labels associated with people with disabilities are just as hurtful as their racial and religious counterparts, but are simply not recognized to the same extent. People with disabilities have been referred to as invalids (not a valid person), handicapped (capable of only begging cap in hand), or disabled (characterizing the entire person as incompetent). Other hurtful labels include crippled, deformed, feeble-minded, idiot, moron, imbecile, mongolism, incompetent, insane, lunatic, maniac, and retard. The same people who would never dream of using the N-word are hardly reluctant to refer to an intellectually challenged individual as a 'retard' or to a person in a wheelchair as a 'cripple' or 'freak.'

Cultural sources of hate

As a cultural phenomenon, racist preferences apparently find inspiration early in life, as children begin to develop the biases that they have learned from dinner-table conversations, family members, friends, and television programs (Levin & Nolan, 2011). In an early study by social psychologists Kenneth and Mamie Clark (Clark & Clark, 1958), preschool children were asked to choose either a black or a white doll with which to play. Surprisingly, the majority of both white and black children preferred to play with the white doll, indicating the early impact of racial subordination and segregation on the psyche of countless minority youngsters. Testimony about the Clark and Clark study was given in the landmark 1954 Supreme Court decision in Brown vs. the Board of Education, which mandated the desegregation of America's schools (Clark & Clark, 1958).

Not unlike racism, anti-Semitism, and homophobia, the negative perceptions of disability are formed very early in the life of a child. The majority of children aged 3–6 are already aware of physical disabilities and have already attributed negative characteristics to those who are not physically able-bodied; they are more likely to learn about psychiatric and intellectual deficits a few years later, when their cognitive abilities have developed enough to think of people who are developmentally different in unflattering terms. Writing in the journal *Mental Retardation*, Laura Nabors (1997) determined that preschool children with disabilities receive fewer positive playmate preference nominations from peers. When able-bodied preschool children were shown pictures of persons with and without disabilities and asked to rate them in terms of whom they wanted to be friends with, the preschoolers showed a marked preference for able-bodied playmates and an aversion to their physically challenged counterparts.

Defensive motivation

Later in life, what began as an aversion may easily be transformed into outright prejudice and hate. From the viewpoint of a perpetrator, the members of some out-group, defined by their physical or developmental difference, represent a threat to his or her economic well-being, cultural or religious values, health, neighbourhood composition, educational opportunities, or physical survival. What we might view as a hate crime is therefore regarded by the perpetrator as a justified act of self-defence. Such defensive hate attacks usually occur in response to some precipitating event that is seen as 'the last resort': a gay rights rally, the first Latino in a college dormitory, a learning disabled student who is mainstreamed into a regular classroom, the opening of a group home for mental patients in a residential neighbourhood, or the like (Wolfe, 1995).

Not unlike the members of racial and religious groups, individuals with physical disabilities have often been the victims of defensive hate crimes when they attempt to relocate into middle-income suburban neighborhoods. A couple in suburban Chicago, both wheelchair users, planned to install a ramp at the entrance of their single-family residence, until neighbours threw rocks through their windows and sent threatening letters saying 'Your kind won't last here.' The couple gave up and moved away. They might have stayed in their home if they had received some support and encouragement from their neighbours and the police, but they did not (Wolfe, 1995).

Defensive hate attacks directed against homeless psychiatric patients have been on the rise during recent years. In October 2008, for example, Matthew Martin, a local resident of a densely populated neighbourhood west of downtown Los Angeles, burned to death John McGraham, a homeless man with a history of chronic depression. Martin doused his victim with gasoline and set him on fire. Three months earlier, the killer was fired from his job at a local barber shop, when his boss learned that he had struck and kicked McGraham in the back. Actually, Martin had had a number of run-ins with homeless men in the area, but his motive for killing McGraham was to get even with the homeless man for his job loss. Being obsessed with cleanliness, he also sought to protect himself from homeless people, whom he regarded as filthy (Leonard, 2010).

Thrill motivation

Not all hate crimes are defensive from the perpetrator's viewpoint. Many attacks are committed for the thrill by groups of young people, teenagers or young adults, who, bored and idle, are looking for a little excitement at someone else's expense (Levin & McDevitt, 2002; Levin & Nolan, 2011). Such thrill hate attacks have few practical consequences for their perpetrators. Instead, they gain bragging rights with their friends, who think that hate and violence are pretty cool. In thrill crimes, there is usually a sadistic leader who has tremendous influence over his peers and a group of friends who may not be hate-filled but are all too eager to be accepted. They go along to get along, hoping to satisfy the demands of their more influential pals by participating in the attack on their victims.

In May 2010, a 19-year-old high school student with a learning disability was brutally attacked on a busy Boston street, in broad daylight, by a group of nine young people, aged 15 to 21 (Boston Channel, 2010). The bloodied victim, who later described himself to police as 'slow and challenged', screamed and pleaded for help, then curled up on the ground, as the perpetrators repeatedly kicked, beat, and choked him. The victim later told police that 'the kids up the street had jumped him.' He had known his assailants from the Dorchester Youth Collaborative, an agency for high-risk teenagers, and they did not like him. But the youthful perpetrators used their shared animosity toward people with learning disabilities as a bonding exercise for the group. The more they shared in bashing their victim, the more cohesive their friendship became.

Retaliatory motivation

Some of the most dangerous hate crimes have a retaliatory motive, encouraging 'tit for tat' in an exchange of violence (McDevitt, Levin & Bennett, 2002). When the motive is retaliatory, an original attack by the members of one group is met by a retaliatory attack, often on a random basis, by the members of the victim's group. In other words, the victim becomes the villain. Retaliatory motivation has been observed to escalate the level of violence between racial and ethnic groups. During the 'troubles' in Northern Ireland, for example, one vicious hate crime directed against a Catholic or a Protestant resident frequently inspired a whole new round of deadly terrorist attacks.

Retaliation has similarly served as the motive for attacks involving people with disabilities. On January 19, 2007, John Odgren stabbed to death his 15-year-old schoolmate, a random victim, in a restroom at Lincoln-Sudbury High School in Massachusetts. The 16-year-old killer was diagnosed, early on, with major depression, Asperger's Syndrome, attention deficit hyper-activity disorder, and obsessive-compulsive disorder. Because of his dis-abilities, Odgren had a long history of having been bullied and had sought to retaliate violently. In third grade, he threatened to shoot some girls who had harassed him. In fourth grade, he jabbed a pencil into another student's chest. He was bullied repeatedly as he bounced from school to school, and then finally got even with his mainstreamed peers by killing an innocent victim. For taking the life of his schoolmate, Odgren was tried and convicted of first-degree murder and sentenced to life in prison without parole eligibility (Valencia, Wren, 2010).

Organized hate

It should be noted that only a very small minority of hate crimes, perhaps 5 per cent, directly involve organized hate groups. Disability hate crimes are no different in this respect. However, it is important to acknowledge that some organized hate groups overtly display their hostility to disabled people in a manner that can easily encourage and support non-members to become violent. In early November 2002, for example, the discussion forum of the white supremacist group Stormfront allocated a section of its discussion forum to eugenics. Among the disablist comments presented online was the following: 'We must put into place social and economic systems that encourage the best genes to dominate in numbers as well as power' (Stormfront, 2002).

Former Nazi skinhead T. J. Leyden took very personally the disablist rhetoric espoused by racist skinheads. He was eventually inspired by concern for the safety of his mother, who had polio as a child and walked with a limp, to give up his skinhead membership and become an ardent anti-racist. Hearing his Nazi colleagues refer to people with disabilities as 'surplus whites,' Leyden became convinced that his mother would be marked for death. This was too much for Leyden to tolerate from his skinhead buddies. For the love of his mother, he rejected his racist views and became a spokesperson for the Simon Wiesenthal Center in Los Angeles, where he took up a fight against anti-Semitism (Leyden, 2008).

Victim responses

Victims of disablist violence learn to respond in any of a number of ways to the maltreatment they are forced to endure. In the face of widespread bias, some people with disabilities come to accept the nasty stereotypes being communicated widely about them and suffer a profound loss of self-esteem. They may see themselves as inferior, incompetent, and totally disabled. Rather than regard their disability as only one of many characteristics they possess, they may instead come to define themselves totally as a person by their most serious disadvantage and give up the struggle for self-improvement in favour of sinking deeply into depression, drug abuse, or alcoholism.

Other people with disabilities refuse to accept the nasty stereotypes that invade their lives and instead seek individually to avoid the nastiest implications of their treatment by segregating themselves in terms of friendship, employment, and dating. Rather than give up, they might attempt to insulate themselves from the insulting behaviour of able-bodied people by selecting friends who have similar disabilities and dating within their own group. Still others seek actively to change the maltreatment they have suffered because of their disabilities. Since the 1970s, members of the Disability Rights Movement in the USA have been involved in boycotts, blocking traffic, protests, marches, and sit-ins. Closely mirroring the civil rights and women's movements of the 1960s, such tactics have effectively aided in the passage of laws helpful to people with physical and mental disabilities and the blockage of policies that would have been hurtful to the group. In the last couple of years, hundreds of people in wheelchairs have demonstrated on the streets of Atlanta, Chicago, Washington DC, and Nashville. In August 2008, the Special Olympics and 21 other disability groups called for a nationwide boycott of the Ben Stiller-directed film *Tropic Thunder* because of what the organizations considered a 'negative portrayal' of learning-disabled people. In March 2009, some 50 adults with learning disabilities and their caregivers marched around the Capitol in Salem Oregon, protesting proposed cuts to social services. They carried coffins as if in a funeral march and raised signs and banners. Some walked, while others were pushed in wheelchairs (Har, 2009; Horn, 2008). Such collective efforts in which people with disabilities participate are important for providing models for what the victims of hate violence might be able to achieve in the future. For now, however, such demonstrations and rallies are typically designed to reduce employment discrimination or to discourage cuts in the budgets for services. The hate crime response has not yet occurred (Har, 2009; Horn, 2008).

Changing minds

Thirty-two state hate crime statutes now protect the 54 million Americans with disabilities, but eighteen still do not (Anti-Defamation League, 2012). At the end of October 2009, President Obama signed the Matthew Shepard and James Byrd, Jr. Hate Crimes Prevention Act, bringing a uniform approach to the protection of hate crime victims that was not formerly possible when matters were left only to the states. The Shepard/Byrd legislation expanded existing federal law beyond race and religion to include also those offences motivated by a victim's disability (as well as gender, sexual orientation, and gender identity). In addition, the expanded version of the law eliminated a requirement that a victim of hate be engaged in a federally protected activity, for example the right to live in the residence of your choice, in order to quality for protection. Thanks to the revision in the federal statute, the vicious crime committed against Jennifer Daugherty qualifies for inclusion (Smydo, 2010). Thus, Americans don't have to change the law, that has already happened; but we must change the thinking of ordinary people who consider only race, religion, or sexual orientation as grounds for bigotry. Many people with disabilities are harmed much more by the way they are treated by others than by their intellectual, psychiatric, or physical disadvantages. Unfortunately, this fact has been widely ignored by otherwise decent Americans. Regarding violence committed against people with disabilities, they might want to focus on hatemongers at the margins of society who wear sheets, armbands, steel-toed boots, or Nazi tattoos. It is easy to forget that hate begins in the silence of ordinary people.

References

Anti-Defamation League (2012) 'Hate Crimes Data Collection and Prosecution'. http://www.adl.org/combating_hate/hatecrimes_qa/hatecrime_qa2.asp.

Boston Channel (2010) 'Nine Boston Teens Accused of Beating Mentally Challenged Man'. May 12. http://www.thebostonchannel.com/news/23526598/detail.html.

Clark, K. B and Clark, M. F (1958) 'Racial Identification and Preference in Negro Children'. Readings in Social Psychology. pp. 169–178.

Farquhar, N (1999) 'Eight are Charged in Tormenting of Learning Disabled Man'. *The New York Times*. February 17.

FBI (2011) 'Hate Crime Statistics,' FBI Hate Crime Statistics, 2010 (2011), Table 13: http://www.fbi.gov/about-us/cjis/ucr/hate-crime/2010/tables/table-1-incidents-offenses-victims-and-known-offenders-by-bias-motivation-2010.xls.

Har, J (2009) 'Adults with Disabilities Protest Cuts Outside Capitol'. *The Oregonian* March 14. http://www.oregonlive.com/politics/index.ssf/2009/03/adults_with_disabilities_prote.html.

Harrell, E (2011) 'Crime Against Persons with Disabilities, 2008–2010 – Statistical Tables,' Department of Justice National Crime Victimization Survey (October).

Horn, J (2008) 'Critics: All's Fair in War and Satire'. *Los Angeles Times*. August 15/ http://articles.latimes.com/2008/aug/15/entertainment/et-protests15.

Kuruvila, M. K & Lee,H. K (2006) 'Religious Hate Seen as Motive for Killing,' SFGate (October 21). http://articles.sfgate.com/2006-10-21/bay-area/17316959_1_coroner-fremont-police-hate.

Levin, J. & McDevitt, J. (2002) *Hate Crimes Revisited*. Boulder:Westview Press.

Levin, J. and Nolan, J. (2011) *The Violence of Hate*. Boston: Allyn and Bacon.

Leonard, J (2010) 'Killer Gets Life Sentence for Burning Homeless Man to Death'. *Los Angeles Times*. April 29.

Leyden, T. J. (2008) *Skinhead Confessions*. Springville: Sweetwater Books.

Martinez, E (2010) 'Jennifer Daugherty: "Friends" Killed Disabled Woman, Forced Her to Write Suicide Note', CBS News (February 12, 2010): www.cbsnews.com/2102-504083_162-6202062.html?tag=contentMain;contentBody.

McDevitt, J., Levin, J. & Bennett, S. (2002) 'An Updated Typology of Hate Crime Motivations', Journal of Social Issues. 58: 303–317.

Nabors, L. A. (1997) 'Playmate preferences of children who are typically developing for their classmates with special needs'. Mental Retardation. 35: 107–113.

Smydo, J. (2010) Pittsburgh Post Gazette, 'Federal Hate Crime Law Now Protects Those with Disabilities'. February 13. http://www.post-gazette.com/pg/10044/1035678-455.stm.

Stormfront, 'White Nationalism or race centric groups hurts the Eugenics movement'. (November 2002): http://www.stormfront.org/forum/t538726/.

Valencia, M. J. & Wen, P. (2010) 'Odgren Convicted of First Degree Murder' *The Boston Globe*. April 29. http://www.boston.com/news/local/breaking_news/2010/04/odgren_jury_sta_1.html.

Wisseman, K. B., Abramson, W.,Emanuel, E., Gaylord, V. & M. Hayden (eds) (2001) 'Impact: Feature Issue on Violence Against Women with Developmental or Other Disabilities'. Impact 13,3 (online).

Wolfe, K. (1995) 'Bashing the Disabled: The New Hate Crime'. *The Progressive*, 59, November.

8 Disabled women and domestic violence
Increased risk but fewer services

Ravi K. Thiara, University of Warwick, UK and Gill Hague, Bristol University, UK

Introduction

The links between disability and domestic violence have largely been neglected within theoretical, research and practice developments in the domestic violence and disability fields in the UK, resulting in the marginalisation of disabled women's experiences of domestic violence and abuse. In particular, there is little research in the UK which documents the experiences of women with physical and sensory impairments who are also affected by domestic violence. However, some recent work has importantly added to this debate by exposing the barriers in help-seeking faced by disabled women in situations of domestic violence (Hague *et al.*, 2008; Radford *et al.*, 2006) and the inadequacy of theorising and of political movements which continue to marginalise abused disabled women (Nixon, 2009). The gaps in research mean that little evidence has been available to support service and policy development. This chapter draws on the findings from the first national study in the UK of the needs of disabled women (with physical and sensory impairments) experiencing domestic violence, and of the services available to meet these needs. Alongside less provision than that available proportionally to non-disabled women is a greater need for focussed and specialist services. In highlighting the complex nature of disabled women's abuse experiences, as well as the inadequacy of professional responses, the chapter concludes that fundamental change is required at multiple levels across different sectors if we are to offer effective support and protection to disabled women.

Conceptual underpinnings

Explanations and definitions of disability have been widely contested by disability activists and writers (see Barnes, 2004; Shakespeare and Watson, 1997). This has served to shift focus away from the medical model of disability, which places emphasis on impairment of individual function, with the accompanying focus on dependency and vulnerability (Oliver, 1990), towards the social model of disability, which locates the problem in the nature of social interaction with 'normal' people and the material environment, resulting in the limitation of opportunities for disabled people. The social model of disability, despite multiple interpretations and more recent challenges (Shakespeare & Watson, 2002), is central to any analysis of the nature and impact of domestic abuse on disabled women and is key to the authors' starting point (see Corker and Thomas, 2002; Swain *et al.*, 2004).

Disabled women's lives are, clearly, marked by multiple systems of discrimination and oppression. Despite considerable conceptual debate over the last 25 years, 'difference' as a conceptual tool for understanding unequal relations within disadvantaged categories has been slower to be utilised in relation to abused disabled women (Thiara *et al.*, 2011). The assertion that domestic violence affects all women regardless of class, 'race'/ethnicity, age, dis/ability and so on has also obscured understanding of these issues for disabled women. This has meant that insights gained from literature emphasising intersections and multiplicity have not, in the main, been utilised, despite the work of some feminists to further our understanding of the complex subjectivity and material location of disabled women along axes of power and disadvantage. For instance, in seeking to place black women within discourses of disablism and sexism and explain multiple oppression, Vernon and Swain have talked about compounded disadvantage (Vernon and Swain, 2002), while Chenoweth (1997) speaks of 'simultaneous discrimination'; and drawing on some of this earlier work, Nixon has coined the term 'compound oppressions' (Nixon, 2009) to refer to the intersection of disablism and other forms of oppression. We argue that 'intersectionality', as a conceptual tool rarely used in the domestic-violence and disability literature, captures the essence of the argument: that the intersection of multiple systems of oppression and domination shapes individual and collective experiences and struggles. Thus, intersectionality is key to any nuanced understanding of, and explanations for, disabled women's experiences of domestic violence. We argue that an intersectional analysis provides an important framework for looking at and understanding the cross-cutting issues for disabled women affected by domestic violence, including social attitudes, marginality within the domestic-violence and disability movements, and responses from service providers. Thus, in considering the experiences of disabled women, it is important to redefine what we mean by domestic violence, the contexts in which it occurs and the perpetration of abuse, as well as the responses to such abuse, since the range of experiences that women have are likely to be particularly diverse and complex.

Women's experiences of abuse

Disabled women are not only susceptible, like non-disabled women, to the possibility of domestic violence/abuse but, given their particular situations as disabled women, the nature of their abuse is likely to be more complex. International research provides important insights and shows that disabled women are just as, and perhaps more, likely to experience abuse, which can take multiple forms, be experienced across a range of settings and be perpetrated by a greater number of significant others (Nosek *et al.* 2001, 2007; Garland-Thompson, 2005). Given inadequate service provision and limited routes to safety, disabled women may be forced to stay in abusive situations for longer (Humphreys and Thiara, 2002). Studies to date suggest that more than 50 per cent of disabled women in the UK may have experienced domestic abuse during their lives (Magowan, 2003), and there is some research evidence that disabled women are assaulted or raped at a rate at least twice that for non-disabled women (Sobsey and Doe 1991). In a subset drawn from the British Crime Survey (BCS), nearly twice as many disabled women had experienced intimate violence compared to non-disabled women (Mirrlees-Black 1999). Based on the 2006 BCS, Jansson *et al.* (2007) also found that having a limiting illness or disability was associated with all types of intimate violence. The national study on which we draw, the first of its kind in the UK, yielded rich but disturbing information from women who related distressing experiences of abuse, especially where the abuser was their carer.

Multiple and complex abuse

That dominant definitions of domestic violence, as intimate-partner violence, are inadequate for explaining the complexity of abuse experienced by disabled women has been amply highlighted (Nosek *et al.*, 2001). Such prevailing definitions were also questioned by women in our study who considered abuse of disabled women to be more wide-ranging than intimate-partner violence and something so pervasive that *'it's uncomfortable for non-disabled people to face up to'*. Disabled women had lived with abuse for several years, often as long as 22 years; the prolonged nature of such abuse is something also identified by other researchers (Young *et al.*, 1997). Severely disabled women with high dependency had sometimes been subjected to abuse for most of their lives. In the face of little or no support, the ongoing effects of abuse took women many more years to deal with.

Those who perpetrated abuse against disabled women ranged from intimate (including same-sex) partners, to paid carers, care agencies and family members. All of the 30 women spoke in detail about physical abuse as well as emotional degradation and humiliation. The most frequent incidents women recounted were being pushed down stairs or across a room, having objects thrown at them, having a hand placed over their mouths while being held down and spat at, having their heads banged on the floor repeatedly, being stabbed, strangled, being held down and stamped on the body, being kicked in the stomach and being dragged by the hair. For some women, such abuse had resulted in severe injuries, including permanent damage to eyes and ears, disfigurement, loss of an arm, loss of babies, fractures, and severe cuts and bruises. Women also spoke about being isolated from other people, being prevented from leaving the house and intrusion into every aspect of their lives.

All of the women said that being disabled affected the abuse they were subjected to and made it worse, and it was evident that abusers frequently used women's impairments to perpetrate specific types of abuse, which typically included insults about the woman's condition. Disabled women were also commonly subjected to sexual violence which many of them had never disclosed to anyone until the interview, where the disclosure was a part of the process of starting to deal with what had happened to them. Women spoke about constant and unrelenting forced sex and repeated rape by partners and sometimes fathers, including sexual assaults in front of children. Despite such violations, women often had to maintain intimate relationships with their abusers, who also performed caring tasks for them.

Care or control – abusive partner-carers

The greater dependence of disabled women on their partner-carers, who use women's impairments as part of their abuse, compounds their abuse experiences and increases the difficulties faced in seeking help. Deliberate neglect at the hands of abusive partner-carers was commonly reported by women who were denied access to vital medicines, sanitary protection, soap and personal washing items. Such neglect was often compounded by the imposed isolation of women by their abusers, where isolating a woman from external carers aimed at creating greater dependency and hence creating greater scope for abuse. Impairment-specific abuse included being denied access to wheelchairs and other mobility aids, being left stranded for hours or days, and being stopped from accessing needed facilities. Women's accounts provide numerous examples of the ways in which abusive partner-carers reinforced women's dependence as a way of asserting and maintaining their control:

> He was the one that charged up the wheelchair. If he didn't charge it, it turned off and if he didn't charge up the wheelchair I couldn't move. Or he didn't help me in the hoist and get me into the chair. He helped me get dressed and helped me go to the toilet or whatever. I was completely reliant on him … But I mean it was like he was making me think I needed him here all the time.

Alongside the physical dependence, women spoke at length about the emotional degradation associated with the impairment to which they were subjected, with the following being typical:

> Oh yes, he would drag me along the floor because I couldn't walk or get away that was how it would start, the way it always went. He'd insult me with all those names, you spassy and so on, who'd want to marry you. And he smashed me against the wall, shouting insults, you cripple, all that sort of thing.

Financial abuse and control was also a common experience for many disabled women who recounted situations where abusive partner-carers took control over benefits and finances or denied them money, sometimes for necessary prescription medication. Some women had to live off child allowance, a woman with a painful condition was made to sleep on the floor because her partner would not spend money on buying her a bed, and another had been forced to leave because she could no longer work.

Women's dependence, alongside the isolation tactics used by abusive partner-carers, made it extremely difficult for women to look for help. When abuse was dressed up as 'caring' but used to exert greater power and control, this made it harder for women to also 'name' abuse and to do anything about it, something that agencies sometimes colluded with:

> I didn't notice it ... he loved doing things for me ... I'd never been taken care of properly ... It was all about caring and it was subtle. It was so subtle I didn't notice it until it had got to a degree of critical ... [Also] I was in the process of getting [my daughter] back [from social services]. I noticed through social services that they left me alone because he was around.

The representation of abusive partner-carers as 'caring heroes', combined with the dominant construction of disabled women as asexual, resulted in women often believing, and being made to feel, that they were undeserving of a relationship and should be grateful – 'for somebody there to look after me, although he didn't'. Feeling unworthy often made women feel ashamed to tell family and friends about the abuse, as well as there being pressure on them to tolerate abuse because 'who else will look after you?' Women in same-sex relationships reported not being believed about their abuse experiences.

The terror of living with an abusive partner-carer on whom they were totally dependent was a reality for many of the disabled women and created huge contradictions in terms of issues of care and control, as highlighted by one woman:

> Physically I suffered ... and all those things about when the phone rings and you just stop or a car would pull up outside and I would just be frozen. You have that moment of absolute terror that it's them ... which is quite hard when you need someone as well.

Abuse by paid carers

Although widespread in disabled women's lives, professional understanding of the relationship of disabled women with paid carers and the nature of the abuse perpetrated by them was considered to be limited (Saxton *et al.*, 2001). Women in our study raised issues about the lack of attention given to mental and financial abuse, abusive invasions of privacy, and the control exerted by some paid carers over disabled women, reported to be pervasive but seldom acknowledged in definitions of abuse and by agencies. Having their privacy eroded and the general intrusion into their lives by paid carers were some of the issues seen to be crucial by women. Fragmentation and privatisation of care services (Ferguson, 2007; Land & Himmelweit, 2010) had compounded the difficulties in some cases:

> It was like, you know, as if I'd done something wrong ... And it is to do with them all being private now. There are less controls and the wages are bad so they get different people and there are fewer checks.

In particular, women who directly employed paid carers found it difficult to critique their poor practice whilst being dependent for care. This was further exacerbated when collusion between care workers and agencies led to the further marginalisation of disabled women:

> There's a lot of relationships between the agencies and you can be left out in the cold, they talk without you and decide ... So they [social services and housing association] were just laughing with the care workers behind my back. What I said didn't count.

In situations where there were profound problems and women needed to take action and ask paid carers to leave, this was found to be difficult in the face of little or no alternative support being available, though this should have been a key role for safeguarding adult services. Instead, the absence of adequate professional support led to a fear among some disabled women that the Independent Living review process could potentially mean their funding being cut, if they disclosed the abuse.

Professional responses

Disabled women in our study often believed they had few routes out of the abusive situation when living with abuse. Our research shows that the wider societal marginalisation of disabled women resulted in less than adequate provision, even within sectors that would be expected to provide support and protection. Some of the barriers to seeking help and effective intervention identified in the literature and reinforced by our findings include: physical accessibility; a lack of knowledge among disabled women about available services; inappropriate skills and attitudes towards disabled women among services which mirror wider societal attitudes; low take-up of domestic violence services and few women disclosing domestic violence to disability organisations; and fear among women that services will be unsupportive and inappropriate places to address their issues (Radford *et al.*, 2006; Magowan 2003).

Leaving an abusive relationship can be particularly problematic for disabled women, who can face obstacles in finding out about available support and

accessing other people for help. They may also experience further difficulties in leaving their home if it has been specially adapted for them with
aids and facilities, or if a care package of home-based community care
services has been organized (Cross, 1999), especially if the abuser was part of
setting this up. Indeed, disabled women who leave violence are likely to have
more complex needs, for accessible accommodation and transport, assistance with personal care or sign-language interpreters, and for specialized
emotional support (Nosek *et al.*, 2001). Further, because of disabling social
attitudes and lack of access or awareness, more general sources of protection
used by non-disabled women (such as criminal justice and legal remedies)
can be less available to disabled women. Available services, including disability organisations, domestic violence services and statutory agencies,
may not be equipped to meet these various needs. These gaps were amply
revealed, both in the two national surveys[1].

Disability organisations[2]

The majority of disability organisations included in our survey rarely considered
domestic violence as 'their' issue and thus did not provide responses to it,
reporting very few abused disabled women approaching them for support.
In some cases, dealing with domestic abuse was seen to be part of wider vulnerable adult policies, or something that was 'automatically' signposted to
specialist agencies. Members of disabled people's organisations rarely asked
about the issue or viewed it as an important matter of concern for women
using their services, and the majority did not offer any specific services on
domestic violence. Lack of staff and funding capacity were given as the
reasons for a lack of development and focus on domestic violence. The
few that were embracing the issue felt that disability organizations needed
to develop an improved awareness of domestic violence, to build links with
existing domestic violence services, and to have the resources to recruit dedicated specialist staff. Only twelve disability organisations (10 per cent) across
the country offered any specialist support, and none provided longer-term
help. The staff of only seven organizations (6 per cent) had attended the
locally provided multi-agency domestic violence training. Disability organisations tended to prioritise disability as the key identity for their service
users over issues of gender and violence, and having to cover a wide range of
services made it difficult for them to address domestic violence. Several
demonstrated very little awareness of gender issues in general, or of violence
against women in particular, and many had only male workers. It is of little
surprise then that very few abused disabled women were approaching them
for support.

Domestic violence services[3]

The survey of domestic violence services (again, context within a given study) showed that some had made efforts to improve their provision for disabled women in recent years. However, specialist services for disabled women across the country appeared to be patchy, and sometimes minimal. Some of the problems identified in accommodating and/or providing services for disabled women included inaccessible old buildings, building regulation constraints, no disability access/adaptations in some cases, and widespread inability to comply properly with British disability legislation, often due to absence of funding. Most were aware of the 1995 Disability Discrimination Act and were making some attempts to make properties accessible, although three quarters were not yet legally compliant. Some projects had specially adapted accommodation or facilities, and a few offered examples of good practice by providing fully accessible housing (e.g. a whole adapted apartment). At times disability access appeared to be interpreted narrowly, solely in terms of wheelchair access.

Overall, some form of specialist services to disabled women was offered by 38 per cent of domestic violence services, though these were primarily 'structural' (accessible accommodation, transport, ramps) as opposed to 'attitudinal' – though a few refuges were able to offer specialized outreach support. Only three services (2 per cent) had disabled workers in posts, and few refuges could offer dedicated carer accommodation for women bringing their care packages and carers with them. An assessment of attitudes within domestic violence services found that while domestic violence services have improved somewhat in recent years, the awareness of disability issues was low. A lack of strategies to reach disabled women and involve them in services was evident in a considerable number of responding organizations. Overall, language use in the surveys displayed a lack of awareness of disability issues and of the implications of the social model of disability. Where some disability equality training was provided (59 per cent), this was found to have assisted with improving attitudes and knowledge about disability, though this depended on the quality and length of the training.

Statutory and other services

Despite the existence of 'safeguarding adults' and 'vulnerable adults' policies, the responses from statutory services to abused disabled women were particularly poor (ADSS, 2005; DoH, 2000). The police, social services/adult services and housing were the top three agencies women had contact with; this was followed by refuges/domestic violence services and disability organisations. When asked if their needs had been met, women almost always said 'no' and when asked which agencies had been most and least helpful, 80 per cent of women mentioned adult social services as least helpful, followed by the police in 50 per cent of cases.

Professionals, focusing only on impairment and women's ability to deal with what was happening in relation to it, generally failed to pick up on the signs of domestic abuse unless women disclosed. Some women who had the courage to disclose a little hoped that professionals would either ask more or take some action, something that rarely happened. Even where the issue could have been easily pursued, professionals were reported to have not followed things up. Not being asked by professionals, coupled with the reluctance of women to disclose, maintained the secrecy of abuse for many disabled women. On the other hand, where abuse had been disclosed, a single professional in a long line of encounters provided a lifeline for women, sometimes through referral to an agency for support or assistance with rehousing issues. Where professionals knew about the dynamics of domestic violence and had been positive to women, this made a crucial difference to the way that some women were able to respond to their situations.

Although police responses varied, women's experiences demonstrated a lack of insight into the nature of their abuse. In a few cases, the police told women to 'leave him until the morning' or 'let him sleep it off' and at times warned women they would have their children taken from them or placed on the child protection register if they continued to live in the situation. Contrary to women's expectations, police officers provided few positive offers of support. Where partners were also carers, police officers assumed that arrests could not be made, illustrating the contradiction for disabled abused women who are often dependent on their abusers for care and thus have limited options. Where a support organisation had alerted them to the potential threat to a disabled woman's life, the police had responded very positively, illustrating the importance of institutional advocacy. Women were particularly positive about the police response where police officers were positive, proactive, and offered helpful options. Indeed, given that many abused disabled women are particularly vulnerable, living in extreme fear, and are scared to disclose, a more proactive response to disabled women was seen to be necessary from the police.

Despite the fact that many disabled women had regular contact with social care professionals, disturbingly our interviewees' experiences of social care/adult services were almost entirely negative. Social workers were largely failing to respond positively to disabled women's situations, and in particular were failing to understand the nature of abuse against disabled women. Where professionals knew about the dynamics of domestic violence and had been positive, it made a substantial difference to the way that the woman concerned was able to respond to her situation. Simply telling a woman they knew what was going on, and doing their best to help to remove her from the situation or putting her in contact with a disability organisation, made a huge difference. 'How would I have ever reached out to anybody if that social worker hadn't have gone out on a limb for me?' was a question posed by one of the women we interviewed. Some minority ethnic women did not trust social workers after having had negative experiences, and some also reported problems with care workers who were unwilling to carry out certain care tasks for a black woman, with this issue being badly dealt with by social care.

Few of the women had accessed disability organisations, and where they had they had not disclosed domestic violence. In those few cases where women had been in direct contact or where professionals had introduced them to a supportive disability organisation, being in a supportive environment enabled these women to become stronger and finally leave the abusive situation at a time of escalating abuse. Similarly, only a minority of the women had accessed domestic violence organisations/refuges and their experiences had varied considerably. Overall, more positive responses were highlighted by women than for disability organisations, and while some positive work had been undertaken, the main difficulty identified with refuges was their lack of accessibility. Women who had accessed a refuge where staff and management had given considerable thought to accessibility issues were extremely positive about the service they had received. Where women had negative responses with refuges, they spoke about the sometimes paternalistic attitude and approach of workers to them as disabled women, and generally felt they were not well equipped to respond to their support needs. Overall, the majority of women in our study had little knowledge about domestic violence services.

Conclusion

Disabled women's accounts of their abuse provide important insights into the complexity and contradictory nature of their experiences which are important to consider in any practice responses. For every one of our interviewees, being disabled had made the abuse worse and perpetrators had used forms of abuse which made use of, or contributed to, the woman's impairment. Given this, the evident lack of adequate service responses among major sectors is concerning. This gap in services and barriers to effective provision are accompanied by the fact that the needs of abused disabled women and their isolation and vulnerability to abusers is often more pronounced. Thus, our findings clearly revealed that substantially *less provision* than that available proportionally to non-disabled women is accompanied by a *greater need* for such focussed and specialist services. Disabled women therefore lose out *on both counts*. In general, the study identified the need for a 'sea change' in the provision of services for abused disabled women across the different sectors and by all relevant agencies. Such fundamental change, required at multiple levels if we are to offer effective support and protection to disabled women, however, can only be achieved if government, relevant statutory organisations, disability organisations and domestic violence services address the issue in a dedicated way.

Notes

1 The research included two national surveys – of domestic violence services and of disability organisations – to establish the nature of services available to disabled women within both sectors.

2 Surveys were sent out to 348 disability organisations (of which 26 had to close during the survey process). After a very lengthy follow-up, a total of 126 responses were received, giving a response rate of 39 per cent. However, 53 of these said simply that they did no work in this area, so substantive responses were received from only 73 organisations.

3 Surveys were sent to 342 domestic violence organisations in England identified through Women's Aid lists and UKrefugesonline. After several follow-ups, the final number of responses was 133, giving a response rate of 40 per cent.

References

ADSS (2005) *Safeguarding Adults: A National Framework of Standards for good practice and outcomes in adult protection work.* Available at *http://www.adass.org.uk/old/publications/guidance/safeguarding.pdf.* Accessed 8/11/11.

Barnes, C & Mercer, G (eds) (2004) *Implementing the Social Model of Disability: Theory and Research.* Leeds: Disability Press.

Chenoweth, L. (1997) 'Violence and women with disabilities: silence and paradox', in S. Cook and J. Bessant (eds), *Women's encounters with violence: Australian experiences.* California: Sage.

Corker, M. and Thomas, C. (2002) 'A journey around the social model', in M. Corker and T. Shakespeare (eds), *Disability/postmodernity: Embodying disability theory.* London: Continuum.

Cross, M. (1999) 'Review of domestic violence and child abuse: Policy and practice issues for local authorities and other agencies', in *Boadicea.* London: GLAD (Greater London Action on Disability).

DoH (2000) *No secrets: guidance on developing and implementing multi-agency policies and procedures to protect vulnerable adults from abuse.* London: Department of Health.

Ferguson, I. (2007) 'Increasing Choice or Privatising Risk? The Antinomies of Personalization', *British Journal of Social Work,* 37(3): 387–403

Garland-Thompson, R. 2005. 'Feminist disability studies'. *Signs,* 30: 21–23.

Hague, G., Thiara, R. K. Magowan, P. and Mullender, A. (2008) *Making the links: Disabled women and domestic violence. Full report.* Bristol: Women's Aid.

Humphreys, C. and R. Thiara. 2002. *Routes to safety: protection issues facing abused women and children and the role of outreach services.* Bristol: Women's Aid Federation of England.

Jansson, K., Coleman, K., Reed, E. and Kaiza, P. (2007) *Home office statistical bulletin 02/07,* London: Home Office.

Land, H. & Himmelweit, S. (2010) *Personalisation: Who Cares-Who Pays.* Available at www.bristol.ac.uk/sps/research/./personalisation100610land.ppt. Accessed 8/11/11.

Magowan, P. (2003) 'Nowhere to run, nowhere to hide: domestic violence and disabled Women'. *Safe: domestic abuse quarterly,* 5, pp. 15–18.

Mirrlees-Black, C. (1999) *Domestic violence: British crime survey self-completion questionnaire.* London: Home Office.

Nixon, J. 2009. 'Domestic violence and women with disabilities: locating the issue on the periphery of social movements'. *Disability and Society* 24, no. 1, January: 77–89.

Nosek M., Foley C., Hughes R. and Howland, C. (2001) 'Vulnerabilities for Abuse Among Women with Disabilities'. *Sexuality and Disability,* 19 (3), pp. 177–190.

Nosek, M. and Hughes, R. (2007) 'Psychosocial Issues of Women with Physical Disabilities: The Continuing Gender Debate', in A. Dell and P. Power (Eds.) 5th Edition,

The Psychological and Social Impact of Illness and Disability, New York: Springer Publishing.

Oliver, M. 1990. *The Politics of Disablement.* Basingstoke: MacMillan.

Radford, J., Harne, L. and Trotter, J. (2006) 'Disabled women and domestic violence as violent crime in practice'. *Journal of the British Association of Social Workers,* 18 (4).

Saxton, M., M. A. Curry, L. Powers, S. Maley, K. Eckels and J. Gross. (2001). 'Bring my scooter So I can leave you: A study of disabled women handling abuse by personal assistance providers'. *Violence Against Women,* 7: 393–417.

Shakespeare, T. W. & Watson, N. (1997). 'Defending the social model'. *Disability and Society,* 12, 2, 293–300.

Shakespeare, T. and N. Watson. (2002). 'The social model of disability: An outdated ideology' *Research in Social Science and Disability* 2: 9–28.

Sobsey, D. and Doe, T. (1991) 'Patterns of sexual abuse and assault'. *Sexuality and Disability,* 9 (3), pp. 243–259.

Swain, J., Finkelstein, V., French, S. and Oliver, M. (eds) (2004) *Disabling barriers – enabling environments.* London: Sage.

Thiara, R. K., Hague, G. with Mullender, A. (2011) 'Losing out on both counts: disabled women and domestic violence'. *Disability and Society, 26 (6) October.*

Vernon, A. and Swain, J. (2002) 'Theorising divisions and hierarchies: towards commonality or diversity?' in C. Barnes and M. Oliver (eds) *Disability Studies Today,* Bristol: Policy Press.

Young, M., Nosek, M. Howland C., Campling, G. & Rintala, D. (1997) Prevalence of abuse of women with physical disabilities. *Archives of Physical Medicine and Rehabilitation,* 78, S34 S38.

9 Disability hate crime

A campaign perspective

Anne Novis, MBE

Introduction

As a community worker, counsellor and chair of a disabled people's organisation (DPO), many disabled people share their experiences with me of being harassed, attacked and reviled. I know in some instances they have tried to report this to social services, police and others but were not believed, or were dismissed. In many cases, there was no monitoring of any reports of crimes against disabled people, therefore disability hate crime did not officially 'exist', and I have personally been told again and again by police that 'as there is no evidence we do not have to respond to it'. In this chapter I share my personal experiences and wider observations as a disabled person campaigning for over 20 years to get disability hate crime recognised, recorded and prevented, and to gain equality of justice for victims. Through my work, for which I received an MBE, I have found that so many disabled people have experienced absolute disbelief and no response from the police. Many disabled people that I have met have no confidence that such reports will be taken seriously in the wider criminal justice system. I will demonstrate how my experiences of victimisation showed me the inadequacies in the criminal justice response and led to my campaigning for change. Persistently, for over 15 years, I have campaigned for monitoring and improved reporting services, and although there have been some achievements, this chapter will identify significant areas of disability hate crime policy and practice that remain underdeveloped.

Some observers might suggest that with Section 146 and the Ministry of Justice Hate Crime Action Plan we are moving in a clear direction of better treatment of disabled people. In recent months, however, after the changeover of government in 2010, the verbal barrage of abuse against disabled people has escalated, media stories increasingly suggest 'non-disabled society' reviles us as fraudsters, a burden on taxpayers, and government ministers state disabled people and their needs are 'unsustainable', as the following ministerial reference suggests:

> In the comprehensive spending review in October 2010, the coalition said there would be a review of DLA: these plans have now become clearer with its announcement that it intends to scrap the benefit and replace it with

personal independent payment (PIP) ... In the executive summary of its DLA consultation document, Maria Miller, minister for disabled people, claims the reason for change is that 'the rising caseload and expenditure is unsustainable'.

(cited in Brennan, 2010)

When the Coalition Government set up a website asking for people's ideas on how to save money, many ideas were given suggesting disabled people should be treated in derogatory ways because of their increasing and unsustainable burden on the state. Repeatedly, myself, members of disabled people's organisations (DPOs) and others complained to the Government. Yet despite the provision of scope for hatred and incitement, the website remained unmoderated and 'the public' were allowed to 'vote' on these ideas, the most popular to be considered by the Government. For many weeks they were not removed and ideas like the one below were highly rated:

> For the Disabled
> End all disability benefits. People who are genuinely unable to work to live or if possible to be rehabilitated in specialized care homes. Those who can work that upon rigorous medical examination turn out to be just thick or bone idle to undertake intesnive [sic] course in employability, where they will learn to be punctual, meticulous, smartly dressed, articulate, and gain working attitude. Those who repeatedly fail the course to be deployed in Afghanistan as IED deterrents.
>
> (by *crunch* on July 09, 2010 at 07:55PM)

Such stereotyping and misunderstandings, as well as targeted hostility, are perpetuating a myth that most disabled people are a drain on society, make no contribution and are somehow less than human (Burleigh, 1991). The recent Equality and Human Rights Commission inquiry into disability-related harassment found that the media had a significant role to play in influencing attitudes towards disabled people (EHRC, 2011; 158). Such portrayals of deserving and undeserving disabled people serve to perpetuate a divisive perception of negative stereotypes leading to hate crime. This issue is so important that I have documented media coverage of disability hate crime, drawing in blogs, forums, articles and online resources to underline how cases are portrayed. The failure to officially recognise the role of the media in accentuating hate or to reduce hostility is a major issue that could reverse many of the advances made in the last 10 years. Quarmby's chapter in this volume explores the role of the media further.

Being a disabled person and being a victim

To become a disabled person is to enter a world of inequality, stereotype, stigma, discrimination and prejudice. That has been my reality from being an active physically well person for 37 years to having a spinal injury and becoming a wheelchair user. No matter what other roles I had in life, I had become one of 'the disabled' and as such was seen by many to have a life less valid. Disabled people suffer multiple and continuous violations of all their human rights through the systems, structures and attitudes of society (EHRC, 2011); as Hollomotz makes clear in this volume, a spectrum of negativity and harms are aimed at people merely by virtue of their being seen as disabled or different. Negative attitudes towards disabled people start before birth, via segregation into day centres, residential homes, special schools (Cook, Swain and French, 2001) and specialist employment, and lead to hate crime, assisted suicides and 'mercy killings' (Warnock and MacDonald, 2008). All ensure many disabled people do not exist, are hidden away, not noticed, not valued, not important.

Evidence shows that hostility against disabled people is commonplace and often goes unchallenged or unnoticed. The recent inquiry into disability harassment found that disabled people experienced many forms of harassment, ranging from being called names to being routinely abused and physically assaulted (EHRC, 2011). These forms of hostility could happen within the home or workplace or in a public place, and be perpetrated by a diverse range of people from different social classes and ages (EHRC, 2011; 86). As a disabled person I have experienced discrimination and prejudice and after raising awareness of disability hate crime for over 15 years you would think I would be prepared for hostility but I was not and do not think I will ever be prepared. The long-term effects of hostility to disabled people are nowhere accounted for in official research.

When I have been attacked, vilified, mocked, threatened, shouted at, stared at, called names, each and every time it is a shock and sickens my soul. I have now changed the way I live to always have someone with me when I go out, try to be unobtrusive and keep out of people's way, and do not go on public transport, all because of the attacks I have experienced. Yet even so the worst attack I experienced was when I was with two people, my personal assistant (PA) and a relative. I was in a busy market waiting outside a shop for my relative to come out, my PA stood next to me. A man started shouting and swearing at me, put his face aggressively in front of mine shouting that I should have been killed at birth and as I was not he was going to kill me. He raised his fists to swing at me, but thankfully my relative ran in front of me, standing between him and me, stopping him hurting me. My PA had frozen in shock; the majority of onlookers did and said nothing. Only one came forth as a witness.

The man ran off when challenged and the police came quickly, within minutes of being called. I reported it as a disability hate crime, yet it took six months before my three witnesses had their statements taken. I was shown photo files and identified the person but the officer with me did not record this and went off long-term sick the next day and when he returned could not recall who I identified. I was not allowed to see the photos again as the

Crown Prosecution Service (CPS) would not accept this as evidence according to the police.

I was let down by my local police due to delays in taking witness statements, mistakes made during the photo-fit and a lack of staff dealing with the case. Yet as an articulate, knowledgeable disabled person wanting justice I faced the same barriers all disabled people face dealing with the aftermath of an attack that in law can only be recognised as 'public disorder' – a term which in no way reflects the nature of the attack, its impact and the denial of justice. This is due to the fact that, unlike racist or religiously aggravated hate crimes, there is no specific offence of disability hate crime. This led to my involvement with the disability charity Scope on their comprehensive report *Getting Away with Murder*, which outlines the numerous ways in which disabled people are targeted and then not assisted in getting justice (Quarmby, 2008).

My work in tackling disability hate crime

As part of a DPO I was in an ideal position to initiate work on disability hate crime. I noted early on that barriers to reporting were one of the key issues facing disabled victims. I saw the potential for 'third-party reporting' to be implemented for disabled people and it became a priority to have this provision available in my local area of Greenwich. Third-party reporting (TPR) is a system where a community organisation can take reports of hate crime and pass them to the police; for me this was an obvious method to promote reporting of disability hate crime for disabled people who risked not being taken seriously in frontline policing and reporting contexts. Third-party reporting had already been initiated for other forms of hate crime as part of the recommendations of the MacPherson report after the racist murder of Stephen Lawrence.

Third-party reporting for disability hate crime raised different questions. Meaningful reporting would mean ensuring a venue that is accessible to all disabled people, which most police stations are not; having disabled people as staff and volunteers who understand the issues and enable accessible communication and hate crime information. All gave a place where other disabled people would share their experience and be encouraged to make formal reports of alleged hate crime. Yet this system takes up staff and volunteer time and the victim often needs support; under current resource constraints no TPR site is likely to be funded as a standalone facility, especially for disabled people who face so many barriers let alone their own health and impairment issues.

It was essential that support was, and is, provided to help disabled people through the procedures and barriers they face in getting a response to hate crime. To this end I sought, and gained, funding from the local authority to set up a Disability Hate Crime Advocacy Project to support third-party reporting. I used the Disability Discrimination Act (HM Government, 2005) duties that give responsibility to local authorities and service providers to eliminate harassment against disabled people to encourage the local authority to provide this funding. Due to all these efforts and knowledge I now advise the British Transport Police, Metropolitan Police and the Ministry of Justice hate crime advisory group on Disability Issues. In this sense, creative use of wider anti-discrimination legislation helped counter the limitations of disability hate crime provisions.

In 2010, Deputy Assistant Commissioner Alfred Hitchcock from the Metropolitan Police Service (MPS) stated, for a report I was writing on TPR, that:

> The MPS support third party reporting by disabled members of the community. We believe that the same benefits which have been valuable in the reporting of racist and homophobic crimes would assist disabled Londoners and provide a route to policing services, which they might otherwise be concerned about accessing directly. At the same time the MPS is improving its direct services via its call centres, the internet and face to face at police station counters.

The Diversity Directorate of the MPS supported Greenwich Association of Disabled People (GAD) as the first ever disabled people's organisation in the UK to launch a TPR site, in 2001. However, the difficulties continue as funding is patchy or non-existent for disability hate crime work. So many larger charitable organisations which were set up to 'relieve the suffering of disabled people' in the last century have been the major influencers of policy for us. These organisations are not solely run by disabled people, do not have only disabled people as members and therefore do not have a mandate to speak on our behalf. Over many years we have tried to get society to understand that absolutely 'nothing about us without us' should be promoted. Yet even now in 2012 it is non-disabled people's organisations who have more funding and are listened to by governments, rather than our own DPOs. Organisations run by disabled people primarily for disabled people ought to be the first port of call for funders in the fight against hate and hostility.

While I focused on getting support for third-party reporting, I also persisted in gathering media information, articles and data to prove the scale of the problem. I faced annoyance, the expected disbelief, apathy and defensiveness, as after all I was quite challenging, stating that disabled people's lives were being lost and ruined due to inaction on this issue. Whilst many disabled people and organisations recognised that their human rights were being violated in all sorts of ways, they have found it hard to use the language around hate crime. This is due to this term not coming from disabled people themselves; we say we have been abused, bullied, attacked, treated as second class citizens. My work helped translate the language from one context to the other and helped gain recognition amongst disabled people to better ensure that they and the criminal justice system were using the same language.

Yet I could see that by using the work around hate crime some of disabled people's experiences could be captured and addressed legally. I must admit to finding the lack of belief and inaction on this from large disability organisations, and institutions, the most frustrating of all. I believe they must be supporters, and at times allies, of disabled people's own organisations in this work, not leaders, for it is often the case that many think they are the experts on our experiences and talk for us, yet are not mandated or elected to do so. We as disabled people through our own organisations are perfectly capable of speaking about our issues and advising on the way forward.

'Nothing about us without us!' is a slogan used by disabled people's organisations (Charlton, 1998) to communicate the idea that no policy should be decided by any 'representative' without the full and direct participation of members of the groups affected by that policy. The term in its English form came into use in disability activism during the 1990s. It has proved hard to impress this principle on many traditional disability charities and the criminal justice system itself.

The Crown Prosecution Service (CPS), the principal agency for ensuring fair prosecution policy and practice in England, also did not engage substantially with disabled people and disability hate crime until 2009. I attended forums with the CPS, and tried to get onto one of their hate crime case panels, but as these local panels set their own priorities, and in most instances still do, often disabled people representing DPOs are excluded and disability hate crime is not addressed. Local hate crime panels still need to improve but I do have confidence now that the CPS will address this. Brookes' chapter in this book offers positive recent evidence of change in some parts of the CPS. There is still, however, a very long and winding road to travel in getting the CPS fully on board with disability hate crime issues.

Magistrates, judges, solicitors and all involved in the justice system need to ensure they are more aware and able to deal with targeted hostility against disabled people in all its forms. Although legislation such as Section 146 of the Criminal Justice Act can increase a sentence for crimes aggravated by hostility due to disability, these enhanced penalties are not always applied in what are clearly disability hate crime cases. I met with Maria Eagle, then Minister of State at the Ministry of Justice, as I was concerned about the need for incitement legislation to include disability. She responded:

> The Government is determined to challenge hatred and discrimination in all its guises. We are working with other Government Departments, police forces, crime and disorder partnerships and local criminal justice boards to ensure that more crimes which are motivated by hatred are reported and more are brought to justice. In relation to disability hate crime, our main priorities are to encourage reporting and to tackle repeat victimisation. There is no question of disabled people having less protection under the law than other targeted groups. We would find that unacceptable.
>
> (Maria Eagle, 2010)

Disabled people have found it unacceptable that we do *not* have equality in law and that successive governments have not addressed this inequality. The failure to engage with the issues of the need for a discrete legislation on disability hate crime and the possibility of an incitement to disablism clause is disappointing for many disabled people as it leaves major legislative gaps in the defences against disablism.

Hope for the future

Organisations like Disability Awareness in Action (DAA) have been recording abuses of disabled people's human rights in the UK, as well as internationally, for decades. DAA were key in getting the UN Convention on the human rights of disabled people formed, and ratified, in the UK. My own personal hope is that this UN Convention will lead to equality of law and justice for disabled people. Yet I doubt I will see this in my lifetime due to the inherent flaws in the structures of justice services that segregate, exclude, and tend to focus on vulnerability, a distraction, rather than equality of legislation and service provision. I am now seeing a slow response and shift in attitudes towards disability hate crime, changes proposed in law, policing and recording of hate crimes, yet the focus continues to focus on 'vulnerability' and separating disabled people into impairment groups, as other chapters in this book make clear. For example, some work has progressed for those with learning difficulties, but other disabled people cannot access the service or get support. For instance, the very good 'Keep Safe Project', which gets local shops and community organisations to be a safe place for those with a learning difficulty to go to if they feel threatened, is not available for other disabled people. This scheme could be broadened to include all disabled people, an equal service that does not separate the experience of disabled people by their impairments but addresses our joint experience of not feeling safe and needing refuge.

I reject this method of approach – in separating us by impairment, more stigma and prejudice is promoted. Prejudice against disabled people is not separated by the type of impairment the victim has, or how 'vulnerable' they may be.

Whilst my campaigning activities have been extremely hard, and at times disheartening, I do have hope for the future due to the slow changes I see now, the acceptance that disabled people do experience hostility due to prejudice. Efforts are being made to initiate national recording of crimes against disabled people in 2011, improve the law and ensure better justice. Yet underlying all this there still remain the negative attitudes inherent in society that demean disabled people in all sorts of ways and allow us to become a target when it is costly or 'inconvenient' to address the inequality of disabled people, let alone give us the same and equal human rights as all people should have in the UK.

References

Brennan, Sharon (2010) 'It's now officially "unsustainable" to support disabled people', *The Guardian* [8 December] available online at http://www.guardian.co.uk/commentisfree/2010/dec/08/disability-living-allowance-cuts.

Burleigh, M. (1991). Death and Deliverance: 'Euthanasia' in Germany, c.1900 to 1945 New York: Cambridge University Press.

Charlton, J. I (1998). *Nothing About Us Without Us.* University of California Press

Crown Prosecution Service. (2007) *Guidance on Prosecuting Disability Hate Crime,* London: Crown.

EHRC. (2011). *Hidden in Plain Sight: Inquiry into Disability-Related Harassment,* London, UK: EHRC. Retrieved October 3, 2011 from http://www.equalityhumanrights.com/uploaded_files/disabilityfi/ehrc_hidden_in_plain_sight_3.pdf.

Quarmby, Katherine (2008) *Getting Away with Murder: Disabled People's Experiences of Hate Crime in the UK,* London: Scope.

Stone, K. (1997) *Awakening to disability: nothing about us without us,* Volcano Press.

Cook, T., Swain, J. and French, S. (2001) 'Voices from Segregated Schooling: Towards an Inclusive Education System', Disability and Society, 16(2), 293–310.

HM Government (2005) Statute: *Disability Discrimination (Amendment) Act.* London: TSO.

UKDPC (2010) Snapshot Report on disability targeted hostility produced by UKDPC: London.

UKDPC (2010) *The Bigger Picture on disability hate crime. UKDPC: London.*

UKDPC (2010) *Action Now on disability hate crime,* UKDPC: London.

Warnock, M & MacDonald, E (2008) *Easeful Death: Is there a Case for Assisted Dying?* Oxford: Oxford University Press.

10 A case for engagement

The role of the UK Disability Hate Crime Network (DHCN)

Stephen Brookes (MBE), DHCN Network Coordinator, UK

This article details the development, scope and function of the award-winning Disability Hate Crime Network. It details the way frustration with disability hate crime policy and practice led to a disability-led network to try to take forward more searching and progressive ideas that would raise the profile and criminal justice response to disability hate crime and also to reduce the incidence of disability hate crime in the future. When Baroness Rennie Fritchie was Commissioner for Public Appointments in the late 1990s and early 2000s, she had a plaque on her office wall which said 'When people who are not used to speaking are heard by people who are not used to listening then real changes can be made.'

In many ways the phrase sums up the aims of the Disability Hate Crime Network by making clear that the often unheard voices of disabled people, their organisations, carers, families, friends, and neighbours need to be a part of the culture of change in reporting and hopefully reducing disability hate crime. The best way of achieving this was seen to be communication in the form of sharing information from, and about, disabled people with those involved in the criminal justice system who the network founders felt were not listening to the voices of disabled people who had experienced, or were experiencing, hate crime. One of the current regular contributors to the Facebook pages of the network makes the point that the criminal justice system fails so many times because 'The problem is that many of us disabled people are not believable. I myself have experienced and reported anti-social behaviour and hate but the Council and the Police did nothing' (Andrew Kirk, DHCN Facebook pages, 7 September 2011).

At the core of the efforts of the contributors to the Disability Hate Crime Network (DHCN) is 'joined up thinking'. Multi-agency work is the only way to combat hate crime as it coordinates the responses of all the agencies responsible for taking disability hate crime cases forward. We believe that by 'spreading the word' about key hate crime messages, more people will gain confidence to report hate crime in future and help other victims as well as themselves. If that means disabled people becoming forceful and proactive to stop stupidity, laziness or institutional ignorance, and therefore stop disability hate crime, then we feel that has to be a key part of your role in establishing the network.

A unified approach: the mission of the network

From the outset the key aims of the network were to:

- share and praise good practice, and identify and criticise bad practice in hate crime resolution;
- avoid the criminal justice system's tendency to falsely separate anti-social behaviour from hate crime;
- probe beneath the surface of hate crimes and publicise crimes which do not appear to have received the fullest response from the criminal justice system.

Any attacks, either physical or verbal, impact on people with a range of impairments, and an 'all disability' approach to challenging hate crime is the driver for the network, although it has to be conceded that those victims with learning disabilities tend to receive a greater and somewhat disproportionate level of publicity in much hate crime policy and practice (CPS, 2007; DoH, 2000; Lamb & Redmond, 2007). As many involved in the work on disability hate crime acknowledge, the turning point in the recognition of disability hate crime as a concept was so eloquently provided by author Katharine Quarmby in her famous report *Getting Away with Murder* (Quarmby, 2008). This recognition was echoed by the then Director of Public Prosecutions (DPP) Sir Ken MacDonald who recognised that disabled people had been historically let down by the criminal justice system. Katharine's massive input to challenging hate crime has been extended by her recent publication 'Scapegoat' (Quarmby, 2011), which is essential reading for anyone who wants to better understand the issues and solutions in disability hate crime.

This work is the baseline for one major facet of the work of the network. That is to question, and request details about, hate crime from established criminal justice authorities. We do seek answers to the discrepancies which all too often occur within the area of Section 146 of the Criminal Justice Act (HM Government, 2003). Section 146 provides a charging option for courts to increase sentences based on aggravation related to disability, but all too often the ability to use this 'tool' fails. As we know, there is no legal definition and therefore no charge which can be specifically prosecuted as disability hate crime. This means that a close watch has to be kept on the criminal justice system, from police officers and prosecutors through to magistrates and judges, to ensure that 'disability hate crimes' are prosecuted 'fairly, firmly and robustly' (CPS, 2009: 2). So, to ensure a consistent and meaningful enforcement of such cases, there needed to be a real engagement of disabled people as key to the process, rather than leaving it entirely to partners in the criminal justice system, and to facilitate this engagement there was a need for a public mechanism and forum to achieve this end.

From small acorns – the growth of the network

The Disability Hate Crime Network was started in 2007 by Robin Van De Hende while he was policy and campaigns officer for Voice UK. Its aim was specifically to provide support for those involved in working with people with learning difficulties. The network was at this stage a very small email contact group which considered issues of hate crime, with an original 37 recipients located in the voluntary sector. However, after a short period, Robin moved on to a post away from the charity and rather than seeing the venture close down, disabled research consultant Stephen Brookes offered to take over the network. Subsequently, having gone through changes and a few blips, the network moved beyond its third-sector and support focus, and over time became much more about sharing information and lobbying for change. The information-sharing aspect of the network was one of the reasons for the coordinators Katharine Quarmby, Anne Novis and Stephen Brookes being given the Crown Prosecution Service/RADAR 'Hate Crime award' at the RADAR 2010 awards event in London. The Disability Hate Crime Network is now Blackpool-based, is free to access and operates on two levels. Having grown to over 6,000 subscribers and contributors nationally (2011), the network is viewed by many in both the statutory and voluntary sectors as the main informational source on disability hate crime. The news and information goes out to disabled people, disability organisations, UK police forces, Crown Prosecution Service staff, local authorities, and housing associations. Politicians, senior CPS, police (including ACPO) and voluntary sector leads are in regular and direct communication with the network. A key feature of the forum, however, is to provide a readily accessible forum for disabled people to share their ideas, observations and concerns.

So as to create a more reactive forum, a Facebook Disability Hate Crime Network was established. This forum consists largely of postings by disabled people reflecting personal views and experiences of disability hate crime. This element has been of great interest to the Equalities and Human Rights Commission (EHRC) in progressing and providing evidence to their inquiry into disability harassment and hostility (EHRC, 2011). What the operators of the network have tried to do is a very difficult task of editing information without censorship. The media experience of the two key coordinators has proven valuable here in getting the balance right – avoiding inflammatory content, but allowing the strength of concern to permeate through. The feedback on the forum's activities highlights the value of the information in terms of good and bad practice, consultation, conferences and news items. Every so often the recognition of the unique use of the network comes from the DHCN's aim to keep up to date. For example, the Office for Public Management, who undertake a range of safeguarding and criminal justice research and events, have written through one of their Principals (Hoong-Sin) to praise our work:

> Just want to thank you and Katharine for all the hard work you've been putting in to ensure that disability hate crime doesn't fall off the agenda. Hate crime is not simply limited to learning disabilities.

Equally, several police forces have found the links and practice helpful, as in this message from Northumbria:

Just a quick thank you for all the useful linked hate crime information. It's much appreciated and helps us keep abreast of what is happening elsewhere.
(Neighbourhood Co-Ordination, Northumbria Police, Sunderland Area Command)

So this is an area where the network has succeeded, simply because the coordinators feel that the most massive issue that needs addressing, as has previously been stated, is about communication. It has become clear, through many of the high-profile cases, that hate crime reporting failures which still occur, despite some official guidance and various ACPO/CPS directives, route back to lack of cross-sector communication, and therefore in such cases there is no confidence for disabled people that there will be joined-up thinking and outcomes, which simply means incidents go unreported. Stephen Brookes, the DHCN coordinator, in his study of communication issues is able to draw on this expertise in working with the Crown Prosecution Service as a member of their Involvement Scrutiny Panels.

These panels exist in the main CPS area, and comprise members of the public from those areas. They review prosecution cases, which means members can and do comment on cases of all types of hate crime. The feedback is reported back to prosecutors, police officers and witness care units for action and where appropriate service improvement. Fortunately for the panels, disability hate crimes are easier to identify than they used to be, not least because of the Crown Prosecution Service and Association of Chief Police Officers (ACPO) definition: 'Any criminal offence which is perceived by the victim or any other person to be motivated by hostility or prejudice based on a person's disability or perceived disability' (CPS, 2010). This definition removes the excuse that a perpetrator had no hate intent toward the disabled victim, for here the key words on which the crime is assessed are 'hostility or prejudice'. The word 'hate' is not included in the definition as it is harder to prove than 'hostility or prejudice'. Prior to this subtle change many disabled people had considered that acts against them were not really 'hate' and therefore had not reported them. It is important to note that the recent Equality and Human Rights Commission inquiry is based on hostility and harassment against disabled people, with no title reference to the term 'hate crime'. The term hate does still however remain in the title of key CPS & ACPO documentation.

Hostility hurts

Hostility against disabled people comes in many forms and has many motivations. The DHCN has case and informational evidence through contributions and links from 'members', showing that major factors influencing disability hostility are:

1) The link between escalating anti-social behaviour and real harassment of disabled people.
2) Inequalities and socio-economic factors, such as those on benefits being viewed as cheats and worthless members of society.

3) The continuing failure of the court system to act consistently in sentences on perpetrators of hate crime offences.
4) The current 'medical model' of the 'safeguarding framework', which turns the victim of a crime into the victim of a social indifference and a statistic with no recourse to justice for their particular issue, rather than an active participant in the solution to the crime which happened to them.

All of these points are identified, commented on and often challenged by the members of the network, as is the recognition of long-term effect on the victim. Criminologist and leading hate crime writer Dr Paul Iganski refers substantially to the long-term harms of hate crime in his book 'Hate Crime and the City' (Iganski, 2008). This aspect is a real concern for some disabled people and for those of us involved in hate crime, as the constant day-to-day discrimination and internalised oppression of disability often means that the victim of a crime doesn't report the event, because it is 'accepted' that hostility goes with the territory of being disabled, something of which I as author of this piece have been guilty.

To many who are, or work with, disabled people, the Fiona Pilkington case is an example of how bad things can be, as it demonstrated the worst outcome of hostility harassment: death. The facts of the case were well publicised at the time – in 2007, Fiona Pilkington killed herself and her 18-year-old disabled daughter after long-term bullying by a gang of youths aged from 8 to 17 years. In the end the accused family were given an ASBO, which was too late for Fiona and her daughter, after over 33 logged complaints to the police and reports to local social services. But it is important to recognise that death is the very worst outcome and most disabled people are 'simply' victims of day-to-day hostility, which while having a massive impact, fortunately does not always lead to such a tragic result. However, in that sentence is the point we need to recognise – the massive impact on disabled people, and their friends' and families' lives, through the constant drip feed of aggression which wears the disabled person down. The DHCN attempts to comprehend and respond to both major cases and people's day-to-day struggles with hate crime.

Third sector – first step

Effective multi-agency community engagement is always a difficult and often costly challenge. Third-sector involvement tends to consist of groups of people who try to undertake advisory/voluntary work at times of the day not always suitable or accessible for disabled people, and which may have funding dictates which affect and limit the range of services offered. It is often forgotten (sometimes conveniently) that being called 'disabled' means people have to carry additional baggage, including the fact that they are viewed as 'different' and 'difficult', which makes it inconvenient to 'employ' them for many tasks or roles. In these politically and financially restricted times, disability is all too often portrayed by many, including the media, as a burden – with disabled people viewed as cheats, scroungers and the great work-shy, which is increasingly leading to verbal abuse (Garthwaite, 2011; Watson *et al.*, 2011). A ComRes survey, commissioned in March 2011 by the disability charity Scope, suggested that the majority of disabled people experience discrimination at least once a week – if not on a daily basis – and disabled people feel that public attitudes towards them have got worse over the past year, through aggressive reporting of disabled people being thieves and fraudsters. According to the survey, 58 per cent of disabled people thought others did not believe they were disabled and half of disabled people feel others presume they are not working. Disabled people have faced greater hostility from the public since the Government launched its controversial benefits reforms, according to the poll.

So it is no wonder that with those issues to fight, the reporting of minor crimes and anti-social behaviour against disabled people does not register high on the table of actions in the activities of people struggling with non-disabled lives. It is important that although we have been anticipating serious national financial reviews and cuts, the community maintain the ability to observe, analyse, and support victims of actions and incidents in whatever format the victim dictates. Disability hostility has differing victims with a range of impairments, but the impact on them and their families when subject to such crime is equally damaging. In many presentations and workshops delivered to unions, police and CJS partners, universities, local-government officers and many official bodies by the coordinators of the network, the discussions have centred on less critical incidents and cases than the Pilkington matter. It is important to put forward the thought that the local statutory and voluntary community, including disabled people themselves, can help by accepting that real cases, no matter how small, must not be accepted as a norm by disabled people. It is all too easy to say that 'they won't do anything about it' if we 'report'. But 'they' (meaning the police and the CPS) cannot do anything if the victim does not report an incident in the first place.

The names of Fiona Pilkington, 38, and her disabled 18-year-old daughter Frankie have already been mentioned in this chapter, and there was a damning verdict at the 2009 inquest into their deaths, after years of hostility and abuse, from neighbours. In October 2007 a jury delivered a verdict of suicide on Fiona and unlawful killing of Francecca. They also decided that police action and social service failures 'contributed' to the deaths, after dozens of unanswered calls for assistance. Of course, the awful result of the case was that the tragic outcome of the constant harassment and bullying could have been prevented by the means of one simple thing, the basis of the work of the network: that of communication between involved agencies. The Pilkingtons had numerous meetings with their neighbourhood watch committee, and there were even more meetings by their social services (over 20) and a similar number of meetings with the police. Everyone who could have helped avoid the matter 'knew the problem existed', and yet nothing was done to stop the abuse. For the network, this was a real indicator of their task – that of emphasising slippage or best practice in overcoming potential hate crime through institutional methods.

Data protection or prevarication

One key barrier to joined-up working and professional communication is the unhelpful imposition of the Data Protection Act. If the police, neighbours, social services, and some NHS staff had all 'communicated' and action been taken, the Pilkington deaths could clearly have been avoided. To quote the Prince speaking to the families and citizens after the tragic death of the two young lovers in Shakespeare's *Romeo and Juliet*, where he accuses everyone of knowing but not doing anything about the disputes, he says to everyone now mourning the deaths, 'All are punished.' All too often the words 'we can't share the information', 'it is confidential' or it 'would breach the data protection legislation' are trotted out as an excuse for failure. In the face of continued and sometimes brutal hate crime, clearly access to information has to be made available.

Communication is the key problem and there are two sides to overcoming that problem. First, getting to the service providers and making them realise that these issues are real harassment and lead to hostility which if allowed to escalate can generate serious problems such as physical and mental health issues. Second, groups of disabled people working together with statutory bodies can jointly set about the task of promoting the fact to other disabled people that they have the right to challenge hate crime. So it is up to the victims, friends, neighbours, housing and care homes, as well as social services, to report incidents – and for the police to listen and take appropriate action. As has been discussed, disabled people must not necessarily assume that hate crime is injury or death. It often isn't, and it is important to remind people that 'reportable incidents' are anything which is based on hostility because of disability.

This is a strength of the network, because it does benefit from looking at a range of matters and cases, major and minor, which reflects on a strong ability to keep focused on hate crime as a concept and not as totally separate strands. It is the essence of those who are involved in the criminal justice system to consider crimes or incidents perpetrated on any group or individual who is being targeted because of what they represent or who they are, which defines hate crime resolution. Work undertaken by members of the network on the subject of hate crime is associated with confidence building and empowerment in minority groups, hopefully leading to an increase in the number of reports and cases brought to the attention of the CJS. Importantly, the network shows that such an initiative can be run outside London, and that real strategic outcomes can be measured by the increasing number of hate crime reports. While these are a welcome improvement, they are still low compared to reported cases involving faith, race, LGBT, as well as those which touch domestic violence and old age. Several voluntary groups and charities mention 'mate crime', describing the abuse of disabled people by individuals who pose as friends. This is why disability hate crime differs from other hate crimes, as often perpetrators are known to their victims, and many of the cases shared by the network demonstrate this added dimension to hate crime. The important issue of mate crime is dealt with elsewhere in this volume.

So many disabled people are 'vulnerable' to situations which put them at risk of abuse, although all too often the term vulnerability puts an inappropriate focus on the weakness of a disabled person and enhances an already negative image of a disabled person being an easy target and being dependent on society protection. It confuses the vulnerability of the situation with the person. The network tries to turn this around by emphasising the victim's right to justice and at the same time challenges the perpetrator's behaviour and prejudice, rather than taking a soft option of looking at the victim's behaviour. There are still some key workers who 'blame' disabled people for being 'there'. This is as hurtful as some of the crimes, and can deter some from reporting. It is essential therefore that the CJS across all areas are trained into a more understanding view of accepting reports of hostility cases with sympathetic treatment.

But if the incident is reported, and maybe is going to court, this is not an activity most people relish. However, the network often looks at how hate crimes come to court and whether they are prosecuted as disability hate crimes, which as we have seen means the sentencing can be severe. That is why the CPS and the police work along with the network to advise on support for victims through witness care, witness support, and where applicable though special measures, all of which are intended to make justice available to disabled people.

An end to hate crime

So, whilst it can be seen that there has been movement toward recognising and responding to hate crime incidents, it has to be accepted that there are a lot of real problems. Very patchy actions in areas of social care, housing associations, local authority and the criminal justice system as a whole do not instil confidence in many disabled people that they are being heard. If one body or group acts in a negative way then an element of confidence is destroyed. If a specific police officer or social service staff member doesn't seem to take notice, then the network has gone on record by demanding action is taken, including simple awareness-raising training. For right-thinking people, every single injury and death of a disabled person is unacceptable, but equally, DHCN know that each targeted theft, each insult, and each hostile action because a person is disabled, is why the network share information and press for change. The Disability Hate Crime Network has independently achieved a measure of success with statutory and voluntary bodies by highlighting the need to get closer to all disabled people through actively engaging with and specifically including disabled people in finding solutions to appalling hate crimes.

References

CPS (2007) *Policy for Prosecuting Disability Hate Crime.* London: Crown Prosecution Service.
——(2009) *Policy for Prosecuting Cases of Disability Hate Crime.* London: Crown Prosecution Service.

——(2010) *Disability Hate Crime – Guidance on the distinction between vulnerability and hostility in the context of crimes committed against disabled people.* London: Crown Prosecution Service.

DoH (2000) *No Secrets: Guidance On Developing And Implementing Multi-Agency Policies And Procedures To Protect Vulnerable Adults From Abuse.* London: Department of Health Equality and Human Rights Commission, Hidden in Plain Sight (August 2011).

Garthwaite, K (2011) 'The Language of Shirkers and Scroungers: Talking about Illness, Disability and Welfare Reform'. *Disability and Society.* Vol 26, No.3 pp. 369–72.

HM Government (2003) *Statute: Criminal Justice Act.* London: TSO.

Iganski, P, (2008) *Hate Crime and the City.* Bristol: Policy Press, 2008.

Lamb, L and Redmond, M (2007) *Learning Disability Hate Crime: Identifying Barriers To Addressing Crime.* London: Care Services Improvement Partnership. Valuing People Support Team.

Quarmby, K, *Getting Away with Murder* (Scope, 2008) available at http://www.scope. org.uk/help-and-information/publications/getting-away-murder. accessed 8/11/11.

——(2011) *Scapegoat: Why we are Failing Disabled People.* London: Portobello.

Scope (2011) *Comres Survey,* available at http://www.scope.org.uk/news/attitudes-towards-disabled-people-survey accessed 8/11/11.

Watson, N (2011) 'Bad News for Disabled People: How the Newspapers are Reporting Disability'. Inclusion London, Strathclyde Centre for Disability Research and Glasgow Media Group. Available at http://www.inclusionlondon.co.uk/domains/inclusionlondon. co.uk/local/media/downloads/bad_news_for_disabled_people_pdf.pdf accessed 8/11/11.

11 Hate crime or mate crime?

Disablist hostility, contempt and ridicule

Pam Thomas, Turnaround, Researcher and Activist, UK

Introduction

The term 'disablist hate crime' is contested; it is used as shorthand for myriad manifestations of hostility, violent attacks, including physical and sexual assault, rape, theft, murder, captivity and damage to property (Thomas, 2011). A common understanding of the term 'hate crime' is hostile actions against individuals with certain characteristics. The actions can involve opportunistic street crime, physical assault and damage to residences, including arson. The perpetrators do not usually have a relationship with their victims, but may be known to live within the same neighbourhood. They are generally considered to be motivated by hatred of a perceived group. There are similarities between these types of targeted attacks against disabled people and people in other identity groups, such as BME communities, lesbians and gay men, and transgender people (Macdonald, 2008). 'Hate crime' is officially recognised (Crown Prosecution Service, 2007).

Earlier critical analysis of 'hate crime' has been developed from knowledge of racist 'hate crime', forming a useful basis from which to develop, but the use of a 'race model' as the template for disablist hate crime policy is seen by some as misplaced (Roulstone, Thomas and Balderston, 2011). For example, a racist attack on an individual may be, or may be taken to be, an attack on a community, and where that community has the capacity there may be reprisals and events can escalate. This is not the case with disablist hostility, since disabled people are often isolated, not part of a community, and possibly even isolated from their own families. Iganski's (2008) study highlighted the opportunistic nature of most racist 'hate crime', everyday conflicts aggravated by racist hostility, often committed by ordinary people going about their ordinary business. The person who is attacked may recognise their attackers as being local. There does not seem to be any attempt to feign friendship in order to carry out this type of attack, nor to steal cash or goods. In comparison there are few recorded incidents of this kind against disabled people. However, there is a growing body of evidence, and growing media interest raising the profile of disablist hostility. There are reports of disabled people being subjected to opportunistic hostility, and of disabled people being singled out and victimised by groups of attackers for repeated harassment and attack near or in their own homes (Sin *et al.*, 2009).

Grattet and Jenness (2001) question the usefulness of a concept of crime which is motivated by perceived difference. They question the benefits of emphasising what could be seen as a 'special needs' approach, since this reinforces, rather than alleviates, cultural differences between individuals in different social and administrative groups. But they also realise that treating people as if they are all the same does not challenge stereotypes and does not equalise people's situation, creating a 'dilemma of difference'. Reducing the issue to an individual level does not convey the influences of cultures, which allow and perpetuate the oppression of certain groups. Acts of hostility against disabled people on the street or in neighbourhoods, bullying and harassment – such as name calling, throwing missiles at individuals, or at their homes, indicate similarities with incidents which are recognised as 'hate crime' against other groups. These acts of hostility against a disabled person may not amount to crime, but nevertheless hurt psychologically and emotionally. A disabled person who has been attacked knows that they are more likely to be targeted again than a person without that characteristic (Macdonald, 2008); the cumulative effect is demonstrated in the case of Fiona Pilkington.

Disablist 'mate crime'

More recently the term 'mate crime', a play on 'hate crime', is appearing. It refers to hostile incidents carried out by one or more people the disabled person considers to be their friends, or by relatives. The term has not been used in relation to any other group that is known to be targeted because of their identity, such as BME groups, lesbians and gay men, or transgender people. It is not the intention of this chapter to suggest more appropriate terms than 'hate crime' or 'mate crime', but to concentrate on concepts not labels. Because disabled people are often isolated from people who care about them, the desire of disabled people for relationships, friendships, company and belonging to a group is a precursor to 'mate crime'. Recently, several projects have been set up to work with people with learning difficulties to build their capacity to reject what has been termed 'mate crime', which is described as: ' ... when people pretend to be friends with people who have a learning disability, but go on to exploit them' (Association for Real Change, 2011).

There is advice for disabled people which emphasises the importance of recognising the difference between real friends, who may sometimes have bad manners, and something more serious:

> when people are clearing out the cupboards and taking the contents with them, drinking all the alcohol, smoking all the cigarettes, and leaving the place in a mess, this is exploitation. When it leads to being asked to steal on behalf of someone, carry a knife, share drugs or threaten someone else – possibly unknowingly becoming a gang member in the process (all

examples that the Safety Net Project has heard about already) – then, clearly, illegal acts are taking place.

(Association for Real Change, 2011)

These issues differentiate hostility toward disabled people from people in other groups who are known to be subjected to 'hate crime'. The Crown Prosecution Service does not use the term 'mate crime', on the basis that it is likely to cause confusion. Certainly there is confusion between 'hate crime' and 'mate crime', but there are also clear identifiable differences (Thomas, 2011). It is important to recognise the differences since there can be assumptions that because someone has family or friends who seem to be supporting them, they are safe.

Indications of hostility

There is little accurate information about what is happening, or the extent of hostility toward disabled people across all impairment groups. There is also a lack of recognition of disabled people as a group in the British Crime Survey – the closest category in major national surveys is 'long-term sick'. Also, disabled people may be reluctant to report hate crime for fear of not being believed, or because asking 'disabled people to define themselves individually as objects of hatred in the eyes of the law demands a great deal in a culture which is often unthinkingly disabling' (Piggott, 2011: 32). The Police and Crown Prosecution Service acknowledge major under-reporting, which in turn will lead to under-recording, but there is also reporting which is also under-recorded, as shown in the case of Fiona Pilkington, where years of reporting was not recognised (Independent Police Complaints Commission, 2011). However, a growing body of evidence of the increased likelihood of disabled people being the targets of violent crime (Balderston & Morgan, 2009; Quarmby, 2008; Roulstone and Thomas, 2009; Roulstone *et al.*, 2011; Sin *et al.*, 2009; Thomas, 2011). Sin *et al.*, 2009) provide a useful analysis showing eight types of incident against people with learning difficulties and people experiencing mental distress. Hotspots were identified, particularly in relation to housing and transport, and also incidents perpetrated by agency staff. Also *Disability Now* has published a dossier of disability 'hate crime', giving brief descriptions of 51 incidents (one of which involved 2 disabled people) of hostility and violence against disabled people. This dossier has many omissions, and is presented as a list of incidents under headings of learning difficulties, physical impairments, sensory impairments, autism and unnamed disabilities; further analysis is not provided. With the addition of two men with learning difficulties who died following targeted attacks, Michael Gilbert and David Askew, a rough analysis shows that in the dossier the largest group were people with physical impairments; this is not surprising since there are many more people with physical impairments than any other condition. Caution needs to be exercised to avoid a hierarchy of impairment and the current media and official attention on incidents against people with learning difficulties could lead to incidents against people with physical and sensory impairments still not being recognised. There were many more men than women – 42 and 12 respectively. It is difficult to draw conclusions from such a small number of people, but this could be related to women being more likely to stay within their biological family than men, who are more likely to live away from family.

Thirteen incidents involved the death of the individual: five murders and one manslaughter. There were 27 incidents of theft and 23 of assault. Fourteen attacks were noted to follow earlier repeated attacks. Ten people were tipped out of their wheelchair or scooter. Nine perpetrators were 'friends' or relatives, and they were most likely to be involved with people with learning difficulties. There are indications that the type of incident may vary according to the type of impairment an individual has. It seems people with learning difficulties were most likely to die and be held captive, whilst wheelchairs users are likely to be tipped out of their wheelchairs and robbed. Only two of the incidents were treated as 'hate crime' by police; in ten cases people were described as vulnerable.

In the USA, Sherry (2010) noted differences in the types of recorded incidents against disabled people; it is noteworthy that rape is 30 per cent higher, and burglary is 11 per cent higher, in disability hate crime relative to other hate crimes. Research into the specifics of disablist hostility within a domestic situation is sparse. However, empirical research commissioned by the Women's Aid Federation to investigate domestic violence against disabled women gives some insight: 'It is important to be aware that, proportionally, many more disabled women are abused than non-disabled' (Hague *et al.*, 2008: 83).

Table 11.1 Very rough analysis from *Disability Now*'s dossier

	Learning disability	Physical impairment	Deaf	Visual impairment	Other	Total
Number of men	13	24	3	4	4	42
Number of women	3	7				12
Tipped out of wheelchair		10				10
Held captive	3					3
Repeated attacks	10	4				14
'Friends'	8			1		9
Money theft	10	14	1	1	1	27
Assault	4	14	2	3		23
Murder	5		1	1		7
Manslaughter	1					1
Death	7	2				9
Hate crime		1	1			2
Vulnerable	4	5			1	10

NB Four people had more than one impairment

Attacks and theft where the perpetrator and victim share domesticity are features of 'mate crime'. Such instances have been included in cases described as 'hate crime' by disabled people's organisations and campaigners; this is similar to conflating street attacks by strangers with domestic violence. Ridicule, contempt, bullying and harassment are features in both, yet there are distinguishing differential features:

> 'Hate crime' – violent attacks which are perpetrated by 'outsiders', not a part of the disabled person's household, or outsiders may enter the home purely to carry out the attack. There is little or no relationship between the perpetrators and the disabled person, they may be recognised as living in the area, but there is no reciprocal arrangement or inter-dependency. The disabled person does not welcome any part of any relationship there may be. These may be opportunistic attacks, or may be long term repeated, sustained attacks. Examples include Francecca Hardwick, Brent Martin, Colin Greenwood, and Christine Lakinski (Scope *et al.*, 2008), David Askew (Jenkins and Naughton, 2010: webpage).

> 'Mate crime' – the hostile acts of perpetrators who are 'insiders', sharing domesticity to some degree, there is a mutual relationship. The disabled person may cling to the relationship, wanting the hostility to stop but welcoming the company and feeling part of a family or group. These situations are not opportunistic, they are calculated. Disabled people in these situations are less likely to complain to the police or other authorities because they consider the perpetrators to be their friends, they may justify the violence. This includes Kevin Davies, Steven Hoskin and Raymond Atherton (House of Lords, 2008: 14), Michael Gilbert (Sugden, 2010: webpage).

> (Thomas, 2011: 108)

Cultivating vulnerability

At an individual level these events seem to be about one person having control over another; there may be a perception of vulnerability which makes certain individuals seem easy targets. However there is the context of a culture that excludes individuals with impairments, a culture that also allows and maintains structures and practices that disable people with impairments; there is a reciprocal relationship between culture and systems and practices. Young (1990) identifies five forms of oppression, exploitation, marginalisation, powerlessness, cultural imperialism and violence (cited in Thomas, 2007: 74–5), these are all relevant to disabled people: 'research and argument also point to the presence of exploitation, powerlessness and violence – with violence involving verbal humiliation and ridicule as well as sexual abuse and physical violence' (Thomas, 2007: 76).

This hostility is motivated by hatred of disabled people (Sherry, 2010); considering perception of vulnerability to be enough of a motivation is superficial: the perpetrator may perceive vulnerability – but this simply makes it easier for them to carry out their acts of hostility (Waxman, 1991). A culture that fosters a society that excludes people with impairments from all areas of life, thus disabling them, also persuades individuals that disabled people are worthy of contempt and hostility. This is illustrated by a comment from one of the murderers of Brent Martin: 'I am not going down for a muppet' (BBC, 2008).

Disablist jokes are still considered good material for high-profile comedy in a way that racist and homophobic jokes are no longer; for example, the recent incident in which stand-up comedian Frankie Boyle poked fun at people with Down's syndrome, including reference to them dying early. The mother of a five-year-old girl with Down's syndrome in the audience took issue with him: 'He tried to laugh it off – "Ah, but it's all true isn't it? Everything I have said is true isn't it?" To which I replied "No, it wasn't." He then went on to say that it was the most excruciating moment of his career but then tried to claw the humour back by saying we had paid to come and see him and what should we expect?' (BBC 2010a). This is part of a culture that accepts impairment as a good target for ridicule. However, a BBC disability correspondent, Geoffrey Spink, wrote:

> It is highly likely, given all of this mainstreaming of disability, that Mr Boyle's jokes about Down's Syndrome will go the way of mother-in-law jokes or sitcoms like *Love Thy Neighbour*. We will probably watch comedy archive programmes in 20 years' time and ask ourselves, 'Did we really used to laugh at that?'
>
> (BBC, 2010b)

Spink cites the presence of disabled people on TV, but presence in itself is not enough if the culture does not change to reflect disabled people's experience. Ridiculing a culture, society and individuals that make life difficult for disabled people challenges, and is uncomfortable for, many non-disabled people; it can also be funny. Disabled people have developed their own form of satire, which finds the humour in all things disablist whilst maintaining a serious note where required, for example Laurence Clark's website (Clark, 2011).

That disabled people are expected to be vulnerable, dependent, and above all grateful, is also a crucial part of our culture, which supports the systems and practices based on care rather than empowerment.

One cannot, therefore, have care and empowerment, for it is the ideology and the practice of caring which has led to the perception of disabled people as powerless (Morris 1997: 54). Current practice in social care conveys an assumption that in order to require social care adults must be vulnerable and dependent, so disabled people may find they need to appear vulnerable, dependent, and grateful in order to get the support they need. Disabled people who are excluded and patronised remain uncomplaining, grateful and accept the status quo for fear of losing support. Meanwhile, disabled people can find that using agency, being assertive and independent can result in losing eligibility for support, whilst gaining a reputation for being demanding and aggressive. This is a Foucauldian situation whereby the power of the medical profession through surveillance arguably keeps people trapped in a life dictated by 'treatment', 'care' and 'welfare'. Combining the widespread exclusion from mainstream life with the expectation that disabled people must be vulnerable and dependent provides a milieu where hostility and exploitation is not extraordinary.

Another aspect of this expectation of vulnerability is that disabled people will have a 'carer' who will take responsibility for them. Carers groups are often outspoken about the vulnerability of the people they are caring for, and that carers save the state a great deal of money. Carers self-organise, for example Carers UK is 'led by carers for carers' (Carers UK, 2011). Some carers are disabled people who may be members, but carers groups do not include disabled people who are 'cared for' in their membership. In the meantime disabled people have fought for choice and control for themselves to live their lives independently, so they do not have to rely on carers (Evans, 2002; Morris, 1997). Anecdotally, disabled people's organisations report that carers expect to be included in their membership.

Undoubtedly, there are some excellent carers. Some carers have devoted their lives to looking after someone; it has become their main purpose and status in life, and they are generally admired for such devotion. There can also be financial reasons for carers to maintain a dependent relationship; they may be reliant on their family member or friend remaining dependent. In the media and in social policy carers are heralded as saviours of disabled people and the social care system, and are rarely criticised. As I have discussed elsewhere (Thomas, 2011), all of this provides a situation that allows carers and pseudo-friends, if they are so minded, to:

Take control of

- Where the disabled person lives;
- Who they live with;
- When they get in or out of bed;
- When they may use the toilet;
- What they wear;
- If they get out of the house;
- Who they are friends with, and when or if they have contact;
- What and when they eat.

Control behaviour or punish by

- Knowingly leaving equipment and other items out of reach;
- Knowingly making the home inaccessible;
- Withholding personal care;
- Withholding medication.

Take advantage of a situation for personal gain; this can include

- Making fraudulent use of blue car-parking badges;
- Making the motability car their own whilst the disabled person does not get to use it;
- Claiming carer's allowance, but not actually supporting the disabled person.

These are all ways for one individual to have power over another, and are not out of the ordinary (Barnes, 2006; BBC, 2011: Hansard, 2008; Hague *et al.*, 2008); they can be done by ordinary people, in ordinary homes. These actions may not be considered unreasonable behaviour by those carrying them out, the disabled person themselves, or others, and many would probably not consider these activities to be crimes. All of the above can easily be carried out without recourse to violence or even argument if the disabled person remains passive, uncomplaining and grateful (see the chapter by Hollomotz in this volume). If the disabled person uses agency and objects, claiming independence and control, then the carer could concede willingly, disabled people do turn things around through gaining control, especially if they secure their own accommodation and an individual budget. However, there may be arguments, verbal and physical violence, the disabled person might back down and not insist for fear of losing the support of their carer whilst having no other means of support, and their home whilst having nowhere else to go. Disabled people may resign themselves to a reality that others will be in control over their lives.

Although the daily terror of being dependent on and living with an abuser was a reality for many of the interviewees, when they regained some power by moving into their own accessible accommodation (with or without their partner), this sometimes made the abuse worse (Hague, 2008: 15). The use of agency is not enough in some situations. There are some carers or pseudo friends who may enact some or all of the above, and combine it with violence regardless of the whether the disabled person is passive or uses agency. A great deal of this is hidden in the privacy of ordinary domestic situations, making the whole matter much closer to domestic violence than to the street or neighbourhood crimes associated with 'hate crime'.

Relationships and domesticity

Relationships give our lives meaning and many of us will compromise on many things to establish and maintain relationships which we value. Empirical evidence indicates that some disabled people allow an element of violence and theft as an acceptable part of receiving 'care' either at home or in an institution. In some instances disabled people defend the perpetrator. A key feature of 'mate crime' is the disabled person's desire for relationships and friendship; this may be the driver for their acceptance of the hostility they endure:

Raymond Atherton seemed to have been 'befriended by groups of teenagers who abused his kind, gentle nature and exploited his vulnerability' ... 'They damaged his [Atherton's] house, took his money and ate his food'. ' ... But because of his vulnerability, he couldn't say no to the people who came to his door, even though he knew he might end up being assaulted or his property damaged. When anything happened he couldn't name the visitors who assaulted him'. Hemingway [the police officer who led the enquiry] says she felt that Atherton would 'rather have their company than no one's'.

(Carter, 2007)

There are strong similarities with domestic violence, which is largely considered to be partner violence by men against women, and to a lesser extent between same-sex partners and women against men. However, disabled women consider their experience differs from non-disabled women since their situation is compounded by impairment, disability and the need for personal care. Interviewees who had been subjected to intensive verbal and mental abuse thought that the service response to physically abused women tended to be more positive whereas, in their case, control issues and threats to harm were not taken as seriously. This was also seen to be part and parcel of the view of disabled women as asexual people who should not be in intimate partnerships, often making women feeling ashamed to disclose to family and friends, as well as there being pressure on them to tolerate abuse ... Interviewees who were in same sex relationships in particular had often been disbelieved and denied help (Hague *et al.*, 2008: 37).

The hostility within domestic situations shows similarities to both domestic violence and 'outsider' 'hate crime' in that the situation is compounded by disablism. The violence happens not just because the women are women, or just because they have an impairment; it is because they are disabled women and can be subjected to abuse from more than one perpetrator, in some cases sexually abused by their father, then partners, but without disclosing it until interviewed by Hague *et al.* (2008). The issue of reliance on others at home for support was particularly marked. The women's narratives extensively illustrate intense and painful vulnerability to, and dependence on, their abusers for everyday tasks. They also emphasised their isolation, inability to leave their abusers (due in part to the limited availability of support services), and also their lack of educational or employment opportunities (Hague *et al.*, 2008, p. 16).

Many of the women interviewed by Hague *et al.* (2008) had never sought help for the abuse they had experienced. They gave various reasons for this, for example:

- not recognising their experience as abuse;
- blaming themselves for the abuse;
- having no other options;
- not trusting agencies to respond effectively;

- fear of losing their independence;
- fear of losing their children;
- pride.

Some of the interviewees needed positive indications that they would be supported before they would disclose to professionals.

Organisational response

The disabled people who have died and whose stories reached the press, and many of those in *Getting Away with Murder* (Quarmby, 2008), may not have been officially known to social services; they would probably be described and considered to have mild or moderate learning 'disabilities', physical or sensory impairments. It is unlikely they would have reached the attention of services because they have not met the eligibility criteria, which have become increasingly more stringent in recent years. Agencies which are meant to act against 'hate crime' may not recognise incidents against disabled people as a problem of the same calibre as those against people with other characteristics (Roulstone and Thomas, 2009). Agencies which are meant to support disabled people can be part of the problem rather than the solution, and be seen as worse than staying with an abusive partner (Hague *et al.*, 2008).

Ruth Bashall commented on *Getting Away with Murder* that the portability of social care packages is essential in moving away from violent home life (Quarmby, 2008: 24). But it is also vital that disabled women get the right support in order to escape abuse, and some may fear their funding would be cut if they reported difficulties in managing personal assistants when in receipt of direct payments. Meanwhile, disabled people's organisations do not pay a great deal of attention to domestic violence, whilst women's refuges do not pay much attention to violence against disabled women. Statutory social care agencies fear that individual budgets with direct payments open up the opportunities for 'mate crime'; certainly there do need to be systems in place to avoid the unscrupulous taking advantage, but also social policies around independent living and personalisation need to emphasise getting the right support in managing personal assistants.

Conclusion

The dominant culture currently allows and supports policy, practices, structures and practices which foster a milieu where 'hate crime' and 'mate crime' are ordinary everyday occurrences. The media needs to take disablism as seriously as racism and homophobia. Disablism or the experience of disability (not impairment) needs to be the butt of jokes. Putting disability comedy into the control of disabled people who ridicule disablism would go a long way to culture change. There needs to be change within the legal and community safety systems toward recognition that hostility toward disabled people, which is triggered by a perception of vulnerability, is just a complication of hatred and is just as serious as uncomplicated hatred. Some current social policy is intended to bring about the changes in practice that are needed. Personalisation and the emphasis on independent living, which puts power and control with disabled people, will go a long way to shift the dominant expectation of dependence. However, this also needs a change in culture and practice in social care agencies as many are still struggling with the concept of handing over control and co-production.

Disabled people's organisations which are controlled by disabled people are well placed to support disabled people to live independently and to resist being drawn into abusive relationships. A key part of this is peer support, capacity building amongst disabled people which will cascade to those not involved in organisations, and send a clear message elsewhere that disabled people are not vulnerable and dependent in the right circumstances (Evans, 2006). The development of disabled people's organisations can also go a long way to shifting the culture of disabled people not being in control. Yet local authorities have hardly started supporting disabled people in this.

References

Association for Real Change (2011)'Safety Net' http://www.arcsafety.net/.

Balderston, S. & Morgan, T. (2009) *Mapping and Tackling Hate Crime in the North East England*. Newcastle: Equality and Human Rights Commission and Vision Sense. Unpublished report.

Barnes, C. (2006) 'Independent Futures: policies practices and the illusion of inclusion – Background notes to a verbal presentation to the November 3rd European Network for Independent Living.'

BBC (2008) 'Disabled man "killed for sport"'. http://news.bbc.co.uk/1/hi/england/wear/7177716.stm. Accessed 11 March 2010.

——(2010a) 'Frankie Boyle criticised for Down's syndrome joke'. http://news.bbc.co.uk/1/hi/england/8611275.stm. Accessed 10 March 2011.

——(2010b) 'Making light of disability'. http://news.bbc.co.uk/1/hi/entertainment/8611391.stm. Accessed 10 March 2011.

——(2011) 'New blue badge disabled parking crackdown in England'. http://www.bbc.co.uk/news/uk-12435529. Accessed 13 June 2011.

Carers UK (2011) website http://www.carersuk.org/. Accessed 13 June 2011.

Carter, H. (2007) 'He couldn't say no'. *The Guardian*, 15 August.

Clark, L. Laurence Clark (2011) website http://www.laurenceclark.co.uk/index.php. Accessed 13 June 2011.

Crown Prosecution Service (2007). *Guidance on prosecuting cases of disability hate crime*. London: Crown Prosecution Service.

Evans, J. (2002) 'Independent Living Movement in the UK' http://www.leeds.ac.uk/disability-studies/archiveuk/evans/Version%202%20Independent%20Living%20Movement%20in%20the%20UK.pdf. Accessed 13 June 2011.

——(2006) 'The Importance of CIL's In Our Movement', presentation, 2nd November 2006; European Network of Independent Living.

Grattet, R. and Jenness, V. (2001) 'Examining the boundaries of Hate Crime Law: Disabilities and the "Dilemma of Difference"' in the *Journal of Criminal Law & Criminology*, Vol 91, 3.

Hague, G., Thiara, R. K., Pauline Magowan, P. and Mullender, A. (2008) *Making the links: Disabled women and domestic violence*. Women's Aid Federation of England.

Hansard (2008) 'Motability: Fraud 6 Oct 2008: Column 67W' [224091].

House of Lords, 'House of Commons Joint Committee on Human Rights' (2008) *A Life Like Any Other? Human Rights of Adults with Learning Disabilities* Seventh Report of Session 2007/08.

Iganski, P. (2008) *Hate Crime and the City*. Bristol, The Policy Press.

Independent Police Complaints Commission, 2011, 'IPCC report into the contact between Fiona Pilkington and Leicestershire Constabulary 2004–2007 Independent Investigation'. Final Report IPCC Reference: 2009/016872.

Jenkins, R. & Naughton P. (2010) 'Footage shows plight of "tormented to death" David Askew'. http://www.timesonline.co.uk/tol/news/uk/crime/article7059812.ece.

Macdonald, K (2008) Sir Ken Macdonald, QC, DPP: 'Prosecuting disability hate crime – Speech October 2008'. http://www.cps.gov.uk/news/press_releases/161_08/. Accessed 6 December 2011.

Morris, J. (1997) 'Care or Empowerment? A Disability Rights Perspective'. *Social Policy & Administration*, 31: 54–60.

Piggot, L (2011) 'Prosecuting Disability Hate Crime: a disabling solution?' in People, Place & Policy Online (2011): 5/1, pp. 25–34. http://extra.shu.ac.uk/ppp-online/issue_1_130411/issue_downloads/disability_hate_crime_solution.pdf. Accessed 13 June 2011.

Quarmby, K. (2008) *Getting Away with Murder: Disabled People's Experiences of Hate Crime in the UK*. London: Scope, Disability Now, UK Disabled People's Council.

Roulstone, A. & Thomas, P. (2009) *Hate Crime and Disabled People*. Equality and Human Rights Commission & Breakthrough UK, Manchester.

Roulstone, A., Thomas, P. & Balderston, S. (2011) 'Between Hate and Vulnerability: Unpacking the British Criminal Justice System's construction of Disablist Hate Crime in Disability and Society. Vol 26 no 3 pp. 351–364.

Sherry, M (2010) *Disability Hate Crimes: Does Anyone Really Hate Disabled People?* Farnham: Ashgate.

Sin, C. H.; Hedges, H., Cook, C., Mguni, N. & Comber, N. (2009) *Disabled people's experiences of targeted violence and hostility*. London: Equality and Human Rights Commission.

Sugden, J (2010) 'Family who tortured and decapitated Michael Gilbert sent to jail'. http://www.timesonline.co.uk/tol/news/uk/crime/article7108473.ece. Accessed 13 June 2011.

Thomas, C. (2007) *Sociologies of Disability and Illness*. Palgrave Macmillan.

Thomas, P. (2011) '"Mate Crime": ridicule, hostility and targeted attacks against disabled people' *Disability and Society* Vol 26. No 1. pp. 107–111.

Young, I. M. (1990) *Justice and the politics of difference*. Princeton: Princeton University Press.

12 Making disablist hate crime visible

Addressing the challenges of improving reporting

Chih Hoong Sin, Principal, Office for Public Management, UK

Introduction

In '*Our Programme for Government*' published in May 2010, the current UK Coalition Government outlined, amongst other things, its commitment to 'promote better recording of hate crimes against disabled, homosexual and transgender people, which are frequently not centrally recorded' (Cabinet Office, 2010: 14). The woeful lack of systematic recording and centralised collation of disablist hate crime statistics has been a recurrent lament by those working in the field (Quarmby, 2008). One of the consequences of under-recording is that it can perpetuate the misperception of low levels of harassment, abuse and violence against disabled people (Sin *et al.*, 2009). Certainly, there is confusion over whether there really is such a thing as 'disablist hate crime' and, if so, what it looks like (Adams-Spink, 2008). Similarly, there is confusion over how we interpret the rise in recorded hate crime (Cox, 2009). This lack of clarity is extremely unhelpful. As Anne Novis, who leads on hate crime issues for the UK Disabled People's Council, puts it, the lack of national statistics means no strategic high-level work to deal with the issue, no appropriate funding, no local initiatives ensured (Pring, 2010).

While the government's declared commitment to improving recording of disablist and other hate crimes is laudable (Cabinet Office, 2010), it is important to recognise that recording comes after reporting. Simply because a disabled person may have reported to relevant authorities does not mean that the incident will be recorded appropriately or at all. The authorities have to take the report seriously and to recognise that the reported incident is a hate crime, before it is actually recorded as such. Even though police forces across England, Wales and Northern Ireland have, since April 2008, been required to collect 'hate crime' data consistently, there are doubts as to whether the data are meaningful. For example, the Association of Chief Police Officers (ACPO) published hate crime statistics for the period January to December 2009 showing a high of 117 disablist hate crimes recorded by Gwent Police to a low of zero for City of London Police, Cleveland Police and Durham Constabulary (ACPO, 2010). Does this mean that there is a higher level of targeted violence and hostility against disabled people in Gwent, and hence is an indicator of wider attitudes in that area; or does it mean that Gwent is better at identifying reported incidence of hate crimes as being disablist in nature, and hence better at recording them as such? For recording to be meaningful as an indication of the prevalence of disablist hate crime, there needs to be better reporting.

In terms of how it is being discussed, the recording of disablist hate crime is represented as a criminal justice issue. Principally, the police have a responsibility for recording. Two issues arise from this representation of, and orientation towards, recording. First, disabled victims are known to under-report to criminal justice agencies (Sin *et al.*, 2009). Recorded incidents are therefore not indicative of the wider sets of experience and the true prevalence of disablist hate crime. Recorded hate crime statistics therefore need to be interpreted with caution. Second, to simply view the police as having the sole responsibility for recording disablist hate crime is to misunderstand the nature of disablist hate crime (See the chapter by Roulstone and Sadique in this volume) and the wider sets of reporting practices. While disabled people under-report to criminal justice agencies, it does not mean that they do not report at all. Yet very little is known about who else they report to, and what happens to this information.

At the same time, however, there are a plethora of national and local initiatives to encourage better reporting of disablist hate crime (Sheikh *et al.*, 2011). While acknowledging the good intentions behind these initiatives, it is important to pause and appraise critically the extent to which models of hate crime reporting are indeed appropriate. After all, the tragic case of Fiona Pilkington and her daughter Francecca Hardwick attests to the fact that reporting, in and of itself, may not necessarily lead to actions being taken (Leicestershire and Rutland Safeguarding Adults Board, 2008). More recently, David Askew, who collapsed and died in his garden, was found to have reported incidents to the police 88 times in 6 years, to no avail (Williams, 2011).

The willingness of the criminal justice system to replicate initiatives, perhaps drawn from the experience of other forms of hate crime, can be based upon unproven assumptions as to the cause of under-reporting of disablist hate crime. For example, the reasons for under-reporting homophobic hate crimes are quite different from those for disablist hate crimes. Dick (2009) has therefore argued against the uncritical expansion of different initiatives to encourage reporting, such as third-party reporting services, in the absence of any critical assessment of their efficacy for different types of hate crime. This chapter provides a timely appraisal of how we may encourage and improve reporting of disablist hate crime. In order to surmount the challenges around under-reporting, there is a need to understand specific barriers to, and experiences of, reporting. These have to be contextualised against the different types of reporting behaviours and motivations. Currently, the evidence base is skewed towards documenting and explaining under-reporting to the police. This rich seam of evidence certainly points to a range of barriers and potential solutions (see Sin *et al.*, 2009 for a review). Yet addressing this set of policing-related barriers will only solve part of the problem. There is a compelling case for developing a much better understanding of the wide range of reporting behaviours by victims of disablist hate crime, many of which are not akin to the formal procedural aspects that we have come to understand reporting by. Without this understanding, strategies that rely solely on the criminal justice system and on third-party reporting centres to encourage reporting will flounder.

Under-reporting to the police

There is already quite a substantial body of evidence on under-reporting of disablist hate crime to the police, and reasons for this. At the risk of over-simplification, these can be grouped under two main categories. The first relates to perceptions and experiences of the police. These may involve specific experiences of reporting to the police, but can also involve impressions formed of the police as a result of other encounters. The second involves more general issues relating to the structural position of disabled people in society and the implications this has for relationships, attitudes and awareness.

Experiences of reporting to the police

While the wider evidence base contains numerous examples of disabled people's experiences of reporting to the police, these tend to be presented as individual case studies (Sharp, 2001). For example, there are experiences of:

- having to wait a long time at the police station to be seen;
- police officers not following usual procedures for responding to incidents, e.g. taking notes or interviewing a person with learning disabilities reporting the incident;
- police officers not listening adequately;
- police officers saying that they cannot do anything about the incident;
- complaints about police response to reporting being handled poorly; and
- police officers being offhand and dismissive of disabled people reporting incidents.

It is, however, difficult to get a good sense of the prevalence of these experiences and the extent to which reported case studies may be typical for disabled people in general or for particular sub-groups. Nonetheless, there seem to be a number of specific barriers to reporting to the police. These are discussed below.

Lack of appropriate support

This manifests itself in a number of ways. There is some evidence that a lack of access to police stations and inaccessible reporting systems can contribute to under-reporting (Cunningham and Drury, 2002). Poor wheelchair access and the lack of interpreters (e.g. British sign language interpreters), inaccessible information and reporting forms and systems, and a lack of disability equality training by frontline staff can create multiple layers of inaccessibility (Gilson *et al.*, 2001). A number of studies have identified a lack of referrals to mental health services, such as counselling and therapy, to support disabled people once they have reported incidents to the police. Anecdotal evidence suggests that referrals to these services are not always given, even where there is a clear need, for example when a victim is self-harming as a result of their experiences (Sequeira, 2006). Access and referrals to mental health services would help victims recognise that the abuse they had experienced was not their fault.

In addition, special measures are not always initiated by the police. Part 2 of the Youth Justice and Criminal Evidence Act (HM Government, 1999) lays down provisions to help witnesses who find giving evidence in criminal proceedings particularly difficult – because they are children, have a physical or mental disability or disorder, or are frightened of retaliation or distressed by the nature of the offence. The special measures to be provided are designed to assist such victims to be able to give evidence, including through the use of approved intermediaries and with the use of communication aids (Home Office, 2007a). Yet a Home Office report found that only between 6 and 12 per cent of 'vulnerable or intimidated witnesses', or those who qualify for special measures under the Youth Justice and Criminal Evidence Act 1999, were identified by criminal justice agencies (Hamlyn *et al.*, 2004). This inadequate response from agencies compounds the problem of under-reporting to the police.

The lack of access to someone who is able to advocate on behalf of disabled victims can compound the lack of other appropriate support being provided. This is an issue raised in the evidence base for both disabled children (Love *et al.*, 2002) and adults (Lewis *et al.*, 2003). This is particularly the case for those with learning disabilities. Advocates are usually not made available, or disabled victims are not consulted as to whom they would like to have act as an advocate for them. The lack of multi-agency working can thus lead to inappropriate support being identified by the police for the victim (Gillard and Wallace, 2004). This can compound the distress experienced by disabled victims, and there is evidence of complaints being dropped because of this. An advocate is important for identifying appropriate support needs as these are not always identified at police stations.

Diagnostic overshadowing

The police's inability, or lack of experience, in identifying appropriate support can be explained in part by the phenomenon of 'diagnostic overshadowing'. This is a term used in the health context to describe the 'tendency to attribute health problems to a person's [disability]' (Disability Rights Commission, 2006: 69). This tendency to explain symptoms or self-reports solely or primarily through the lens of a person's impairment finds resonance in the criminal justice system, where the victim's disability overshadows the crime that has been committed:

There is a risk that sometimes, services including the criminal justice services see someone has a learning disability and think it is their learning disability that has to be dealt with rather than the crime.

(Joint Committee on Human Rights, 2008, p. 69)

This form of diagnostic overshadowing is manifested in instances where standard procedures are not followed. For example, there is evidence that some people with learning disabilities who are victims of sexual abuse do not have medical checks carried out. This departs from the standard procedures and can mean that there is a paucity of medical evidence that could be used to prosecute the offender. There is also evidence of victims not being referred to Victim Support, again demonstrating a departure from standard practice (Gillard and Wallace, 2004).

Lack of disability awareness

Diagnostic overshadowing is just one of the symptoms of a more general lack of disability awareness. The police can make ill-informed decisions based on a lack of understanding of disability and or specific impairments. This can often be influenced by a range of unexamined and implicit assumptions. For example, the following testimony by a person with a visual impairment has been reported:

It's pointless [reporting abuse], because I've tried reporting it to the Community Police and the first thing they say to me is, could you recognise him?

(Action for Blind People, 2008: 11)

There are other examples pointing to the police not recognising that the victim has learning disabilities, or treating learning disability and mental conditions as similar. The police can therefore make ill-informed judgements about disabled people and how best to respond to them as a result of stereotypes and a lack of awareness about individual needs. The lack of awareness can combine with diagnostic overshadowing to doubly disadvantage disabled people. This double jeopardy has been described for people with learning disabilities:

On the one hand, police are unlikely to identify whether people have LDs, and therefore are unlikely to provide appropriate support to assist them in reporting crime and harassment. On the other, the police may become aware that the person has learning disabilities through the reporting process and then not follow through with the report as they would with another person.

(Sharp, 2001: 90)

Disabled people not having their accounts taken seriously

There are several dimensions to this. First, the police may not think that the incidents reported are serious enough to warrant action or to follow up. It is quite common to find experiences being described pejoratively as 'low-level incidents'. Yet as Iganski (2008) demonstrated powerfully elsewhere, there is no such thing as a low-level incident. So-called low-level incidents have been shown to have high impact on the disabled victims. Lamentably, Sin *et al.* (2009) and others have reported examples of the police not wishing to deal with perceived low-level incidents reported by disabled people, despite the fact that these may be prevalent. As a disabled victim remarked:

> The police want to be dealing with serious crimes. That is their business. When you decide you want to be a police officer, you want to deal with bank robberies.
>
> (reported in Sin *et al.*, 2009: 66)

Certainly, the Serious Case Review following the Pilkington tragedy found that there were 19 reported anti-social behaviour incidents from 1997 to 2006, with a clear sign of escalation. Of the 19 reported incidents, 10 were in 2004. In 2007, there were 13 incidents. According to Leicestershire Police's grading of the seriousness of incidents, none of those reported by Fiona Pilkington and her family were categorised as Grade 1: those requiring the speediest responses (Leicestershire and Rutland Safeguarding Adults Board, 2008). The police management report notes that only 66 per cent of the incidents received either a telephone contact or a visit. Similarly, Hinckley and Bosworth Borough Council, in response to complaints from Fiona Pilkington, felt that 'there was no indication ... that this was anything other than low level nuisance behaviour' (Leicestershire and Rutland Safeguarding Adults Board, 2008).

This careless description of incidents being 'low level' trivialises the impact they had on Fiona Pilkington and her family. It overlooks the fact that the persistent and corrosive effect of prolonged exposure to this so-called 'low level nuisance' can be devastating. This emphasis on the more serious end of the spectrum of incidents creates significant challenges for disabled people as it may not reflect the reality of their everyday lives. Second, there is evidence that stereotypes about disabled people can not only lead to dismissive responses from the police, but also to negative behaviours in some instances. This seems to be particularly so for people with learning disabilities and/or mental health conditions, where reports of victimisation or low-level harassment by the police exist. There can be a perception, by the police, that those with mental health conditions or learning disabilities are more likely to be offenders than to be victims. During interviews, police officers can give the impression that the victim is in the wrong or that the police do not believe the victim (Voice UK All Party Parliamentary Group, 2007). It is unsurprising that studies of people with mental health conditions who have experienced disablist hate crime report that they are more likely to be dissatisfied with the overall response of the police to their reports (Wood and Edwards, 2005, MIND, 2007).

Third, there is evidence that the police can doubt the credibility of victims of disablist hate crime. Various negative stereotypes around the capability and competence of disabled people can lead to them being seen as unreliable or 'lacking'. It may be assumed that the disabled person is not able to give evidence or that it will be too stressful for them to do so. For example, police officers have been found to be reluctant to pursue cases that rely on the testimony of a person with learning disabilities or with mental health conditions because they are thought to be unable to remember accurately and reliably, or to vocalise their experiences (Voice UK APPG, 2007; Burgess and Phillips, 2006; Marley and Buila, 2001). The negative assumptions around disabled people's ability to provide credible accounts mean that the police may think there is a reduced likelihood of successful prosecution. Hence a case may be dropped (Joint Committee on Human Rights, 2008). This issue gained attention following a ruling by the High Court in 2009 that the Crown Prosecution Service (CPS) were wrong to drop a prosecution of a case involving a victim with mental health conditions (referred to as FB) because the CPS believed that the victim would not be a credible witness (EHRC, 2009).

It is important to note that the assumptions behind what constitutes the ability to provide credible and reliable accounts is clearly underlain by complex ideologies and social constructions of what 'normal' and 'competent' constitute (Sin, 2005). 'Competence' is not 'all-or-nothing' (Gilhooly, 2002) and there can be no universal set of criteria for ascertaining competence. Instead, competence is task-specific (Beauchamp, 1991). However, the adversarial style of questioning used in the criminal justice system has been found to be inappropriate, and can cause distress and confusion (Hatton *et al.*, 2004). Assumptions about reliability and credibility can lead to a tendency for professionals to speak with other people instead of listening directly to disabled people (Cooper, 2007: 1).

Previous experiences of, and confidence in, the police

Under-reporting, as the preceding discussion shows, can be due to past experiences of reporting and unsatisfactory responses. However, particular sub-groups of disabled people are more likely to specifically avoid reporting to the police because the police are actual or perceived perpetrators of violence, abuse and harassment against them. Most prominently, people with mental health problems can have poor relationships with the police. For example, black men with mental health conditions report negative prior experiences with the police 'stopping and searching' for no apparent reason. Sin *et al.* (2009: 35), for example, reported the following anecdote:

> I told them [the police] I had multiple disabilities and wanted to see a doctor, but they just saw a big black man who was a bit drunk. It was a horrible experience. It was the first time I felt completely

voiceless ... There is a fear of us and them – for black men because our experience of the police has been quite negative in the 80s and 90s. We both have negative stereotypes of each other. We need to integrate more and break down barriers.

Such experiences, while not related to disablist hate crime, subsequently affect reporting practices around disablist hate crime (MIND, 2007). More generally, disabled people have been found to have lower levels of confidence in the criminal justice system compared with non-disabled people. Quarmby (2008), for instance, reported that only 35 per cent of disabled people had confidence in the criminal justice system to bring about justice. This is compared to 41 per cent of the general population. As discussed previously, disabled people often feel that they will not be listened to or taken seriously (Cunningham and Drury, 2002). There is also a concern that they themselves may get into trouble (Home Office, 2007b; Sin *et al.*, 2009). Dissatisfaction with responses can lead to breakdown in the relationship between disabled people and the police, stemming from a loss of trust. Disabled people are also reported to lack confidence in agencies such as the police to resolve problems reported by them. This is fuelled by a more general perception among disabled people that statutory agencies are unwilling to intervene on their behalf (Disability Rights Commission and Capability Scotland, 2004).

Other reasons for under-reporting

For the barriers identified above, there are thankfully ways in which reporting may be encouraged through specific actions. These include more appropriate and timely training in disability equality among criminal justice personnel; better partnership working with a range of disabled people's organisations and other agencies; better outreach and communication with disabled people; improved information provision and accessibility; and more effective use of existing instruments and provisions to support victims and to enable access to justice. Many of these involve interventions aimed at the way the police and other criminal justice agency partners operate. On their own, however, these do not solve the problem of under-reporting. Over and above the relationship between disabled people and the police, there are a number of other key reasons explaining under-reporting of disablist hate crime. These have very different implications for effective interventions to improve reporting, and are discussed below.

The relationship between the perpetrator and the victim

Just as victims of domestic violence confront barriers to reporting due to the fact that offenders are often current partners or spouses (Walby and Allen, 2004), victims of disablist hate crime can also be prevented or discouraged from reporting due to complex sets of relationships within which they are enmeshed. Attempts to encourage reporting will need to take into account the relational context within which disabled people are positioned. Issues of unequal power, dependency and the lack of viable alternatives can constrain the ability of the disabled victim taking actions to improve their lives. For victims of disablist hate crime, three particular types of relationship can conspire to discourage reporting: close interpersonal relationships (e.g. familial or friendship ties); relationships between disabled people and their carers or personal assistants; and more distant relationships that may be near home-based settings (e.g. neighbours and others living nearby).

In the context of perpetrators being carers, or individuals with whom the disabled person has a close personal relationship, the disabled person may fear grave personal harm if they make a report (Petersilia, 2001; Joint Committee on Human Rights, 2008). The issue of 'mate crime', for example, has become increasingly apparent – see the chapter by Thomas in this volume. Due to the multiple exclusions experienced by many disabled people (Williams *et al.*, 2008), some can find it difficult to form supportive and sustainable social networks. People with learning disabilities and/or mental health conditions, in particular, have been found to be susceptible to being 'befriended' by people who then exploit them. Disabled people may put up with acts of cruelty, humiliation, servitude, exploitation and theft from those whom they regard as 'friends' (Thomas, 2011). As Hunter *et al.* (2007: 14) noted, for some disabled people, 'out of desperation to end their social isolation: they believed that this was the way to "win" friends, led on by a "bad crowd" who were exploiting the lack of social understanding'. This was certainly so in the case of Steven Hoskin, who found his bedsit increasingly being used for a range of anti-social behaviour by people who claimed to be his 'friends' (Flynn 2007: 24). Hoskin himself was subjected to acts of violence and abuse, some of which are of shocking brutality, that led eventually to his tragic death.

In other relationships where family members or others may be involved in caring, Saxton *et al.* (2001: 408) reported that disabled people

> constantly reported weighing the pros and cons of a relationship that turned abusive, which is very similar to the way that [non-disabled women] respond to abuse. Included in this equation are factors such as repeated difficulty in finding and keeping quality PAS [Personal Assistance Service] providers, fear that the next provider might be worse, the lack of emergency back-up PAS, and the risk of being admitted to a nursing or foster home and/or losing custody of children because of not having an assistant.

Victims of disablist hate crime often describe 'keeping it bottled up inside', particularly if the perpetrators are family members, relatives or people close to them. This weighing of the pros and cons of reporting also applies in the case of perpetrators who live in the same neighbourhood or who are familiar to the disabled person by sight. Victims of disablist hate crime can be hesitant to tell other people because they are fearful of reprisals from the perpetrator:

> I could not report because they threatened me that if they saw the police coming, they would know that it would have been me, and will therefore put myself in further danger.
>
> (Hunter et al., 2007: 66)

These considerations around likely adverse impacts of seeking help through reporting to the police are often accompanied by a more generalised fear of 'losing control' that manifests itself in different ways. Central to this fear is that disabled people often have no idea what will happen to the information they provide and whether actions will be taken without their consent, and even well-intentioned actions may actually exacerbate their circumstances. These act as formidable barriers to reporting. As Sin *et al.* (2009) reported, victims can find it difficult to initiate a conversation with somebody to report the experience. They report finding it easier to tell somebody if asked directly, rather than having to initiate that conversation themselves. This has important implications for how we think about and operationalise reporting procedures. The conventional models of reporting, including formal third-party reporting, are predicated on victims initiating contact to articulate the experience of disablist hate crime through formalised channels. The extent to which these are effective in meeting the needs of all victims of disablist hate crime can therefore be doubtful.

Lack of awareness about human rights

Many disabled people are not aware of their rights under a range of international and domestic human-rights and equality legislation (e.g. the Human Rights Act, the UN Convention on the Rights of Persons with Disabilities, the Equality Act 2010, and so on). They are therefore unlikely to seek to rely on these legislative frameworks when complaining to the police, let alone in taking legal action (Perry, 2004). This lack of awareness manifests itself in a perception among many disabled people that hate incidents and hate crimes are 'part of everyday life'. The Joint Committee on Human Rights, for example, cited evidence that people with learning disabilities sometimes do not know that what is being done to them is a criminal act and that their rights have been violated by the abuse that they have experienced. It is thus important to raise awareness, amongst disabled people, about their human and legal rights.

Confusion over what 'hate crime' is

The language of 'hate crime' can confuse and obscure a diverse range of incidents experienced by disabled people (Perry, 2004). Disabled people's interpretations of what constitutes a 'hate crime' can lead them to downplay the 'everyday' experiences. Wrong 'labelling' of incidents can exacerbate the under-reporting by encouraging the victim to change their behaviour instead of taking action and reporting incidents to police. A lack of awareness around hate crime increases the chance that disabled people will not see the terminology as relevant to their personal experiences and may not use existing tools to their best advantage in seeking redress. There is evidencing suggesting that despite attempts by ACPO and the CPS to clarify the definition of hate crime, there is still widespread misunderstanding that something can only be defined as hate crime if we can demonstrate that it was motivated by 'hatred'. The Criminal Justice Act (2003) recognised hate crime against disabled people, enabling redress through the courts through Section 146. Section 146 is designed to ensure that offences aggravated by *hostility* based on disability are treated seriously by the courts. Evidence of hostility, as opposed to 'hatred', is necessary to prove disablist hate crime. The CPS published guidance to help clarify appropriate handling procedures relating to disablist hate crime. For example, the CPS policy for prosecuting disablist hate crime states that:

> when prosecuting cases of disability hate crime, to help us apply our policy on dealing with such cases, we adopt the following definition: 'Any criminal offence, which is perceived, by the victim or any other person, to be motivated by hostility or prejudice based on a person's disability or perceived disability'.
>
> (CPS, 2010)

This draws attention to two key issues. First, the burden of proof is in establishing hostility or prejudice. This presents a lower evidential threshold than to establish hatred as the motivation behind the crime. Second, the definition of hate crime is victim-centred. As Perry (2009) explained, this shifts the power to identify 'what happened' from criminal justice agencies to victims and witnesses. This should shape how police forces prioritise and respond to hate crime and how they respond to victims and witnesses generally. Unfortunately, within the disabled population, there are still very low levels of awareness of the victim-centred approach to defining hate crime. Recent research by Sheikh *et al.* (2011) attest to the fact that such lack of awareness similarly exists within a number of police forces in England.

Reporting behaviours and the challenges around encouraging 'third party' reporting

While we know that there is under-reporting of disablist hate crime to the police, there is much less understanding around other forms of reporting behaviours. The limited data in this area often relate to specific groups, and are often out of date. For example, data from Scotland suggest that 90 per cent of disabled victims of hate crime in Scotland have told someone about the incident, with friends and family being the most likely people to have been informed. 41 per cent of disabled people in the study reported the incident directly to the police (Disability Rights Commission and Capability Scotland, 2004). Other research carried out with visually impaired people found that the majority of those who experienced verbal and physical targeted violence tended to turn to their family and friends for support (Action for Blind People, 2008). Primary research conducted by Sin *et al.* (2009) similarly pointed to the fact that people with learning disabilities and/or mental health conditions who have experienced hate crime have a tendency to tell third parties such as social workers, health professionals and others, as opposed to the police.

There is specific evidence on reporting by people with mental health conditions and those with learning disabilities that confirms the above picture (e.g. Berzins *et al.*, 1993; Burgess and Phillips, 2006; MIND, 2007). For example, Sin *et al.*'s (2009) study reported that those with mental health conditions were more likely to have reported their experience through statutory complaints systems compared to those with learning disabilities. These include reporting to the environmental health department at the local council in the case of experiences of anti-social behaviour, or to the complaints department at the hospital in the case of incidents perpetrated by statutory agency staff. Healthcare staff (particularly those in hospital settings), general practitioners and mental health workers, appear to play an important role as a result of increased contact with healthcare workers due to the deterioration of mental health following experiences of hate crime.

In comparison, Mencap (1999) reported that while a substantial proportion (75 per cent) of people with learning disabilities do report incidents to another person, only a small proportion (17 per cent) do so directly to the police. It was more common for incidents to be reported to medical or support staff (54 per cent). Similarly, Sin *et al.* (2009) identified the importance of support workers in relation to reporting by victims with learning disabilities. Other useful third parties include advocates, teachers and housing officers. In comparison with those with mental health conditions, people with learning disabilities are more likely to tell someone they already know, such as support workers.

It is amply clear that while it is important for criminal justice agencies, particularly the police, to encourage better reporting and to improve the recording of disablist hate crime, this is insufficient if we are to truly understand the prevalence and nature of such crime.

The paradox of hate crime reporting is that while the policymakers and practitioners lament the 'under-reporting' of such incidents, the evidence demonstrates that disabled victims of hate crime do 'report' to someone. However, what constitutes a 'report', and to whom these are made, are key barriers to the formal understanding of hate crime reporting. The evidence suggests that 'reporting' to third parties is widespread, although lamentably understudied. The policy and practice focus on the criminal justice system has meant that the critical role played by other individuals and organisations has been overlooked. While formal third-party reporting systems and organisations do exist (e.g. Stop Hate UK) and are used by victims of disablist hate crime, the evidence relating to 'reporting' practices of victims to third parties indicate that these are far more informal. In fact, the term 'reporting' may not accurately represent the processes and dynamics involved. For example, Sin *et al.* (2009) found that such 'reporting' can often occur through informal conversations with support workers, teachers or healthcare professionals. The topic of conversations may not be around hate crime. Instead, it is usually through discussion of some other issue (e.g. a health problem) that an experience of hate crime is mentioned, often incidentally.

Unfortunately, such 'reports' do not often get passed onto the police. For example, evidence demonstrates that victims of hate crime often experience worsening physical and/or mental health (Iganski, 2008). Yet, primary research by Sin *et al.* (2009) identified that when victims presented with health issues, health professionals focused on symptom treatment even in cases when the disabled victim had discussed experiences of hate crime. Similarly, the case review into the death of Steven Hoskin stated that

> What is striking about the responses of services to Steven's circumstances is that each agency focused on single issues within their own remits and did not make the connections deemed necessary for the protection of vulnerable adults and proposed by No Secrets.
>
> (Flynn, 2007: 21)

The issue, therefore, is not simply about whether disabled people report. It is about how and whether various individuals and agencies recognise that a disablist hate crime has been reported even when it may not be a formal report of a hate crime. It is also about whether these individuals and agencies do anything with that information. It is an oversimplification to claim that these numerous third parties do not report the information onwards. There are examples of third parties who had reported incidents to the police on behalf of the disabled person. These, however, tend to relate to instances where a more 'straightforward' crime has been committed, such as a burglary. This draws our attention to lay understandings of what hate crimes are, and different implicit assessments of what constitutes a 'crime' and whether this is 'serious enough' to warrant attention by the police. The confusion in these assessments has been reported by Sin *et al.* (2009: 59):

> One of the main problems of the language of hate crime for disabled people and other targeted groups is that it obscures the evidential requirements for Section 146 to apply. Section 146 simply requires evidence of hostility which has dictionary definitions of 'unfriendliness' or 'antagonism'. Disabled people, the police and CPS all might suffer confusion in this area. The separate issue is that crimes experienced by disabled people more generally get mislabelled as 'abuse', 'bullying' so that the police do not perceive the incidents to be the business of the criminal justice system.

This finding has been supported by evidence reported more recently by Sheikh *et al.* (2011) in their study of 14 police forces' practice in handling disablist hate crime. Such confusion is compounded by inconsistent and confusing terminology across different organisational and sector boundaries. For example, within the social work setting, terms such as 'bullying' or 'abuse' may be used to describe incidents that the police may regard as 'crime'. These may be treated as internal matters, within day centres for example, rather than being reported on to the police. Decisions around reporting to the police are not simply informed by having the requisite knowledge of what constitutes a disablist hate crime. They are also influenced deeply by an individual's and society's attitudes towards disability and disabled people. Disabled people are often conditioned by their carers and family members, and by wider society, to accept and ignore negative behaviour targeted at them. Sin *et al.* (2009: x) reported the following two anecdotes:

> 'My auntie tells me to ignore it if people say bad things to me. When I ignore them, she says I have done the right thing.'
> 'They [learning-disability support workers] also told me not to stare at people and to go another way if I see big groups of young people and to ignore them. I think that advice is useful. You don't get into as much trouble if you don't answer back. It's better to ignore them. I would give the same advice to other people.'

These examples demonstrate the pernicious effect of wider conditioning by those people and organisations around disabled people, and by society, leading to acceptance that disabled people cannot and should not expect to lead fulfilling lives. While some of this may be well-intentioned, the welfarist and protectionist assumptions underpinning such responses mean that the focus is on harm avoidance and risk minimisation through the disabled person changing his or her behaviours and routines (Sin *et al.*, 2011). The message is that we, as a society, are in favour of disabled people self-excluding rather than doing anything to prevent such unacceptable behaviour from occurring. The structures and attitudes that perpetuate these negative behaviours towards disabled people are thereby reproduced and sustained.

In order for third-party reporting to be effective, therefore, we need concerted efforts at raising awareness among key partner agencies, disabled people, and the general public, not only about what hate crime is, but that we should not tolerate it and that all of us can do something about it.

Conclusion

Lack of involvement in community safety action and criminal justice interventions, poor awareness of rights and routes to redress, lack of appropriate response by others, together with the internalisation of low expectations by disabled people all contribute towards under-reporting. For safer, stronger communities to exist it is essential that all citizens have confidence in the programmes and institutions set up to keep them safe or to provide redress. Disabled people are not only at higher risk of crime but also suffer higher rates of victimisation (Sin *et al.*, 2009). Despite this, they tend to lack trust in the criminal justice system and repeatedly report their experiences of disablist hate crime being dismissed as insignificant or their credibility as witnesses being questioned. While there are promising developments afoot, there is still low institutional and operational priority and investment in ensuring that disabled people have equal access to justice. A condition of genuine citizenship is that everyone should be assured of equal access to justice, irrespective of locality and living arrangements, with continuous and effective support as victims and as witnesses. Despite the existence of a number of legislative instruments and policies that offer protection and potential redress for victims of disablist hate crime, these are not being utilised fully and effectively (Perry, 2004).

The criminal justice focus of disablist hate crime means that the true scale and nature of reporting frequency and behaviour has been underestimated and under-researched. Despite evidence that disabled people have a tendency to report incidents to third parties rather than to the police, there is a gap in our understanding in relation to these third parties. For example, we do not as yet have a comprehensive picture of the range of third parties, choosing instead to think instinctively of third-party reporting centres. We also lack understanding of what types of experiences get reported to which types of third parties. There is also a glaring gap in our understanding of disabled people's experiences of, and rationale for, reporting to the various third parties.

This is not to dismiss the valuable and vital work being undertaken by third-party reporting centres such as StopHate UK. Similarly, the ongoing mapping of third-party reporting services by RADAR is also very much welcomed. Nonetheless, for third-party reporting to be effective, we need to look beyond the formal structures and processes that currently exist. Instead, we need to develop a far more sophisticated understanding of what third-party reporting actually means in practice from disabled people's perspectives. The most effective means of encouraging reporting must surely be underpinned by a person-centred approach, designed in collaboration with disabled people and reflecting their motivations and preferences for reporting.

Formal initiatives to encourage reporting, such as third-party reporting centres, should work in tandem with the more informal and routine 'networks of practice' within which disabled people interact with other individuals and agencies. For example, would it be possible for a third-party reporting centre such as StopHate UK to raise awareness among general practitioners (GPs), care providers, housing officers and others about recognising signs that their clients may be experiencing disablist hate crime, and to teach them what to do about it? Can material be provided in GP surgeries and other locations well used by disabled people to signpost people to third-party reporting and other support services?

It is clear that more research looking into the role of various third parties and their role in promoting reporting is required. There are likely to be different sets of opportunities and challenges in relation to disabled people's experiences of reporting to various individuals and agencies. The issues go beyond the current narrow criminal justice focus. As we develop our understanding and practice around third-party reporting, however, we must not lose sight of the fact that the police can still take actions to encourage direct reporting. Sheikh *et al.*'s (2011) research documents a number of innovative practices from police forces that have had demonstrable impact in encouraging direct reporting. This shows that the documented tendency for disabled people to avoid reporting to police may not, in itself, be an insurmountable barrier.

These targeted actions need to be complemented by sustained long-term investment in promoting genuine disability equality. While it is important to encourage reporting, we need to acknowledge that this is a reactive approach (Essex Coalition of Disabled People, 2011). The safety and security of disabled people can only be achieved if the structures and prejudices reproducing such crimes are dismantled. The disablist nature of such hate crimes point to the unequal structural positions occupied by disabled and non-disabled people in society. We require a culture change that shifts our understanding of the issues away from a simplistic focus on trying to understand the 'vulnerability' of disabled people and the characteristics that make them 'prone' to experiencing hate crime. Instead we need to examine how disablism reproduces the conditions that manifest themselves as hate crime; and how it erects barriers throughout the arduous journeys that disabled people undertake to seek justice.

References

Action for Blind People (2008) *Report on Verbal and Physical Abuse Towards Blind and Partially Sighted People across the UK*, London: Action for Blind People.

Adams-Spink, G. (2008) 'Does disability hate crime exist?' 19 August 2008, available at http://news.bbc.co.uk/1/hi/magazine/7570305.stm.

Association of Chief Police Officers (ACPO) (2010) *Total of Recorded Hate Crime From Regional Forces in England, Wales and Northern Ireland During the Calendar Year 2009*, London: ACPO. Available at http://www.acpo.police.uk/asp/policies/Data/084a_Recorded_Hate_Crime_-_January_to_December_2009.pdf.

Beauchamp T.L (1991) *Philosophical Ethics*, (2nd ed.). New York: McGraw Hill.

Berzins, K., Petch, A. and Atkinson, J. M. (2003) Prevalence and experience of harassment of people with mental health problems living in the community, *British Journal of Psychiatry*, 183 (12), 526–533.

Burgess, A. W. and Phillips, S. L. (2006) Sexual Abuse, trauma and dementia in the elderly: A retrospective. *Victims and Offenders*, 1(2), 193–204.

Cabinet Office (2010) *The Coalition: Our Programme for Government*, London: The Cabinet Office.

Cooper, S. (2007) 'Was Westminster another Climbie?' *Children Now*, 21 February 2007, 12–13.

Cox, S. (2009) 'How real is the hate crime rise?' BBC News, 26 November 2009, available at http://news.bbc.co.uk/1/hi/uk/8378817.stm.

Crown Prosecution Service (CPS) (2010) *Policy for Prosecuting Cases of Disability Hate Crime*, London: CPS. Available at http://www.cps.gov.uk/publications/prosecution/disability_hate_crime_leaflet.pdf.

Cunningham, S. and Drury, S. (2002) *Access All Areas. A Guide for Community Safety Partnerships on Working More Effectively with Disabled People.* London: Nacro.

Dick, S. (2009) 'Homophobic hate crime: findings from the Gay British Crime Survey 2008', *Safer Communities*, 8(4), 35–42.

Disability Rights Commission (2006) *Equal Treatment: Closing the Gap. A Formal Investigation into Physical Health Inequalities Experienced by People with Learning Disabilities and/or Mental Health Problems.* London: DRC.

Disability Rights Commission and Capability Scotland (2004) *Hate Crime Against Disabled People in Scotland: A Survey Report.* Edinburgh: DRC and Capability Scotland.

Equality and Human Rights Commission (EHRC) (2009) CPS 'wrong' to drop prosecution where victim had a history of mental illness, London: EHRC, available at http://www.equalityhumanrights.com/news/pre-june-2009/cps-wrong-to-drop-prosecution-where-victim-had-a-history-of-mental-illness/.

Essex Coalition of Disabled People (2011) *Disability Hate Crime. Lived Experiences Report*, Essex: ECDP.

Flynn, M. C. (2007) *The Murder of Steven Hoskin. A Serious Case Review.* Cornwall: Cornwall Adult Protection Committee.

Gilhooly, M. L. (2002) *Quality of Life and Real Life Cognitive Functioning*, ESRC Award Reference Number L480 25 4029.

Gillard, D. and Wallace, C. (2003) 'No way to handle assault'. *Community Care* 20 November 2003, 46–47.

Gilson, S. F., Cramer, E. P. and DePoy, E. (2001) Linking the assessment of self-reported functional capacity with abuse experiences of women with disabilities. *Violence Against Women*, 7(4), 418.

Hamlyn, B., Phelps, A., Turtle, J. and Sattar, G. (2004) *Are Special Measures Working? Evidence from Surveys of Vulnerable and Intimidated Witnesses*, London: Home Office.

Hatton, C., Johnson, S. D. and Kebbell, M. R. (2004) Witnesses with intellectual disabilities in court: what questions are asked and what influence do they have?, *Legal and Criminological Psychology*, 9(1), 23–35.

HM Government (1999) *Statute: Youth Justice and Criminal Evidence Act.* London: TSO.

Home Office (2007a) *Achieving Best Evidence in Criminal Proceedings: Guidance for Vulnerable and Intimidated Witnesses, Including Children*, London: Home Office.

——(2007b) *Learning Disability Hate Crime: Good Practice Guidance for Crime and Disorder Reduction.* London: Home Office.

Hunter, C., Hodge, N., Nixon, J., Parr, S. and Willis, B. (2007) *Disabled People's Experiences of Anti-social Behaviour and Harassment in Social Housing: A Critical Review.* London: DRC.

Iganski, P. (2008) *Hate Crime and the City*, Bristol: The Policy Press.

Joint Committee on Human Rights (2008) *A Life Like Any Other? Human Rights of Adults with Learning Disabilities.* London: House of Lords, House of Commons Joint Committee on Human Right; HL paper 40-I HC 73-I session 2007–08.

Leicestershire and Rutland Safeguarding Adults Board (2008) *Executive Summary of Serious Case Review in Relation to A and B*, Leicester: Leicestershire and Rutland Safeguarding Adults Board.

Lewis, L., Gillard, D. and Franklin, K. (2003) Taken with a pinch of salt. *Community Care* 10 April 2003, 46–47.

Love, S., Joslin, E., Cerrone, P., Franklin, K., Priestley, C. (2002) A botched investigation? *Community Care* 10 October 2002, 42–43.

Marley, J. A. and Buila, S. (2001) Crimes against people with mental illness: Types, perpetrators and influencing factors, *Social Work*, 46(2), 115–124.

Mencap (1999) *Living in Fear. The Need to Combat Bullying of People with a Learning Disability*. London: Mencap.

MIND (2007) *Another Assault*. London: MIND.

Perry, J. (2004) 'Is justice taking a beating?' *Community Care* 1 April 2004, 44–45.

——(2009) 'At the intersection: hate crime policy and practice in England and Wales'. *Safer Communities*, 8(2), 9–18.

Petersilia, J. R. (2001) Crime victims with developmental disabilities: a review essay. *Criminal Justice and Behavior*, 28(6), 655–694.

Pring, J. (2010) *Campaigners attack government over hate crime delay*, 23 April 2010, available at http://www.bhfederation.org.uk/federation-news/item/605-campaigners-attack-government-over-hate crime-delays.html.

Quarmby, K. (2008) *Getting Away with Murder: Disabled People's Experiences of Hate Crime in the UK*. London: Scope, Disability Now, UK Disabled People Council.

Saxton, M., Curry, M. A., Powers, L. E., Maley, S., Eckels, K. and Gross, J. (2001) 'Bring my scooter so I can leave you: A study of disabled women handling abuse by personal assistance providers'. *Violence Against Women*, 7(4), 393.

Sequeira, H. (2006) 'Implications for practice: research into the effects of sexual abuse on adults with intellectual disabilities'. *Journal of Adult Protection*, 8(4), 25–34.

Sharp, H. (2001) 'Steps towards justice for people with learning disabilities as victims of crime: the important role of the police'. *British Journal of Learning Disabilities* 29 (3) 88–92.

Sheikh, S., Khanna, M., Pralat, R., Reed, C. and Sin, C. H. (2011) *Hate Crime Research for Stand By Me Campaign*, London: OPM for Mencap.

Sin, C. H. (2005) 'Seeking informed consent: reflections on research practice', *Sociology*, 39(2), 277–294.

Sin, C. H., Fong, J., Momin, A. and Forbes, V. (2007) *The Disability Rights Commission's Formal Investigation into Fitness Standards in Social Work, Nursing and Teaching Professions: Report on the Call for Evidence*. London: DRC.

Sin, C. H., Hedges, A., Cook, C., Mguni, N. and Comber, N. (2009) *Disabled People's Experiences of Targeted Violence and Hostility*, Research Report 21, London: OPM for EHRC.

——(2011) 'Adult protection and effective action in tackling violence and hostility against disabled people: some tensions and challenges', *Journal of Adult Protection*, 13(2), 63–75.

Thomas, P. (2011) 'Mate crime': ridicule, hostility and targeted attacks against disabled people, *Disability and Society*, 26(1), 107–111.

Voice UK All Party Parliamentary Group (2007) *Disability Hate Crime*. London: Voice UK All Party Parliamentary Group; 14 November 2007 meeting notes.

Walby, S. and Allen, J. (2004) *Domestic Violence, Sexual Assault and Stalking: Findings from the British Crime Survey*, Home Office Research Study 276, London: Home Office.

Williams, B., Copestake, P., Eversley, J. and Stafford, B. (2008) *Experiences and Expectations of Disabled People*, London: ODI.

Williams, S. (2011) *Executive Summary of the Serious Case Review in Respect of Adult A*, Tameside: Tameside Adults Safeguarding Partnership.

Wood, J. and Edwards, K. (2005) Victimisation of mentally ill patients living in the community: Is it a life-style issue? *Legal and Criminological Psychology*, 10(2), 279–290.

13 Civil courage, civil societies and good samaritans

A response to disablist hate crime

*Toby Brandon, Northumbria University,
UK and Sarah Keyes, Edinburgh University,
The Lawnmowers Independent Theatre
Company, UK*

Introduction

Hate crime and our responses to it are fundamentally concerned with what kind of communities and societies we wish to live in. If we wish them to be 'good' or 'civil' what exactly are we prepared to risk, or do, to create them? Hate crime, and in particular disablist hate crime, is a relatively new concern in the UK. What makes its experience unique is the sense in which it is both devaluing to the victim themselves and also to the group (i.e. ethnic, sexuality or disability) to which they belong. This chapter draws directly upon the work and ideas of a group of people with learning difficulties, The Lawnmowers Independent Theatre Company. In terms of hate crime they have numerous personal examples to call upon, ranging from being called 'spaz' on the street and being pushed around at college, right through to having battery acid thrown in their faces. In this chapter, we do not focus on these experiences or their effects but rather The Lawnmowers' collective challenge to disablist hate crime, through the powerful media of Theatre for Change.

Over a series of months, discussions took place with The Lawnmowers, including the design and piloting of a workshop in response to hate crime. As the chapter progressed, its constituent ideas were repeatedly taken back to the Lawnmowers for further development. They responded with group discussions, small vignette theatre pieces and role-plays. What arose out of this collaboration went further than their simple descriptive work around hate crime and any connected legal debate to the construction of the kind of society that people with learning difficulties would like to live in. The following discussion begins by exploring the concept of a 'civil society' before introducing the ideas behind the 'Bad Samaritan' and 'civil courage' as direct responses to disablist hate crime. Throughout the discussion, descriptions of the work done by The Lawnmowers will illustrate the points being made.

The construction of disablist hate crime

The social construction of disablist hate crime is often complex and confused. The normative perception of 'learning difficulties' is often synonymous with 'vulnerability' and the associated language of 'bullying', 'an easy target' and 'abuse', as opposed to 'hate', 'assault' and 'hostility'. Sir Ken Macdonald, Director of the Public Prosecution Service, accused the relevant authorities of seeing disabled people as 'easy targets' of crime, rather than as people who had been victimised due to their impairments. He asserted that this was a 'scar on the conscience of criminal justice' (Macdonald, 2008: 1).

This is a powerful idea of disenfranchised people within our society looking around for the first person who is 'fair game' to vent their aggression on. This poses the question as to whether this is a true expression of hatred of a specific group (Sherry, 2010), being driven by disablism. That is, the belief that disabled people are inferior, invalid and of less value within society. Hatred itself involves impersonal intense feelings of dislike for a group, which as a motivator for crime intensives/amplifies its meaning (Iganski, 2008). It can be offensive to the disabled person in the immediate or long term, and also to the wider disability community. It therefore has the potential to be a joint attack on both group and individual identity.

The Disabled People's Movement is a collective response to the barriers to meaningful inclusion in society faced by disabled people, including challenges to the assumption that disability is synonymous with vulnerability. Vulnerability is created by numerous social factors, including poverty and social exclusion. It is important to contextualise it away from disabled people's 'identity' to the particular 'situations' we may find ourselves in. This avoids the totality of vulnerability as a patronising identity for all disabled people. In terms of the social model of disability, this approach also challenges the locating of any problem with disabled people, not society. That is, the emphasis being on the disabled person having to change, be trained, restricted or moved, and thus become less vulnerable. Sir Ken MacDonald again stresses that we must in crime clearly distinguish between the meanings of 'vulnerability', 'hostility' and 'senselessness' to avoid shifting responsibility away from the assailant onto the victim in any way (Macdonald, 2008).

The reality for disabled people can be a harsh one; Mencap (Living in Fear, 2000) reported that 90 per cent of people with learning difficulties had experienced bullying and harassment. The Disability Rights Commission survey report 'Hate Crime Against Disabled People in Scotland' (2003) stated that disabled people in urban areas are more likely to be scared of attack; 73 per cent of respondents had reported being frightened or attacked, or had experienced verbal abuse. For both reports, hate crimes were mostly likely to occur in public places: 'The attacks had a major impact on disabled people: around a third have had to avoid specific places and change their usual routine. One in four have moved home as a result of the attack' (Macdonald, 2008: 4). Two thirds are bullied on a regular basis and almost a third experience bullying on a daily or weekly basis. The Mencap survey suggests that 'the bullying of people with learning disability is institutionalised throughout society' (2000: 1). In a similar vein, Roulstone and Thomas (2009, xii) state that the under-reporting of hate crime is significant: 'Disabled people continue to face unique institutional forms of hate crimes in residential and nursing home contexts. Some of these crimes may be very hard to identify.' This reality encouraged the UK Equality and Human Rights Commission (*Guardian*, 2010) to want people in the UK to report disablist hate crime, threatening to act against any public body, including councils, police or schools, which it finds to be at fault.

The Lawnmowers Independent Theatre Company

The Lawnmowers Independent Theatre Company, based in Gateshead, Tyne and Wear, is an organisation of learning-disabled actors whose performance work reflects their own concerns in terms of service delivery, and personal issues faced by themselves and others with learning difficulties. Their work combines humour with songs and movement as they tackle contested contemporary concerns. They formed in 1986:

> The Company is dedicated to the research and development of new ways of working and supports places where people with learning disabilities can explore their ideas and help plan and take control of their future ... through all its work and its members will continue to work towards a future, just and equal society honouring and developing the culture of people with learning disabilities.
>
> (company website)

Much of The Lawnmowers' work is based on the use of Legislative Theatre, also known as Theatre of the Oppressed or Theatre for Change. Two of the actors from the group describe this interactive model which enables audiences to engage with and suggest alternatives to issues of importance to people with learning difficulties:

> we have a scene, say it's a bad scene, we do that, and then we ask the audience how they would change it, then we get them to step into our shoes and see if it'll change the scene, and also it'll change people, what they view, and how they feel ... If anyone in that audience has similar problems, then they get good ideas of how they can sort themselves out. And it really helps them with their lives.
>
> (Keyes, 2010, p. 156)

The Lawnmowers' work is situated within a worldwide movement of Theatre groups who use Theatre for Change to communicate their experiences of oppression and to campaign for changes, both within society and in relevant policy (Boal, 1998). The Lawnmowers' work, therefore, forms links 'between the largely disenfranchised world of the learning disabled and policy makers' (Price and Barron, 1999: 822).

As a group of people with learning difficulties using this powerful way of communicating the discrimination which they face, the Lawnmowers' Theatre for Change work has links with both the self-advocacy movement and the disability-arts movement, both of which are effective examples of empowerment through participation, bringing about social change (Mitchell *et al.*, 2006; Goodley and Moore, 2002). Thus, the workshops and forums facilitated by The Lawnmowers on the issues surrounding disablist hate crime highlight its existence in the direct experience of disabled people, including core members of their Theatre Company. Their work goes beyond that, too, in equipping audiences with solutions to specific situational concerns. This collective challenge to disablist hate crime is therefore an ideal and effective medium for communicating how disabled people wish their societies and communities to improve. The Lawnmowers' work also equips other groups of people with learning difficulties, their supporters, service providers, policymakers and the general public with tools to challenge disablist hate crime.

The civil society

In general terms we can view a society as the totality of informal and formal relationships and arrangements between citizens, organisations and the state. Plato's ideal state has as a central tenet the civic virtues of wisdom, courage, moderation and justice. Daly and Howell (2006) point out that there is no single clear explanation of civil societies but the competition of different interpretations of public worth. Civil societies are born from collective or common-good actions which put the personalisation or individualisation agenda to one side and push for a more civil or perhaps 'bigger' society. The civil society is an expression of positive democracy with a consideration of respect, trust, tolerance, freedom and social capital. The now disbanded Centre for Civil Society at the London School of Economics (website) defines the civil society as:

> the arena of uncoerced collective action around shared interests, purposes and values. In theory, its institutional forms are distinct from those of the state, family and market, though in practice, the boundaries between state, civil society, family and market are often complex, blurred and negotiated. Civil society commonly embraces a diversity of spaces, actors and institutional forms, varying in their degree of formality, autonomy and power. Civil societies are often populated by organisations such as registered charities, development non-governmental organisations, community groups, women's organisations, faith-based organisations, professional associations, trades unions, self-help groups, social movements, business associations, coalitions and advocacy groups.

The Lawnmowers' place in this is clear, and they state that in order to create a civil society, the most significant changes need to be in people's attitudes. Edwards (2009) proposes that the development of a civil society is threefold: the association of social capital between voluntary associations; good society in terms of shared positive values; and a space for public debate. Thus, the discussion moves on to explore these three concepts in relation to changing people's attitudes in order to reduce, and eventually eradicate, hate crime against people with learning difficulties in the UK. We will look at each of these in turn.

The association of social capital between voluntary associations

Social capital, according to Putman (2000: 19), 'refers to connection among individuals – social networks and the norms of reciprocity and trustworthiness that arise from them'. In that sense, social capital is closely related to what some have called 'civic virtue'. The Lawnmowers are a voluntary association linked both nationally and internationally into a network of organisations which collectively strive to develop further positive associations of people with learning difficulties and their supporters. They are part of a Community of Practice (CoP), including the Centre for Excellence for Teacher Training for Inclusive Learning (Brandon and Charlton, 2011) based at Northumbria University. CoPs strive towards shared goals, according to Wenger (1998), by the negotiation of meaning and knowledge within communities. Wilkinson and Pickett (2009), in their book *The Spirit Level*, map social capital to different notions of inequalities for different groups. The Lawnmowers recognise that it is not just disabled people who experience hate crime; people can be targeted on the basis of ethnicity, gender and many other characteristics. They see the key to challenging hatred and changing society as residing within the education of children in schools.

Shared positive values

It is important to note that The Lawnmowers' response to disablist hate crime is a collective response, grounded in an affirmative group identity. Within the context of a group workshop focussing on developing this chapter, The Lawnmowers spoke about collective positive identity when socialising as a group, and alongside groups from other minorities who have experienced hate crime and/or other forms of discrimination. Group members spoke about the strength drawn from being together, and stated that most instances of hate crime had been experienced when alone in public. Mutual support has been conceptualised previously within the co-construction of a model of peer support which outlined positive effects of meaningful interpersonal interaction within the group, including: an ongoing mentoring process; the reclamation of dignity and respect; fulfilment of ambitions and breaking down barriers to inclusion (Keyes 2010). The strength of this support, alongside an emphasis on self/group advocacy, provides a firm foundation for The Lawnmowers' response to disablist hate crime.

A space for public debate

The strength of working together to promote positive values is the basis on which The Lawnmowers would create a space for public debate. In order to explore what this 'space' might look like, the group worked at devising an outline for a workshop that would communicate the issues surrounding hate crime to a wide range of audiences. It was felt that the workshop should be aimed at members of the general public as well as within educational settings such as schools, and also in public places where hate crime is particularly prevalent, such as areas where drinking often leads to violence. Part of citizenship education (Kerr *et al.*, 2007) programmes might be The Lawnmowers and other such organisations raising awareness of hate crime issues within educational and other settings. This connects with ideas of communitarianism (Etzioni, 1995) where people are actively involved in their communities. This has more recently been rebranded as the 'Big Society', although it is still unclear what this actually means in practice for different groups. Hoban and Beresford (2001) explore how local people mobilise themselves into groups in response to particular issues, such as disablist hate crime. Daly and Howell (2006: 25) state that 'although the government underlines how citizens can better engage with the state, it has given less importance to how citizens can better engage with each other.'

The workshop devised and piloted by The Lawnmowers included interactive opportunities for those taking part to be challenged about their personal and collective response to disablist hate crime. The scene was set for discussion by exercises that encouraged people to think about when they had been bullied, as well as instances when they had bullied others. The use of songs and actions within a second group exercise provided a space for reflection on the dynamics of positive group leadership. The use of role plays, in situations where service providers (in this case owners of a bar) had ignored or even encouraged hate crime, enabled those taking part to challenge the service providers by asking questions, and ultimately deciding what sanctions should be placed on the bar owners. Finally, a piece of forum drama outlined a 'night from hell' in which a series of events occurring during a night out led to one of the actors being beaten up in the street. Following the first presentation of this 'night from hell', the audience were asked to take each of the scenes and act out changes that could have resulted in a more positive ending to the night.

Daly and Howell (2006, p. 26) state that 'Studies of civil society have shown that what often matters most to people is the extent of the personal security, respect, understanding and acts of kindness that they experience in their everyday lives.' Having explored aspects relating to a civil society, The Lawnmowers workshop provides a model for public and private challenges to hate crime which enables the development of a civil society. Work done by

The Lawnmowers can also be considered to be driven by the principles of civil courage.

Civil courage

Civil courage is concerned with standing up or speaking out for others in an attempt to create a more civil society. It was first referred to as the German 'zivilcourage' coined by Bismarck in 1864 (Zivilcourage 21 website). It is a kind of public advocacy in the sense that it is concerned with representing someone else's interests as if they are your own. In practice it could take the form of whistleblowing on a service (Thomson in Hunt, 1998) or intervening in a threatening situation in the street. Courage can be considered in terms of the personal, social and political. It can also be constructed in terms of enhanced participation, autonomy and the engagement with cultural, social change and compassion. It can be framed as an act of civil disobedience and/ or protest which is considered more than simple 'prosocial' helping behaviour, as it involves anticipated negative social consequences for the actions, such as being attacked for stepping in to protect someone else. It is seen as deriving from a 'form of value-rational social action; more precisely, it can be characterised as an action, which is inspired by ideal interest, which is carried out irrespective of its chances of success, and which entails a conflict, typically by challenging a law or a convention' (Swedberg, 1999: 517).

In terms of a response to hate crime we can refer to the work of Greitemeyer *et al.* (2007: 115): 'We define civil courage as brave behavior accompanied by anger and indignation which intends to enforce societal and ethical norms without considering one's own social costs.' The Lawnmowers propose that a civil society needs people to act with civil courage to reduce disablist hate crime. The question then arises as to how societies and their constituent communities can encourage or even insist upon their citizens to act with courage against hate crime.

Bad and Good Samaritan laws

To an extent, the encouragement of civil courage is enshrined in law in certain countries including Brazil, France and Germany. This means that if a disablist hate crime is committed in public, people are obliged to act, either by alerting the authorities or by intervening in the situation. These laws make citizens act to help the state; they are omissions laws as they work on actions that should be taken. Legislation such as this is referred to as Bad Samaritan Laws, as they intend to force people into acting for the protection of others. Within Britain you may be under moral pressure to save a drowning child but there is no legal obligation. Vranken (1998: 1) writes that 'At common law there is no legal duty to go to the rescue of strangers ... Extreme examples include "malicious failures to warn a blind man of an open manhole, to lift the head of a sleeping drunk out of a puddle of water"'.

Malm (2000: 1) asks the question 'whether this moral obligation ought to be enforced by the criminal law'. If yes, three obstacles need to be overcome. Malm describes these: first, to show that the moral duty to go to the aid of others is proper for legal enforcement. Second, that this duty to aid someone can be defined in a way that can be enforced by the court, and third, that the benefit of such an enforced law is worth the effort. Malm argues that these cannot be met: 'Our current efforts toward Bad Samaritan laws may appear more like psychological venting in response to a few dramatic cases than sincere efforts to effect a good' (Malm, 2000: 1).

The citizen's duty to the state is not unproblematic; it is reminiscent of the current government's intended development of the 'Big Society'. Are the citizens of a country bound by a social contract and therefore obliged to help the government in enforcing the law, over and above paying taxes? Similarly, does the Big Society mean those citizens are obliged to create a more civil society? Malm (2000: 3) argues that 'We have ample evidence that people are willing to aid others in the absence of a legal obligation to do so and sometime in the presence of great risk to themselves.'

All interventions, even if just reporting crime to the police, can carry risk. The use of laws to socially engineer societies into acting, or even caring, in certain ways, is a problematic one. This involves the complex relationship between internal moral norms and external development of social norms:

> if we really wanted to affect people's attitudes, we could make efforts to encourage, publicize and perhaps even reward acts of good samaritanism (or maybe even decent samaritanism). A reward system, which doesn't have to be monetary and could focus on something as simple as 'citizen of the month', could send the same symbolic message about community and what we as a society value as would a prohibition-based system, and could do it without moral problems and costs.
>
> (Malm, 2000: 16)

One member of the Lawnmowers described how he had been picked on by someone at a bus stop and a woman not known to him presented herself as his mother in his defence. When we explored the topic they were, as a group and individually, interested in standing up for other people in society. A number of the group had stood up for other people and paid the price of being assaulted themselves. As a result they agreed that you cannot force people to stand up for others through the use of a Bad Samaritan law and other means. They also expressed an appreciation that hate crime is not just against disabled people but against other groups. The realisation that people with learning difficulties are not alone in their experience of hate crime is an important one. Associated with this, the role of self/group advocacy in supporting people to challenge disablist hate crime was seen as significant.

Conclusion

We began this chapter by stating that hate crime and our responses to it are fundamental to the societies and communities we wish to live in. We propose that by enacting civil courage and developing civil communities, hate crime can be challenged. To do this we need to directly listen to people with learning difficulties, how they envisage the societies they wish to live in, and how they might be realised. This means that there is a difficult balance/tension between viewing people with learning difficulties as vulnerable and needing protection under the law, and the desire to increase personal empowerment, enable choice and facilitate autonomy. The Lawnmowers dismiss the introduction of Bad Samaritan laws, believing that citizens should not be forced into taking risks. They do suggest that Good Samaritan actions can be encouraged and this is in line with the aims stated in their publicity material, to create a 'just and equal society'. This intention goes beyond the current personalisation agenda to a group agenda of 'honouring and developing the culture of people with learning disabilities'. Roulstone and Thomas' (2009) examination of approaches to practice around hate crime in the North West of England provides a useful frame of reference. Key points from the work included the need to improve the understanding of disability in relation to hate crime. Statutory bodies and policy initiatives need to work in partnership with organisations of disabled people so a better understanding of the practical context of discrimination can be gained. The Lawnmowers are not alone; organisations like Inclusion North (a website) have attempted to increase the reporting and awareness of hate crime. On a local level, supported Keep Safe schemes for people with learning difficulties have been spreading. Locations such as Boots the chemists are designated as help points with a 'Keep Safe' sticker, and staff at these points have been instructed on ways to support people with learning difficulties. In some areas local councils have issued people with learning difficulties with small cards which hold information about them and who to contact if they need help.

There is no single way to tackle hate crime. Roulstone and Thomas (2009) report that any action needs to include increased work around reduction – proactive campaigns, education, management, liaison, and better reporting options. The work of the Lawnmowers agrees, and they state there is a need to challenge and change the culture that fosters hate crimes within our communities. We would argue that history and culture for people with learning difficulties is not one of hatred but more one of overwhelming devaluation, characterised by the great confinement of the nineteenth century through to the Mencap report of institutional disablism in the NHS – *Death by Indifference* (2007). Within this the avoidance of what can be termed victimology is important. This has a tendency to assume disabled people are victims of their own impairments; however, historically they have not only been passive vulnerable victims, they have protested through many means, including songs of resistance (Brandon, 1990). The Lawnmowers and similar organisations are part of rewriting a more affirming disability history. Further research needs to be conducted into disablist hate directed not only at disabled people but also at their supporters, carers and paid staff. In addition, The Lawnmowers wish to engage with perpetrators and ask them why they hate and commit the crimes.

Civil courage would not be needed in truly civil societies; it's concerned with what societies should be like, not what they are like now. The Lawnmowers do not characterise civil courage as isolated individual actions by people with learning difficulties and/or their supporters. They see how collective action can inspire and be mutually supportive for disabled people, their supporters and the communities we all live in. The development of civil societies goes hand in hand with the development of self-respect for disabled people. The Lawnmowers believe and demonstrate that we should have civil courage in all that we do.

References

BBC News (2010) Disability hate crime action to be investigated by EHRC. Available at http://www.bbc.co.uk/news/10304445. Accessed 4 April 2011.

Boal, A. (1998) *Legislative Theatre: using performance to make politics.* London: Routledge.

Bismarck, O. 'Zivilcourage 21' http://www.zivilcourage21.info/aktuell.html. (visited: 20 March 2011).

Brandon, D. (1990). *Strange Places: experiences in mental handicap hospital* University College Salford.

Brandon, T. and Charlton, J. (2011) 'The Lessons Learned from Developing an Inclusive Learning and Teaching Community of Practice in England' *International Journal of Inclusive Education.* 15(1), 165–178.

Centre for Civil Society http://www2.lse.ac.uk/CCS/home.aspx (visited: 5 March 2011).

Daly, S. and Howell, J. (2006) *For the common good? The changing role of civil society in the UK and Ireland.* Fife: Carnegie UK Trust.

Disability Rights Commission (2003) *Hate Crime Against Disabled People in Scotland: A Survey* http://www.leeds.ac.uk/disability-studies/archiveuk/DRC/Hate%20Crime%20report.pdf (accessed 10 April 2011).

Edwards, M. (2009) *Civil Society* (2nd Edition) Cambridge: Polity Press.

Etzioni, A. (1995) *The Spirit of Community. Rights responsibilities and the communitarian agenda,* London: Fontana Press.

Equality and Human Rights Commission (*Guardian*, 14 June 2010) http://www.bbc.co.uk/news/10304445 (visited: 4 April 2011).

Goodley, D. and Moore, M. (2002) *Disability arts against exclusion. People with learning difficulties and their performing arts.* Kidderminster: BILD.

Greitemeyer, T., Osswald, S., Fischer, P. and Frey, D. (2007) 'Civil courage: Implicit theories, related concepts, and measurement'. *The Journal of Positive Psychology* 2 (2), 115–119.

Hunt, G. (1998) (ed.) *Whistle blowing in the Social Services: Public Accountability & Professional Practice,* London: Arnold.

Kerr, D., Lopes, J., Nelson, J., White, K., Cleaver, E. and Benton, T. (2007) *Vision versus Pragmatism: Citizenship in the secondary school curriculum in England.* (DfES Research Report 845). London: DfES.

Keyes, S. (2010) *Mutual Support. An exploration of peer support for people with learning difficulties.* Unpublished PhD thesis, Northumbria University.

Iganski, P. (2008) *Hate Crime and the City.* London: Policy Press.

Inclusion North Stop Hate Crime 'Learning together training pack' available at http://www.inclusionnorth.org/about-us.asp (visited: 11 March 2011).

Malm, H. M. (2000) 'Bad Samaritan laws: harm, help, or hype?' *Law and Philosophy* 19(6) 707–750.

Macdonald, K. (2008) *Prosecuting Disability Hate Crime* http://www.cps.gov.uk/news/nationalnews/dhc_dpp_speech.html (visited: 10 April 2011).

Mencap (2000) *Living in fear* http://www.mencap.org.uk/document.asp?id=12069&audGroup=&subjectLevel2=&subjectId=9&sorter=1&origin=subjectId&pageType=&pageno=&searchPhrase= (visited: 10 April 2011).

Mitchell, D., Traustadottir, R., Chapman, R., Townson, L., Ingham, N. and Ledger, S. (eds) (2006) *Exploring Experiences of Advocacy by People with Learning Disabilities: Testimonies of Resistance.* London and Philadelphia: Jessica Kingsley.

Roulstone, A. and Thomas, P. (2009) *Disabled People and Hate Crime* Manchester: Equality and Human Rights Commission.

Putman, R. (2000) *Bowling Alone: The Collapse and Revival of American Community.* New York: Simon & Schuster.

Sherry, M. (2010) *Disability Hate Crimes Does Anyone Really Hate Disabled People?* Farnham: Ashgate.

Swedberg, R. (1999) Civil courage (Zivilcourage): The case of Knut Wicksell. *Theory and Society* 28 (4), 501–528.

The Lawnmowers Independent Theatre Company http://www.the lawnmowers.co.uk/company/index.php (visited: 05 March 2011).

Price, D. and Barron, L. (1999) 'Developing Independence: the experience of the Lawnmowers Theatre Company', *Disability and Society*, 14 (6), 819–829.

Vranken, M. (1998) 'Duty to rescue in civil law and common law: les extremes se touchent' *International & Comparative Law Quarterly* 47(4), 934–942.

Wenger, E. (1998) *Communities of Practice. Learning, meaning and identity* Cambridge: Cambridge University Press.

Wilkinson, R. and Pickett, K. (2009) *The Spirit Level Why Equality is Better for Everyone* London: Penguin books.

Zivilcourage 21 (2011) Das Kreuz mit der Zivilcourage: Otto Von Bismarck. Available at http://www.zivilcourage21.info/aktuell.html. Accessed 20 March 2011.

14 After disablist hate crime

Which interventions really work to resist victimhood and build resilience with survivors?

Susie Balderston, Lancaster University, UK

Background and context

This chapter aims to be relevant to policymakers, user-led disabled people's organisations (ULOs), criminal justice workers, funders, rape crisis and victim groups, which have an interest in providing evidence-based interventions after disablist hate crimes. It outlines the rationale and recommendations from a user-led pilot in the North East of England (Balderston & Roebuck, 2010), which mapped local need, pathways and gaps in victim services after hate crime, informed by service-user experiences and international evidence on intervention efficacy. Several large-scale studies have already suggested a pressing need for accessible interventions with disabled people after violent crime. This is particularly significant for disabled women are between twice (Smith, 2008) and four times (Martin *et al.*, 2006) more likely to experience sexual assault and domestic violence than non-disabled women, repeat victimization in these crimes is at 38 per cent (Home Office, 2009a) and there is even greater harm and victim impact after hate crimes (Iganski, 2008). Given the escalating nature of disablist hate incidents, effective prevention and early intervention is crucial to prevent further distress, particularly after rape (Resnick *et al.*, 2005).

Yet significant institutional barriers and structural inequalities (Young, 2009) exist when disabled people try to access mainstream victim services, which often results in inappropriate responses, particularly with disabled women after domestic violence (Hague *et al.*, 2010) and violent crime. The mainstream resources for victims in England and Wales are predominantly shaped on troubled neo-liberal, individual model designs, contrary to accepted sociological research in the area; interventions centre on ineffectual counselling by volunteers (Rose *et al.*, 1999), thorny empowerment (Riger, 1993), and problematic target hardening (Hope, 2008); evaluations show that statutory sexual violence services may be seen as less independent and less victim-focussed than third-sector services (Robinson & Hudson, 2011, p. 530). In contrast, proven collective group methods to resist victimhood, described by activists and criminologists in the USA and UK (Kelly and Humphreys, 2001, Chesney-Lind, 2006), build on approaches from feminism and, perhaps surprisingly, may be up to five times more successful in gaining conviction outcomes from reported cases after rape than mainstream provision (Robinson & Hudson, 2011). User advocacy models from the disabled people's movement may also assist disabled and Deaf people after hate crime to resume independent living, inclusion and recovery (Lowicki and Pillsbury, 2004). The author argues that these feminist approaches may be adaptable, relevant and successful in work with disabled and Deaf women who have experienced disablist or audist hate crime, including targeted sexual violence. In user-led settings, the space and access can be provided in which people can take back their own agency, self-organise, tackle barriers and enable themselves and others to more successfully move on with life after violent attacks.

Introduction: an accessible pathway for disabled victims?

In the first decade of the new millennium, activism, research and progressive journalism has tried to raise awareness of disablist hate crime in the UK; this important work has exposed the problem by reporting disabled people's experiences and numbers of attacks and improved policy, as the preceding chapters in the book demonstrate. This is essential work (especially in the early stages of any movement seeking social justice), but the pathway of support for the victim herself may end abruptly in the short term after she has reported the crime, is no longer a focus for media interest, after a prosecution has been dropped or after the first days and weeks of crisis following an attack. Disabled women are amongst the worst hit and experience higher rates of violence than both non-disabled women and disabled men, and are still largely invisible in the mainstream agenda; for example, disabled women only enjoy one passing mention in the current Home Office action plan, designed to end violence against women and girls (Home Office, 2009b: 6).

Conversely, despite being ignored or labelled 'hard to reach' by mainstream agencies, our user-led, disabled people's organisations (ULOs/DPOs) at street level regularly witness the escalation or continuation of attacks, the medium-term consequences of violence and the long-term harm for the victim, their family and community, who may have been silenced, or invisible for years (IPCC, 2009). Prevention is a timely concern, especially when resources are scarce. Criminologists expect to see hate crime become more common and more violent in times of recession, where groups victimise 'unwelcome outsiders' which they perhaps perceive (incorrectly) as unfairly challenging their cultural or economic status (Chakraborti & Garland, 2009), a phenomenon known as 'economic threat theory' (Frost, 2008). Good community-relations work, in building links and reducing tensions *between* groups in communities, is a crucial strategy to ensure that people and places are safer (Harris & Young, 2009). Projects like the pilot being discussed here work intersectionally with groups (for example, recognising that people are not in 'silos' of disability or gender or ethnicity or religion or sexual orientation) and can assist us to support each others' campaigns, find allies to work with to improve services, and ultimately build safer communities.

So, this chapter will introduce some practical support strategies which have been shown to be effective (and critique the not so useful) in a range of public, private and third-sector projects which may be made inclusive or accessible with disabled or Deaf people after violent, interpersonal attacks. Here, the preferred term is 'interpersonal violence' (Hepburn, 1973; Powers *et al.*, 2002) as this comprehends domestic violence, harassment where the perpetrator provides or withholds personal care or support, either at home or in an institution, hate crime, rape or other violent attacks by a stranger. This term resists the homogenisation of 'hate crime' and recognises the increased harm of targeted injury or escalating harassment over time (Iganski, 2008). The term, 'disablist hate crime' is the preferred hate crime term as it recognises that it is the targeting by a perpetrator that is the risk to disabled people.

Why do we need interventions?

International studies show that the long-term effects of interpersonal violence and abuse include negative physical, psychological, financial, and sexual consequences, with the victim then being more likely to experience further neglect, abuse and violence during their lives (Pritchard, 2001). When an attack is perpetrated on the grounds of hostility, prejudice or hate, against the victim's identity (so-called hate crime) the harm is even greater (Iganski, 2008), with particular psychological ill-effects for the victim (Herek *et al.*, 1999). The effects of the crime may be exacerbated by fear of repercussions, which may in turn lead to subsequent under-reporting (Disability Rights Commission, 2004; Mind, 2007). But for women, there are particular impacts after violent crime. Reliable research shows that women are more likely to experience post-traumatic stress disorder (PTSD), especially when there was direct threat to their life, or rape (Resnick *et al.*, 1993). Women victims are also more likely to subsequently use alcohol, have depression, anxiety and risk their health in other ways (Steketee & Foa, 1987), particularly if they had been repeatedly victimised (Ullman & Brecklin, 2002). This is important in the UK, where even taking into account the under-reporting in official figures, repeat victimisation in interpersonal violence is at 38 per cent (Home Office, 2009a). In addition, disabled women may be less able to leave perpetrators, due to access barriers and dependency on support (Milberger *et al.*, 2003). Young disabled women are more at risk of intimate-partner violence (Brownridge, 2006) than other disabled or non-disabled women and disabled women are more likely to be victims of violence related to alcohol or drug use than disabled men (Li, Ford, and Moore, 2000), so a suite of diverse approaches, resisting standardised services, is recommended to reflect the diverse manifestations of harm. In addition, the effects of these experiences appear at different stages along the victim's journey and not only immediately after the attack. This is problematic given that interventions such as Cognitive Behavioural Therapy

(CBT) are promoted as effective mostly over the first 7–10 days and early weeks after the attack (Foa *et al.*, 1995; DoH, 2009). Following a random unaggravated property crime, a victim may recover in between two weeks and six months, but the effects of hate crime take 28 per cent longer than in other crimes. Rape effects, meanwhile, can last from 17 to 34 years (Barnes & Ephross, 1994; Marhoefer-Dvorak, 1998). Alongside this evidence, the work of Sacks *et al.* (2008) paints a worrying picture of invisibility and need in mainstream services.

Does individual victim counselling work?

But if there is need, why can't disabled people just use the same victim support, counselling or other mainstream services set up for victims of crime? Even after fifteen years of legislation to promote equality of disabled people in the UK, disabling institutional barriers and structural inequalities (Young, 2009) in mainstream victim services can render them inaccessible or ineffective, having a significant effect on outcomes of justice and recovery for disabled or Deaf victims. Despite the work of some committed individuals, there is currently no register of accessible victim support facilities. Although the service offers home visits instead of appointments at inaccessible offices, one volunteer in our pilot study explained how difficult it can be for someone who is distressed after an attack to advocate for her own access requirements in a coherent way, or to access this offer if their abuser lives with her or provides her only support (Balderston & Roebuck, 2010: 19). It has long been understood that trying to ignore the memory of a rape, or places linked to it, is damaging and can lead to depression (Cohen & Roth, 1987), so support is essential. But lack of understanding of the evidence can be damaging; in our North East study of barriers after hate crime, one trans woman had been told by a well-meaning victim support volunteer to 'get on with things' (Balderston & Roebuck, 2010, p. 18), which had increased her distress after the hate crime.

Can we make disabled people safer at home?

What might reasonably be dubbed the 'victim industry' in the UK spends millions of pounds in 'Target hardening' – for example, the fitting of locks, cameras or alarms after domestic violence or burglary. However, this practice may not be accessible or effective, especially for disabled people. Some international evidence disputes the value of this intervention (Hope, 2008; Casey *et al.*, 2004) and criminologists are suspicious of new technologies being marketed to crime victims and agencies (Radford & Gill, 2006). Even victim support's own UK evaluation of target hardening (2005) fails to demonstrate reduced victim anxiety after attacks or improved victim outcomes. Although it may seem 'natural' for a victim to want to secure his or her home after burglary, clinical psychology tells us that safety-seeking behaviour such as this can result in negative feelings being unintentionally reinforced.

Salkovskis found that target hardening can also reduce responsibility for safety in the future, encourage checking (Salkovskis, 1996: 53) and help unpleasant thoughts become even more persistent (1996: 62), thus preventing recovery. Participants in our pilot project discussed that, for disabled people with rigid thought patterns or compulsive behaviours, the imposition of well-meaning measures involving yet more checking and locks or cameras after a crime might be even more disabling. Returning disabled people to institutions after hate crime may be considered appropriate by paternalistic social workers, but evidence shows that disabled people are overwhelmingly more likely to experience violence, neglect, rape and abuse in institutions than in the community (Sobsey & Mansell, 1994; Healthcare Commission, 2007; BBC, 2011).

Are services culturally competent and accessible?

Despite improvements in Public Protection Units and excellent reports of some police officers who investigate reports thoroughly, taking disablist hate crime seriously, a lack of victim-centred skill was also seen in some police services. One Action Learning Set member from the North East pilot study said:

> Often, the Police will know the name of the perpetrator in a case, but not the name of the victim. That sends a powerful message that they don't care or understand the impact on the victim or the dignity [needed] in the process.
>
> (Balderston & Roebuck, 2010: 19)

Some learning-disabled women who had been raped talked of being interviewed in nursery rooms, with dolls and cartoon characters on the walls, and expressed their hurt at the lack of age-appropriate and dignified support available to them. If a disabled victim is happily one of the few for which the case may progress to prosecution stage, they should benefit from special measures if they require them (HM Government, 1999). Special measures can include evidence given by a television link and intermediaries to ensure witnesses understand proceedings, so that victims and witnesses, including disabled people, can give their best evidence in court. However, Burton *et al.* found that only 1 per cent of disabled victims and witnesses (compared to 18 per cent who were eligible for them) had been identified by the Police, CPS, Courts or Victim Support as needing special measures (2006: 22); this study showed an even greater barrier for disabled people accessing justice than other groups of so-called 'Vulnerable and Intimidated Witnesses'. Since this report, in the North East and North West of England, some work has been undertaken in partnership with disabled people's user-led organisations and prosecutors, to tackle these barriers, but inconsistencies across the UK still remain.

Another significant barrier to effective interventions with disabled people after hate crime or rape, which permeates across criminal justice, health and social-care services, is the problem of a diagnosis-led approach. As Scott explains, pressurised staff may ask 'What's wrong with this woman?' rather than 'What has happened to this woman?' (2004: 256). This is prevalent, not only in context of Scott's research in prisons, but in mental health services, where experience of crime is not advocated as part of initial or Care Programme Approach (CPA) assessment (Robinson & Spilsbury, 2008; NICE, 2011). In some criminal justice services, awareness of autism and Asperger's Syndrome is now promoted (Browning & Caulfield, 2011), in a way that is puzzlingly at odds with the lessons of 30 years of social model theory which focuses on barriers rather than personal deficits. Rather than attempting to label each victim or offender by diagnosis, or locate them as 'vulnerable' (Hollomotz, 2009), user-led organisations, including some small third-party reporting centres and refuges, identify disabling barriers in their services and systematically work to remove them. In addition, mainstream providers may find it difficult to understand how disabled people may be differently affected by body-image issues, particularly after rape or abuse, and how psycho-emotional disablism (Reeve, 2004) may be worsened by victim labelling and hate-crime experiences. If a disabled person is gay or lesbian, barriers in mainstream organisations may be compounded where even an organisation's own guidance asserts that LGBT (sic) 'Are less likely to report crime or request our services' (Victim Support, 2006).

Schneider *et al.* (2009) found that people significantly underestimated the length and severity of actual aftereffects of rape survivors, particularly in their understanding of the impact on Asian women. The authors emphasised the need for cultural sensitivity regarding expectations of families from ethnically diverse backgrounds connected to rape victims, as well as understanding from service providers and policymakers who may cap provision. However, it may not only be disabled or Deaf people experiencing hate crime that volunteer counselling does not assist. In the first large-scale, randomised control trial of its type with victims after violent crime in the UK, Rose *et al.* (1999) found that there was no significant effect of debriefing on victims' symptoms when they were followed up. This is consistent with the findings of Kilpatrick & Resnick (1993). One question, therefore, is whether the role of evidence-based practice could be expanded in victim services in the UK today, given the spending of £49 million on victim support alone (Victim Support, 2010). The individualised victim-counselling approach may lead some victims to gain a sense of empowerment (particularly after burglary), but there is little evidence in the UK that they actually demonstrate outcomes which may linked to being empowered by, for example, improving resources, employment or being safer (Riger, 1993) in the longer term, or in the particular case of work with hate crime victims.

Different problems arise when Deaf people who identify with a capital 'D' – Deaf as a linguistic and cultural minority, rather than as disabled – struggle to access mainstream counselling and support services after crime, as British sign language (BSL) is a scarce resource in the criminal justice system. Services not delivered in the victim's chosen sign language can even unintentionally exacerbate paranoia (Gahir, 2006), result in poor recovery outcomes (Foster, 1998) and further exclusion (Young *et al.*, 2000). In counselling, people who do not use BSL, attempting to provide services to people who do, can be at best ineffective in delivering therapeutic outcomes (Vernon & Miller, 2001). Lack of cultural competence to work with Deaf people's values (Glickman & Black, 2006), often leads to a failure to deliver an equitable service (Tugg v. Towey, 1994: 1001). At worst, services can even be damaging (Ubido *et al.*, 2002; Hindley & Kitson, 2000; Steinberg *et al.*, 1998), to the extent that they may not prevent a Deaf person taking their own life (Turner *et al.*, 2007). Following the 'Towards Equity and Access' report (DoH, 2005), North East NHS Commissioners have enabled Deaf-led training for some Deaf people and health staff in the North East, to improve Deaf patient outcomes, particularly helpful after abuse. This research appears to strongly support the efficacy and value of Deaf-led initiatives, in which trained Deaf people, who are culturally competent and delivering accessible native BSL use, deliver services for Deaf people. Currently, few Deaf groups are funded to deliver support to Deaf victims after crime and, especially where there is only a small population who require intervention in each region, with increased reports of Audist hate crime, the impact on Deaf individuals may be disproportionately high (Nayak, 2003), particularly as Deaf people are largely invisible, either as providers or users of the services.

So, what can we do about disablist hate crime?

Criminal justice?

First, an important area of work, prioritised by disabled victims and survivors, is the prevention of attacks and the tackling of revictimisation, both crucial to prevent further distress and escalation, particularly after rape (Resnick *et al.*, 2005). This may be done most effectively in communities by addressing the underlying causes of high crime rates in deprived (often urban) areas in which poverty (Rayburn *et al.*, 2005), homelessness, unsettled, poor-quality housing and tensions from segregation of communities may worsen crime levels (Grover, 2008). In New York City, high crime rates were tackled by police, housing agencies, schools and businesses working with residents' groups to regenerate areas. In addition, they 'Rediscovered policing, as opposed to law enforcement, and prevention, as opposed to case processing' (Kelling & Bratton, 1998: 1230); this is a contemporary theme emerging in the UK in conversations with Forces and communities through Crime and Disorder Reduction Partnerships (CDRPs), where services may be unable to prosecute a hate crime effectively if the evidence (such as witness statements, graffiti, CCTV footage, knowledge of control of the victim – perhaps including stolen money prior to the attack) is not collected meticulously because police officers are not confident in understanding the witness, or may prejudge that he or she is 'unreliable' or not be trained to recognise a hate attack.

Even in racist hate crimes, where there is greater experience than in disablist hate crime, we still only see 1 prosecution for every 35 crimes (Gadd, 2009: 757) and applying Gadd's method to disablist hate crime figures, this may be as high as 1 in over 300; this may suggest that victims and survivors may not benefit from criminal justice-linked interventions. If they do, the services may not be culturally competent, or may be inaccessible to deal with the particular after-effects of 'hyper-violent, hyper-sexual' (Sherry, 2010, p. 100) disablist hate crime, and particular worries occur for families or victims with no recourse to public funds.

Prevention is better than cure

As community groups working to promote social justice and rights, we can prepare ourselves to work to stay safe. There are refreshing, user-led approaches to security, such as the Better Days training developed in the North East of England for other user-led disabled people's groups (Inclusion North, 2009). In the USA, an evidence-based study worked to teach students how to recognise rape perpetration risks and how to intervene safely if they saw a potential or actual attack, taking the blame away from the victim. Foubert & Langhinrichsen-Rohling (2010) found that students who had taken the Women's Program showed greater willingness to help and had less acceptance of rape myths than the control group. This has interesting parallels with work invoking Bismark's notion of civil courage, for example by the Lawnmowers, a company of disabled actors and musicians in the North East of England who use drama to train people to stay safe and tackle disablist hate crime on the streets (See Brandon, in this volume). But whilst prevention programmes are important, it is interventions for people who have been attacked which are crucial in reducing the long-term devastation of victimisation.

Inter- and intra-sectional approaches

Of course, people do not belong to identity groups in silos; a person may be Black-British, disabled, gay and young, for example. Intersectional work (Crenshaw, 1991) across identity groups can be important to improve the life chances of young people who experience racist hate crime, before their education and employment chances are hurt by the hostility and consequences of attack. For example, holistic work in the West End of Newcastle, by the Angelou Centre and several member groups which meet there, ensures that women and children (Mullender *et al.*, 2003) from black, minority ethic and refugee communities access culturally competent services to prevent repeat victimisation, but also so that they can be involved in training, education, social events and employment activities to ensure their life chances are repaired after hate crime and to resist social isolation. So, specific skills, cultural knowledge and experiences exist with women's aid groups, refuges and other third-party reporting centres in the community, usually already tackling and supporting people after racist or homophobic hate crime, but in many, disabled survivors may be invisible or unable to access services. Historically, many established LGB and T projects have had their meeting places upstairs, with buzzer entry, to ensure protection for service users who can also often safely report homophobic hate crime there, but this makes them unintentionally inaccessible to many gay, lesbian, bi and trans disabled men and women.

In a 2009 pilot, the Gay Advice Durham and Darlington Criminal Justice Worker and a group of trans women who had experienced hate crime came together with Vision Sense, a user-led organisation of disabled people, to tackle hate crime together and work with mainstream agencies, such as ARCH (a reporting project), the Equality and Human Rights Commission and Victim Support in the region. This reciprocal work, through an action learning set approach (Balderston & Roebuck, 2010), built alliances and gave a more nuanced understanding to mainstream organisations of the varied experiences of hate crime, to resist a 'one size fits all' interventional approach. For example, despite their excellent work and transformative results, some women's refuges may need support to negotiate the barriers experienced by women when the abuser also provides their personal support (Saxton *et al.*, 2001). Intersectional approaches after Crenshaw (1991) are crucial, but intrasectional acknowledgement (McCall, 2005) shows development in recognition of cultural barriers in between categories which are more than simply additive gendered and disabled experiences. Working with disabled people's organisations, LGB and T and Q groups have supported us to better understand how to be proud to be disabled people, how to fight hate crime and overcome barriers in criminal justice; we have shared reciprocally how to tackle disabling subcultural constructs of the body beautiful (Atkins, 1998) and the stigma which may desexualise disabled people, as well as practical access provisions for buildings, staffing and events. So, inter- and intra-sectional approaches are useful at different times in addressing barriers experienced by victims of crime and in promoting a cultural pride in diversity, respectively.

Evidence-based and collective approaches after hate crime

In addition to helping survivors adjust after rape and interpersonal violence (Chang *et al.*, 2003; Ullman & Filipas, 2002), altruism in helping others (Straub, 2010) or impacting positively on the community can influence individuals to thrive (Peterson and Seligman, 2004), whilst establishing and maintaining these connections is a key attribute also identified by Mitchell and Correa-Velez (2010). Rape crisis centres and women's refuges have built effective services on women helping women for years; they offer support to family members, including the children of victims, and work with survivors immediately fleeing violence, but also provide advocacy, often many years after the initial trauma (Coy, Kelly & Foord, 2007). In addition, women's advocacy groups also work to prevent future violence and support women experiencing revictimisation, or who have been criminalized themselves through being abused (Chesney-Lind,

2006). Excellent examples of this approach are the work of Powerhouse (Morris, 1991) and 'My Sister's Place' in Middlesbrough. Although the latter project began simply as a necessary and valuable crisis refuge, it now offers support, training and advocacy to a wider range of women and their families in the local communities, with older women and disabled women supporting each other to live independently and safely.

The community concept of a safe, supportive collective is mirrored too in the disabled people's movement, where peer advocacy groups, led, staffed and controlled by disabled people, have formed over the last forty years by people who have been abused, institutionalised and segregated, to gain access to, or resume, independent living inclusion and recovery (Lowicki and Pillsbury, 2004). More recently, projects are developing in Manchester (the Breakthrough UK *Working Through It Together* project) and Tyne and Wear (Vision Sense Survivors against Hate Crime and Better Days training sessions about hate crime for learning-disabled people). This approach is distinct to that of often non-disabled 'professionals' setting out to, 'empower' service users; instead, disabled people, who are the experts from their own experiences of the barriers they have encountered, support each other along their journeys and the groups create the space where people can take their own agency, choice and control to move on from the victimisation or segregation.

Person-centred, user-led services – more than just a victim project.

The benefits of collective approaches are evidenced convincingly and may be particularly important with disabled people after hate crime and abuse, especially where the perpetrator relied on the isolation of the victim in order to carry out the violence or abuse. In disabled people's organisations, rather than being isolated, or having few contacts who are not professionals engaged in someone's personal care or support, disabled people after hate crime in these settings can be integrated into a circle of support or a social network which provides 'A sense of purpose, belonging, security, as well as recognition of self-worth' (Kawachi and Berkman, 2001, p. 459). This is a compelling reason for interventions to be delivered within disabled people's organisations in the community and not separate victim support organisations; engagement with other projects and activities, with the support net of a related and specialist crime project, allows a consistent pathway out of victimhood which may prevent a disabled person after hate crime, rape or domestic violence slipping back into revictimisation and isolation. At Breakthrough UK, for example, disabled people accessing the hate crime project can also progress to work or access advocacy for independent living and deliver training to criminal justice workers. At Vision Sense in the North East of England, disabled people can also access accredited training and support to constitute their own social enterprises if they wish to deliver services for others, alongside or after their hate crime advocacy involvement. These inclusive settings are important, as social inclusion, safety from violence and access to economic resources have been identified as three key elements strongly linked to mental health and well-being (Keleher and Armstrong, 2005). Ensuring the intervention meets the needs of the person can be achieved by disabled people including safety and security in our support plans. By gradually introducing a disabled person into a new area through regular contact with people in the area in social and community environments and building a workable circle of support before the person moves into supported or independent living, problems of isolation and risk of harm can be substantially reduced and prevented. Circles of support, popularised in Canada, allow people, not only support workers, to formalise the parts they play in a disabled person's life, and to problem-solve (Gold, 1994). This can extend opportunities for managed risk, reduce isolation and victimisation, prevent the need for expensive crisis intervention and enable a person to fulfil their aspirations. In addition, interventions in which bereaved families develop campaigning and resistance in organisations can have important roles in supporting other families and survivors in tackling the barriers which perpetuate hate crime. No chapter about interventions after hate crime would be complete without a recognition of the work of Doreen Lawrence or Sylvia Lancaster, both mothers who have fought to right systemic wrongs after the murders of Stephen and Sophie, respectively.

Having demonstrated that a range of culturally competent and accessible interventions are needed to address victim harm after hate crime and rape and that one size does not fit all, the consideration of greater voluntary sector provision and the use of individual victim budgets to purchase the support, although problematic if appropriated by neo-liberalism, may provide the personalised choice and control over evidence-based interventions that disabled victims and survivors really require to transform their own life chances after hate crime and rape. It is noted that by involving the victim and the wider community of identity, and reducing tension between groups, the wider harms of hate crime may be prevented and tackled in a more evidence-based way than with individualistic and standardised mainstream services.

Conclusions

This chapter has shown that collective, user-led work through disabled people's and survivors organisations, after (or during repeated) hate crime, rape or domestic violence may produce some of the most effective, sustainable and cost-effective outcomes for victims, Survivors and communities. Compelling research supports what disabled people's and women's organisations have known anecdotally for many years; control over the process helps survivors adjust more effectively after violence and rape (Chang *et al.*, 2003; Ullman & Filipas, 2002). Although Survivors of violent hate crime and rape must lead design, delivery and evaluation of services (Morris, 1991). That is why our movement banners say, 'Nothing about us, without us' – we call upon our allies in criminal justice, health, housing, education, social care, academia and communities who are committed to social justice and equity, to work with us to prevent, expose, tackle and eradicate disablist hate crime, using evidence-based, accessible and culturally competent approaches. Surviving problems in this way will save money, help us transform our life chances and build the safer future of our communities, whilst we work together between generations to change the attitudes and segregation that reproduce disablist hate crime. In our last conversation before she died, Rowan Jade, the Chair of Equality 2025 said to the co-editor of this collection Alan Roulstone and myself, 'I don't care what you call [disablist hate crime], I just want to know what we are going to do about it.' In working to meet Rowan's priority and turning to address the barriers and promote transformative models, might we be able to demonstrate evidence-based and effective interventions, which lead to recovery with disabled and Deaf survivors?

Bibliography

Atkins, D. (1998) *Looking Queer: Body Image and Identity in Lesbian, Bisexual, Gay and Trans gender Communities*. Binghamton: Haworth Press.

Balderston, S. Roebuck, E. (2010) *Empowering Victims to Tackle Hate Crime* http://www.equalityhumanrights.com/key-projects/good-relations/empowering-people-to-tackle-hate-crime/ [Accessed 8 July 2011].

Barnes, A. Ephross, P. H. (1994) 'The Impact of Hate Violence on Victims: Emotional and Behavioral Responses to Attacks'. *Social Work* May 1994, pp. 247–251.

BBC (2011) *Panorama, Undercover Care: The Abuse Exposed*. BBC One 31 May 2011 21:00 BST.

Brandon, T. (2010) 'Civic Courage'. Paper given at Hate Crime Seminar, DeMontfort University.

Browing, A. Caulfield, L. (2011) 'The prevalence and treatment of people with Asperger's Syndrome in the criminal justice system'. *Criminology and Criminal Justice* 11 (2), pp. 165–180.

Brownridge, D. A. (2006). 'Partner violence against women with disabilities: Prevalence, risk, and explanations'. *Violence against Women*, 12(9), pp. 805–822.

Burton, M. Evans, R. Sanders, A. (2006) 'Are special measures for vulnerable and intimidated witnesses working? Evidence from the criminal justice agencies.' London: Home Office On-Line Report No. 01/06. Accessed from: http://www.homeoffice.gov.uk/rds [Accessed on 14 April 2011].

Casey, C. Bhavani, P. R., Jacka, S. (2004) *Evaluation of the Target Hardening Pilot Programme*. Wellington: Ministry of Justice.

Chakraborti, N., Garland, J. (2009) *Hate crime, Impact, Causes and Responses*. London: Sage Publications.

Chang, J.C., Decker M., Moracco, K. E., Martin, S.L., Petersen, R., Frasier, P.Y. (2003) 'What happens when health care providers ask about intimate partner violence? A description of consequences from the perspectives of female survivors'. *Journal American Medical Womens Association*. 58(2), pp. 76 81.

Chesney-Lind, M. (2006) 'Patriarchy, crime, justice: Feminist criminology in an era of backlash'. *Feminist Criminology*. 1(1), pp. 6–26.

Cohen, L. J., Roth, S. (1987) 'The Psychological Aftermath of Rape: Long-Term Effects and Individual Differences in Recovery'. *Journal of Social and Clinical Psychology* 5 (4), pp. 525–534.

Coy, M., Kelly, L. and Foord, J. (2007) *Map of Gaps: The Postcode Lottery of Specialised Women's Support Services*, London, End Violence Against Women.

Crenshaw, K. (1991) 'Mapping the Margins: Intersectionality, Identity Politics, and Violence against Women of Color' *Stanford Law Review*, 43(6), pp. 1241–1299.

Deninger, M., Couthen, A. J. (1983). *Managing cultural conflict in schools for the deaf: Focus on the organizational level*. Winnipeg: The Convention of American Instructors of the Deaf.

Disability Rights Commission (2004) *Hate Crime Against Disabled People in Scotland*. Edinburgh: DRC.

Foa, E. B.; Hearst-Ikeda, D., Perry, K. J. (1995) 'Evaluation of a brief cognitive-behavioral program for the prevention of chronic PTSD in recent assault victims'. *Journal of Consulting and Clinical Psychology*, 63(6), pp. 948–955.

Foster, S. B. (1998). 'Communication as social engagement: Implications for interactions between deaf and hearing persons'. *Scandinavian Audiology, 27* (49), pp. 116–124.

Foubert, J. D., Langhinrichsen-Rohling, J. (2010) 'Effects of a rape awareness program on college women: increasing bystander efficacy and willingness to intervene'. *Journal of Community Psychology*, 38 (7), pp. 813–827.

Frost, D. (2008) 'Islamophobia: examining causal links between the state and "race hate" from "below"', *International Journal of Sociology and Social Policy*, 28 (11/12), pp. 546–563.

Gadd, D. (2009) 'Aggravating Racism and Elusive Motivation'. *British Journal of Criminology* 49 (6), pp. 755–771.

Gahir, M. (2006) 'High Secure Care for Deaf People in England and Wales'. in Austen, S. Jeffery, D. (eds) *Deafness and Challenging Behaviour 360° Perspective*. Chichester: John Wiley and Sons.

Glickman, N. S. Black, P. A. (2006) 'Demographics, Psychiatric Diagnoses, and Other Characteristics of North American Deaf and Hard-of-Hearing Inpatients' *Journal of Deaf Studies and Deaf Education* 11:3.

Gold, D. (1994) 'We don't call it a "circle": The ethos of a support group'. *Disability & Society*, Vol 9(4), pp. 435–452.

Grover, C. (2008) *Crime and Inequality*. Cullompton: Willan Publishing.

Hague, Gill; Thiara, R. and Mullender, A. (2010) 'Disabled Women, Domestic Violence and Social Care: The Risk of Isolation, Vulnerability and Neglect', *British Journal of Social Work*, 40 (6).

Harris, M., Young, P. (2009) 'Developing community and social cohesion through grassroots bridge-building: an exploration', *Policy and Politics*, 37, 4: 517–534.

Healthcare Commission (2007) *A life like no other: A national audit of specialist inpatient healthcare services for people with learning difficulties in England*. London: Healthcare Commission.

Hepburn, J. R. (1973) 'Violent Behavior in Interpersonal Relationships'. *The Sociological Quarterly* 14 (3), pp. 419–429.

Herek, G. M., Gillis, J. R., Cogan, J. C. (1999) 'Psychological Sequelae of Hate Crime Victimization among Lesbian, Gay and Bisexual Adults'. *Journal of Consulting and Clinical Psychology*. 67(6), pp. 945–51.

Hindley, P., Kitson, N. (2000) *Mental Health and Deafness: A Multidisciplinary Handbook*. Chichester: Wiley.

HM Government (1999) 'Statute: Youth Justice and Criminal Evidence Act'. London: TSO.

Hollomotz, A. (2009) 'May we please have sex tonight?' *British Journal of Learning Disabilities* (37) pp. 91–97.

Hope, T. (2008) 'Dodgy evidence: fallacies and facts of crime reduction'. *Safer Communities*: Volume 7:4.

Iganski, P. (2008) *Hate Crime and the City*. Bristol: Policy Press.

Inclusion North (2009) 'Learning Together Training Pack'. Accessed 16 February 2011 from http://arcsafety.net/page7/assets/Hate%20Crime%20Learning%20Together%20Training%20Pack.pdf.

IPCC (2009) 'Independent Police Complaints Commission report into the contact between Fiona Pilkington and Leicestershire Constabulary 2004–2007', Report 2009/016872. London: IPCC.

Kawachi, I., Berkman, L. F. (2001) 'Social ties and mental health', *Journal of Urban Health: Bulletin of the New York Academy of Medicine*, 78 (3), 458–467.

Kelly, L. & Humphreys, C. (2001) 'Supporting women and children in their communities: outreach and advocacy approaches to domestic violence.' In Taylor-Browne, J. (2001) *What works in domestic violence? A comprehensive guide for professionals*. London: Home Office.

Keleher, H., Armstrong, R. (2005) *Evidence-based mental health promotion resource*. Melbourne: Department of Human Services and VicHealth.

Kelling, G. L., Bratton, W. J. (1998) 'Declining Crime Rates: Insiders' Views of the New York City Story'. *The Journal of Criminal Law and Criminology* 88 (4) pp. 1217–1232.

Kilpatrick, D. G., Resnick, H. S. (1993). 'Posttraumatic stress disorder associated with exposure to criminal victimization in clinical and community populations'. In Davidson, JRT. Foa, E. B. (eds) Post-traumatic Stress Disorder: DSM-IV and Beyond, pp. 113–143. Washington: American Psychiatric Press.

Li, L., Ford, J. A., Moore, D. (2000). 'An exploratory study of violence, substance abuse, disability, and gender'. *Social Behavior and Personality*, 28, pp. 61–72.

Lothian CIL (2006) 'Counselling disabled people and training disabled people in counselling – the LCIL experience'. Accessed from www.lothiancil.org.uk/fileuploads/writing-up-resources-version2—may-06-3185.doc+working+with+disabled+people+counselling&hl=en&gl=uk. [Accessed March 10, 2011].

Lowicki, J., Pillsbury, A. A. (2004) 'Supporting Young Refugees' Participation In Their Own Protection And Recovery: Lessons Learned', *Refugee Survey Quarterly*, 23 (2), pp. 72–88.

Marhoefer-Dvorak, S., Resick, P. A., Kotsis Hutter, C., Girelli, S. A. (1988). 'Single vs. multiple-incident rape victims: A comparison of psychological reactions to rape'. *Journal of Interpersonal Violence* (3) pp. 145–160.

Martin, S. L., Ray, N., Sotres-Alvarez, D., Kupper, L. L., Moracco, K. E., Dickens, P. A., et al. (2006). 'Physical and sexual assault of women with disabilities'. *Violence against Women*, 12(9), pp. 823–837.

McCall, L. (2005) 'The Complexity of Intersectionality'. *Signs: Journal of Women in Culture and Society*. 30 (3), pp. 1771–1800.

Milberger S, Israel N, LeRoy B, Martin A. (2003) 'Violence against women with physical disabilities' *Violence and Victims* 18 (5), pp. 581–91.

Mind (2007) *Another Assault*, London: Mind.

Mitchell, J. Correa-Velez, I. (2010) 'Community development with survivors of torture and trauma:an evaluation framework'. *Community Development Journal* 45 (1) pp. 90–110.

Morris, J. (1991) *Pride Against Prejudice*. London: Women's Press.

Mullender, A. Hague, G., Imam, U. F., Kelly, L., Malos, E., Regan, L. (2003) *Children's Perspectives on Domestic Violence*. London: SAGE Publications Ltd.

Nayak A. (2003) *Race, Place and Globalization : Youth Cultures in a Changing World.* Oxford: Berg.

Peterson, C., & Seligman, M. E. P. (2004) 'Character strengths and virtues: A handbook and classification' Washington, DC: American Psychological Association.

Powers, L. E. et al. (2002) *Interpersonal Violence and Women with a Disability.* http://vawnet.org/Assoc_Files_VAWnet/AR_WomenWithDisabilities.pdf. Accessed 6 December 2011.

Pritchard, J. (2001) *Good Practice with Vulnerable Adults.* London: Jessica Kingsley Publishers.

Radford, L. and Gill, A. (2006), 'Losing the Plot? Researching Community Safety Partnership Work Against Domestic Violence'. *The Howard Journal of Criminal Justice.* 45 pp. 369–387.

Rayburn, N. R. Wenzel, S. L.; Elliott, M. N.; Hambarsoomians, K., Marshall, G. N., Tucker, J. S. (2005) 'Trauma, Depression, Coping, and Mental Health Service Seeking Among Impoverished Women'. *Journal of Consulting and Clinical Psychology,* 73(4), pp. 667–677.

Reeve, D. (2004) 'Psycho-emotional Dimensions of Disability and the Social Model' in *Implementing the Social Model of Disability: Theory and Research* edited by Barnes, C. & Mercer, G. Leeds: The Disability Press, pp. 83–100.

Resnick, H. S., Kilpatrick, D. G., Dansky, B. S., Saunders, B. E.; Best, C. L. (1993) 'Prevalence of civilian trauma and posttraumatic stress disorder in a representative national sample of women'. *Journal of Consulting and Clinical Psychology,* Vol 61(6), pp. 984–991.

Resnick, H., Acierno, R., Kilpatrick, D. G., and Holmes, M. (2005) 'Victims Description of an Early Intervention to Prevent Substance Abuse and Psychopathology' in Recent Rape Behaviour Modification 2005; 29; 156.

Riger, S. (1993) 'What's wrong with Empowerment'. *American Journal of Community Psychology,* Vol. 21, No. 3, 1993.

Robinson, L., Spilsbury, K. (2008) 'Systematic review of the perceptions and experiences of accessing health services by adult victims of domestic violence'. *Health & Social Care in the Community* 16 (1), pp. 16–30.

Robinson, A., Hudson, K. (2011) 'Different yet complementary: Two approaches to supporting victims of sexual violence in the UK'. *Criminology and Criminal Justice* 11: 515.

Rose, S. Brewin, C. R., Andrews, B., Kirk, M. (1999) 'A randomized controlled trial of individual psychological debriefing for victims of violent crime'. *Psychological Medicine* 29 (4), pp. 793–799.

Roulstone, A., Thomas, P. & Balderston, S. (2011) 'Between hate and vulnerability: unpacking the British Criminal Justice System's construction of disablist hate crime'. *Disability and Society.* 26 (3), 351–64.

Sacks R., Keeling S., Heke S., Braybrook H., Cybulska B., Forster G. (2008) 'Referral of Young People Attending a Sexual Assault Referral Centre to Mental Health Services'. *International Journal of STD & AIDs,* 19 (8), pp. 557–8.

Salkovskis, P. M. (1996) *Frontiers of Clinical Psychology.* New York: Guildford Press.

Saxton, M., Curry, M. A., Powers, L. E., Maley, S., Eckels, K. and Gross, J. (2001) 'Bring My Scooter So I Can Leave You: A study of disabled women handling abuse by personal assistance providers', *Violence Against Women,* 7, 4: 393.

Schneider, L. J., Mori, L. T., Lambert, P. L., Wong, A. O. (2009) 'The Role of Gender and Ethnicity in Perceptions of Rape and Its Aftereffects'. *Sex Roles* (60) 5–6, pp. 410–421.

Scott, S. (2004) 'Opening a Can of Worms? Counselling for Survivors in UK Women's Prisons'. *Feminism and Psychology* 14 (2), pp. 256–261.

Sherry, M. (2010) *Disability Hate Crimes: Does Anyone really Hate Disabled People?* Farnham: Ashgate.

Smith, D. L. (2008). 'Disability, Gender And Intimate Partner Violence: Relationships From The Behavioral Risk Factor Surveillance System'. *Sexuality And Disability*, 26 (1), pp. 15–28.

Sobsey D., Mansell S. 'An international perspective on patterns of sexual assault and abuse of people with disabilities'. *International Journal of Adolescent Medicine & Health* 1994; 7 (2), pp. 153–78.

Steketee G, Foa E. B. (1987) 'Rape victims: Post-traumatic stress responses and their treatment: A review of the literature'. *Journal of Anxiety Disorders* 1 pp. 69–86.

Tugg v. Towey (1994) p. 1001, quoted in L. J. Raifman and M. Vernon (1996) *Professional Psychology: Research and Practice* 1996, Vol. 27, No. 4, 372–377.

Turner, O., Windfuhr, K., Kapur, N. (2007) 'Suicide in deaf populations: a literature review'. *Annals of General Psychiatry* 6 (26).

Ubido. J, Huntington., J., Warburton, D.(2002) 'Inequalities in access to healthcare faced by women who are deaf'. *Health & Social Care in the Community* 10 (4), pp. 247–253.

Ullman, S. E. & Brecklin, L. (2003). 'Sexual assault history and health-related outcomes in a national sample of women'. *Psychology of Women Quarterly*, 27, pp. 46–57.

Ullman, S. E. & Filipas, H. H. (2001). 'Correlates of formal and informal support seeking in sexual assault victims'. *Journal of Interpersonal Violence*, 16, 1028–1047.

Vernon, M., Miller, K. (2001) 'Interpreting in mental health settings: issues and concerns'. *American Annals of the Deaf* 2001; 146 (5): 429–434.

Victim Support (2005) *Investigating the practical support needs of burglary victims.* London: Victim Support.

——(2006) *Guidance on developing services for LGBT victims of crime.* (internal document) London: Victim Support.

——(2010) *Annual Report and Accounts.* London: Victim Support.

Young, A. M., Ackerman, J., Kyle, J. M. (2000) 'On Creating a Workable Signing Environment: Deaf and Hearing Perspectives' *Deaf Studies* 5:2.

Young, I. M. (2009) 'Structural Injustice & the Politics of Difference'. In Grabham, L., Cooper, D., Krishnadas, J., Herman, D (eds) *Intersectionality & Beyond.* New York: Routledge Cavendish.

Index